DEDI
MR. ROBERT SHELTON

OLD TUCSON:

The Biography of a Movie Studio

PAUL LAWTON

TABLE OF CONTENTS

INTRODUCTION

In penny arcades, peep shows, Kinetoscope parlors, the machine's flickering moving pictures entranced the young and old. A penny in a slot, the crank grinding, the light on, naive comedies and erotic vignettes danced before the customer's eyes.

By 1895 there were those trying to combine the magic lantern principle with the Kinetoscope to throw a larger-than-life-size image on a wall or other white surface. Meanwhile, the Kinetoscope parlors offered Kinetophones, which gave the viewer the chance to hear music or sound effects while watching.

The Koster and Bial's Music Hall in New York invited the Kinetoscope Company's managers to put on the first public showing of "motion pictures." On the morning of April 24th, 1896, the New York Times reported that "an unusually bright light fell upon the screen [in the Music Hall]. Then came into view two precocious blond persons of the variety stage, in pink and blue dresses, doing an umbrella dance with commendable celerity. Their motions were all clearly defined." The movies were born.

Cripple Creek Barroom, 1898, featured a jug of red-eye in a prominent place along with a cast of the usual saloon western types in an authentic Old West vignette; produced in Edison's "Black Maria" studio in West Orange, New Jersey.

George Melies, the owner of the Théâtre Robert-Houdin in Paris, applied the camera to his art around 1900. In the process, he either invented outright or accidentally discovered almost the entire bag of tricks now used in most movies; double exposure, stop motion, fast and slow motion, fades, dissolves, and animation.

He followed this with the first Western movie: *The Great Train Robbery, Crime in the Far West*, featuring the telegrapher's daughter bound by the robbers, the engineer forced to uncouple his locomotive, the escape into the "badlands," which in this case were woods. The often-repeated scene of crooks and robbers spending their loot in a saloon, shooting at the feet of a tenderfoot who must dance for them. For some unexplained reason, at the end of the film, one of the characters draws his gun and fires directly at the audience.

The first Westerns were generally one-reel films with little more than a chase scene and a fight; most of the men who made and appeared in them knew nothing about the west they portrayed. The landscape of the West drew them. *The Gunfighter* had already been made in 1916. William S. Hart, himself a seasoned real-life cowboy and ranch hand who thought the earlier West of Broncho Billy Anderson too theatrical. He created the character of the "good, bad man." The moral reformation of an outlaw became a new fare for moviegoers.

This book is a look at the history of Old Tucson Studios. It covers the history of movies in Tucson and the building of the studio. Also covered is eighty years of studio filming from the Movie *Arizona* (1940) to *Five Mile Cave* (2019). Additionally, covered are music and band celebrations, Wild West doins', and Special presentations.

All the movie names are listed in Italics, while book titles and live shows are in quotations.

I want to express my appreciation to the following people: Robert Shelton for his stories about the history of Old Tucson, Marty Freeze for his insights into the films shot at Old Tucson, Sandy Schantz for information about the Jaycees, Mary Davis for her help in editing the manuscript, Rob Jensen for his support in researching the live-action shows, Jack Young for his stories about the early stunt shows, Carolyn Shelton for access to Bob's photographs, and my wife Karen for her support.

All photographs, except those marked differently, are from the Robert Shelton photo collection.

CHAPTER ONE:
Tucson Pre Old Tucson

In 1910, two film distributors broke away from their parent company in Chicago and started the American Film Manufacturing Company. This was the first studio to film in Tucson. American Film did not stay long, maybe four months. Long enough to crank out five Westerns, including at least one filmed in front of Mission San Xavier Del Bac.

The Western Lubin Stock Co., a troupe of about 20 performers and crew, under the direction of Wilber Melville, arrived in March 1912. They left July 11th and shot six pictures, spending $6,172.30 in salaries and supplies. Filming out of a studio at 315 N. Stone Ave, a canvas awning was rigged over it to control the light from the brilliant Arizona sunshine. Inside the studios were located all the costumes, props, and paint shop.

The one, two, and three "reeler's," lasting about 15 minutes a reel, were then sent back to the company's Fort Lee, New Jersey lab for processing.

The first movie made use of San Xavier Mission for the "Renunciation." This film was Tucson's financial baptism into the economic benefits of the movie-making business. The silent one-reelers made by the Lubin people were shot in a matter of days, using local backgrounds and people. Of course, they were silent and were shown to the public with dialogue indicated on "titles." Many theaters preceded the film with a projected slide admonishing the moviegoers to "Please read the titles to yourself. Loud reading annoys your neighbors".

Then, as now, many local Tucsonans participated as "extras," and such popular tourist attractions as San Xavier del Bac and Tucson streets and buildings were used as settings for the films. Events as common as a ball game provided the storyline for some of the "productions." But even then, the scripts had the "Hollywood" touch. In the ball game film, the "dudes" played the "cowpunchers," and when an unwilling umpire made a bad decision against the cowboys, they hanged him. The cast consisted of regular local teams and spectators with a few Lubin players in key roles. The company filmed the action during the time between the two games to not disrupt the regular games.

The most significant Lubin production in Tucson was "The Sleeper." It had a gold rush scene in which 400 residents, dressed in their roughest clothes and carrying packs, bedrolls, and mining tools, boarded a borrowed Southern Pacific Railroad train at the end of the depot and chugged a short way down the track before unloading. The "goldfields" were near Sentinel Peak ("A" Mountain), where a temporary tent city was set up. Several hundred Tucsonans brought wagons, buckboards, mules, horses, and mining equipment for the elaborate scene. An old prospector found gold in the mountains, and when the news Tucson, a great rush to the fields took place. In this case, the pictures were taken in "old town" to show Tucson as it was years ago. Then the shooting was transferred to the scene of the strike, and another town would be established there, built of tents and adobe houses. The old man who first made the strike is then supposed to wander off, and in the meantime, his family is reduced to want. They were turned out in the streets, and the next scene is 20 years later when the old couple is shown in the newer section of the city. Pictures of the business section will be shown as well as the residents' area. Romaine Fielding directed "the Sleeper." The film finished July 7th, 1912 and, the movie company left town in July with promises to return in the fall to establish winter quarters and a permanent studio.

When it left Tucson, the Lubin Company went to Prescott. The American Ranch, about 12 miles out of Prescott and one of the famous shelters for settlers in times of Indian uprisings was used as a scene of the Indian period.

In mid-November 1912, Fielding took his troop to Nogales and created a new headquarters in an old sanitarium, and built a stage. They stayed six months and made a total of 24 movies in Arizona.

Lubin lost almost all its prints in a devastating fire at its New Jersey Headquarters in 1914.

The American-Eclair Movie Company arrived in Tucson on November 15th, 1913, with 13 players plus William Collison as manager.

They rented a house, the Sorin mansion, at 430 North Main St. as an office and to contain a stage. The mansion had ten rooms, dressing rooms, business offices and the backyard contained a 30 ft.[2]

stage, which faced south with a muslin top and diffusion side curtains. The stable was to the west. Scenes painted on the side of the fence served as backdrops.

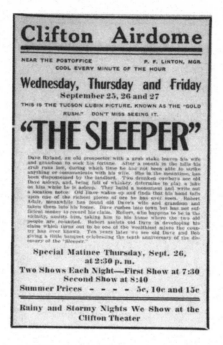

Advertisement for "The Sleeper" showing at Clifton Airdome. 1912
(Az Daily Star)

They would concentrate on O. Henry stories since they obtain the rights to six of the Westerns. Éclair filmed *The Dupe, When Death Rode the Engine,* and *Caballeros' Way* (the world's first Cisco Kid movie) on Tucson and Sabino Canyon's location. The production, *The Girl Stage Driver,* is a splendid story filmed at the foot of Sentinel Peak ("A" Mountain). It is the only Tucson movie from this period known to exist.

In little more than a year, the Éclair Film Company would churn out more than 70 films in the Tucson area. The company and scenery sailed forth from New York to New Orleans, and then came overland on the Southern Pacific Railroad. At its height, Eclair had as many as six units filming around town simultaneously, each turning out a movie in a matter of days.

Two local kids, who made it to billing credit with the stars, were Ann– Eve and Leonor Mansfeld, the young daughters of a prominent pioneer family living near the studio. Ann Eve, the older by ten months, was spotted by someone from the studio, remembers her sister Leonore Williamson. "They asked mother if she could be in the movies. That's how I got in too," says Williamson, now deceased. Ann Eve Johnson died in 1981. Always accompanied by their mother or grandmother, in eight months, they made more than 30 pictures between them, including *Dead Men's Tales* and *The Price He Paid*.

For its Westerns, the studio could draw upon its stock, including as many as 30 horses housed in a studio property corral. Rounding out the menagerie were an American Eagle, three squirrels, one-horned toad, and a silver fox. It was the animal farm – and a few offended noses – that may have hastened the company's departure for Southern California. Considered to be a "fashionable residential section of town," the studio, or rather its corral, began drawing complaints from the neighbors.

At which point, Webster Cullison, the studio's local manager, announced the company's move to Los Angeles. "It seems that the company of actors of the Eclair Motion Pictures, located at the Old Pueblo are raising a kick on the high prices being charged them for certain necessities in making the pictures, and are contemplating a move to some other city. Eclair is leaving Tucson due to the hard feelings caused by a few prominent citizens who do not want the film company in Tucson. They have gotten merchants to charge excessive fees for goods. This would cost the city about $150,000 annually from the loss of the movie company", stated the Arizona Daily Star. (January 22, 1915)

A month later, feathers on both sides appeared to be considerably less ruffled as the Star reported Cullison's last kind words regarding the city – and a parting gift of four traffic signs, which were prominently placed along downtown intersections. Making the trip to the coast were five baggage cars, including one filled with horses, three Bobcats, and the Fox. Financial difficulties, however, soon led to the company's demise in California.

On August 15th, 1915, a group of citizens met at the Teatro Carmen to form the Cuauhtemoc Film Company. Also, around the same time, the Tucsonence newspaper ran ads announcing shows at various theaters around Tucson. Cuauhtemoc incorporated as Cuauhtemoc Feature Film Manufacturing Company and capitalized at $5000. The main studio was located at 300 North Court St. The location to have the film processed and edited was located at the Mission studio on Congress Street.

The first regular movie filmed by Cuauhtemoc is called *Adventures of Avilas*. Filmed downtown and made in 14 scenes as a comedy with Manuel Sanchez as the Main director.

The company's main reason was to film the Stratten Mining Company, located in the Catalina Mountains. This way, the 300 stockholders who were unable to visit the company's property in the Old Hat District on the north side of the range could get a first-hand idea of what the company and the new road appeared.

A local advertisement said, "A local film will be shown at the Broadway Theater tonight, and was produced by the Cuauhtemoc

Film Company. It showed the university students completing the "A" on Sentinel Peak, laying the cornerstone of the Allianza Hispanic – Americana building, and confirmation of children at the Cathedral on Easter Sunday."

On December 4th, attempts by the Cuauhtemoc Company to take pictures of the Indians fiesta for a scenario which they were producing came to naught when the Indian dancer who was the piece de resistance of the feast, refused to shake his rattlesnake bound ankles when he sighted the camera and fled into the mission.

On February 5th, 1916, the government announced that a movie actress and general tied to the Cuauhtemoc Company might be deported. Senorita Trujillo is said to be a spy for the Villa revolutionaries. Because immigration authorities were detaining her on two charges, Senorita Bellin Trujillo, a pretty and talented young Mexican actress, could not work at the Cuauhtemoc film company studio. It was probable that her absence ruined a six-reel production which was almost complete. The young woman was taken into custody by immigration authorities in the company of General Luis Hermosillo, a prominent Vallista general who has been sojourning in this country. It was at Nogales, it is said, that Hermosillo and Señorita Trujillo became acquainted, and the man followed her here. He is married and has a wife who resides in the city of Hermosillo. $35,000 in Mexican money was found in their possession. When the company folded, there were a lot of hard feelings.

Several movie houses were in Tucson. A couple of these showed films outside and were referred to as "airdomes."

Newspaper advertising a movie at the Arizona Theater. 1914 (Az Daily Star)

On September 20th, 1913, *Dead Men's Tales*, filmed in Tucson, was shown at the Garden Airdome Theater located at Fifth Avenue and Congress Street.

The Western and its conventions had become entrenched by 1918, a year that saw *Out West* released, a parody of cowboy clichés starring Roscoe "Fatty" Arbuckle and Buster Keaton. Also filmed was *Light of the Western Stars*, starring Dustin Farnum, filmed at La Osa Ranch, southwest of Tucson.

In 1924, Sol Lesser, of the Principle Pictures Corporation, paid $90,000 in one check as the first payment for the picture rights to several Harold Bell Wright's books, among these books was the "Mine with the Iron Door." He agreed to film in the authentic setting of the Canyon Del Oro on the Catalina Mountains. It was the first big outdoor picture of its kind made. The movie company made its headquarters in Oracle, and there was much local interest in this, and hundreds of people visited its location around Oracle. One scene called for a flash flood in the Canyon Del Oro River, and the film was purposely filmed during the monsoon to take advantage of a storm that would fill the river with water.

Eventually, it rained, and a real gully washing mountain storm arrived. The company got its flood shots alright but very nearly drowned from a wall of water while they were filming.

Part of the movie's hype was an old-timer who showed some gold samples, stating he had found the real "Mine with the Iron Door." He described that the mine had buried treasure in it, and he presented specimens which supposedly came from this mine, which he stated had an iron door. The payoff came when he stood on the national capital's steps chatting with President Coolidge in front of a battery of cameras and received congratulations from the president on uncovering the historic "Mine with the Iron Door."

Principle Pictures and western writer Wright joined forces again in 1925 to make *Son of His Father* with Warner Baxter, Bessie Love, and Raymond Hatton. The press releases for *Son of His Father* played heavily on the stories of dangerous wild Mexican bandits. The Mexican authorities and Tucson Chamber of Commerce were outraged, but no one paid attention to their denials. The cast and crew packing 18 days to the movie location and had food parachuted by biplanes.

With the advent of sound on film motion pictures, in 1928, several silent film companies found themselves shutting down production because they could not compete with the new generation of "talkies." The new talkies were little more than shallow vehicles to get the latest scientific breakthrough, talking pictures, and much like 3-D films of the 1950s. These talkies offered little in the way of artistic expression or cinematography.

In Old Arizona (1928), the movie starring Warner Baxter and Edmund Love was filmed in Tucson and won the Academy Award for best actor by Warner Baxter. Not because of its excellent acting or script, but because it was the first one to be an all-talking picture. The movie was shot primarily outdoors. *In Old Arizona* made the Cisco Kid, an early 20th century folk hero.

Warner Baxter returned here in 1931 for *The Cisco Kid*, in which Tucsonan Chris-Pin Martin made his first appearance as Pancho (he was referred to as Gordito in this picture), a role he would play in eight more Cisco Kid movies. The Cisco Kid became known as the Robin Hood of the West, a good guy who palled around with Pancho, getting into all manner of harmless adventures. But that is a far cry from the cold-blooded white man first imagined by O. Henry in his classic story, published in 1907. The first sentence of the book states: "The Cisco Kid had killed six men in more or less fair scrimmages, had murdered twice as many (mostly Mexicans), and had winged a larger number whom he modestly did not count."

Lobby card for the "Cisco Kid". 1931 (Author's collection)

Tucson's first 100% talking picture was shown at the Rialto Theatre in Tucson for a week commencing Sunday, March 24th. Roy Drachman, the manager, announced.. In *Old Arizona*, the opening feature was especially fitting for the occasion as the plot was acted out near Tucson. There will be a slight change in the policy at the Rialto when talking pictures were presented. The regular prices will be $.60 for the lower floor, $.40 for the balcony, and $.10 and $.25 for children.

Perhaps the first crime scene to be filmed occurred on October 21st, 1932, when a private citizen filmed Prohibition Agents making a raid in the Tortilito Mountains, north of Tucson. They used the film as evidence.

While in town filming *Blonde Bombshell*, Jean Harlow was made an official Deputy Sheriff of the Pima County Sheriff's Department by Sheriff John Belton on September 21st, 1933. This contemporary film is a writer's concept of what a tobacco spitting, gun-toting female Deputy Sheriff was like. A portion of this MGM movie's outside shooting was filmed at a "famous cactus garden" east of Tucson. No hint was given as to the exact location of the cactus garden.

Tucson's casual and haphazard wooing of the motion picture industry changed in 1934 when Nick Hall arrived to manage the Santa Rita Hotel. Hall liked having his lobby full of movie people, and he went all out to get them. He hired photographers to search out and photograph picturesque ranches and impressive mountain and desert scenery. Hall found out who owned each piece of property and who could give permission for its use. Hall persuaded local businessmen to cater to the movie makers by supplying any unlikely item at any unlikely time. He knew the "right" people in Hollywood and kept them reminded of Tucson by gifts of steaks cut from champion steers. He offered privacy or publicity, as they wished when they stayed at his hotel. The big payoff for his efforts came in 1939 when Columbia Pictures came to build the Old Tucson movie set for the film *Arizona*. All of this brought recognition to Nick Hall, the Santa Rita, and, of course, to Barney Goodman, the owner of the Santa Rita Hotel.

Goodman's entry into Tucson was important and helped improve our economy when the town was suffering badly. The entertainment at the Santa Rita hotel boosted the morale of the community.

Old Tucson's Mayor Nick Hall died in Long Beach, California, on December 23rd, 1960, with his boots on.

An ornate document bearing the Seal of the State of Arizona signed by former Gov. Robert Jones and dated October 1st, 1939, proclaimed him Mayor of Old Tucson.

On June 2nd, 1934, three faiths joined in the fight against film content. The Tucson Diocese acted in the drive against indecent pictures. Protesting vigorously against block booking and listing eight recent movies as "violating the producers" own code of decency," the Tucson diocese joined a national movement to clean up motion pictures.

Bishop Gercke says, "the Catholic Church has been on the liberal side of the amusement question. We have not opposed, for example, baseball or theatrical performances on Sunday. We are not supporters of blue laws. We encourage clean, wholesome recreation at all times for our people and shall continue to do so." He did not condemn theatre owners because their hands were tied by blind blocking and other producers' practices. (Blind blocking was selling a group of films as a block, with no choice as to the movies included).

Decency pledges have been sent around the state and were signed by more than 100,000 Catholics.

Starting on July 14th, 1935, newsreels were shown, shot in the South West by Jack McFarland. He filmed fourteen scenes in the last eight months for national distribution. Each release went to an audience of 35 million theatergoers. Filming included a large cattle round-up at Gil Brothers Ranch in Sasabe (Universal), Wild horses crossing the border at Sasabe and Naco, Arizona (Paramount), Notre Dame University stops for practice at the University of Arizona. Also shown were Japanese farmers bombed at Salt River Valley, the Robles Kidnapping arrest, and "Ghost Town Comes to Life..., Tombstone, Arizona (Paramount).

A Hollywood troupe of approximately 75 actors and technicians, headed by Nino Martini, singing star, and Ruben Mamoulian, director, arrived in Tucson, July 24th, 1936. He began filming local exterior scenes for The Gay Desperado, a modern Mexican gangster story set somewhere below the international border. The company filmed four scenes in the Mexican quarter, with activities centering on South Myers Street at the old Royal Theater, the side of which has been done over by the company's carpenters and painters to represent the world cinema house in Mexico. Desert exteriors were filmed on-site near San Xavier Mission and Northeast Tucson, near the Catalina foothills base.

The company's production schedule called for a six-day stay here, but a fortnight would be consumed if the heat slowed down work. Martini is featured in the story as a singer kidnapped by Braganza, the music-loving bandit leader, played by Leo Carrillo (when the Cisco Kid moved to television, Leo Carrillo played the part of Pancho). Braganza later kidnaps a honeymooning American couple (Ms. Lupino and James Blakely), and from there on, the plot thickens.

San Xavier Mission was again in the spotlight in *The Gay Desperado*, a gangster/Mexican bandito comedy starring Ida Lupino that also boasts tantalizing glimpses of our barrio streets. They shot other scenes on South Meyer Street and The Cactus Forest (in the Tucson Mountains). The New York Times Film Critics Circle named Rouben Mamoulian the best director of the year for *The Gay Desperado*. Among the cast was Chris-Pin Martin, who was born in 1893 on Meyer Street in Tucson. His given name was Ysabel Ponciana Chris-Pin Martin Piaz. He was described as a "Dark-complexioned, roly-poly comic actor in Hollywood films of the 30s, 40s and early 50s, in whose 80-or-so screen appearances he usually speaks in a fractured Mexican accent."

Downtown Tucson during the filming of "The Gay Desperado". 1932
(Author's Collection)

A Paramount unit arrived Monday, June 12th, 1938, and Coast Studio would film a Zane Grey story in Tucson. Transported from Hollywood in circus-style, a company of motion picture actors and technicians in addition to three carloads of equipment arrived in Tucson. On Tuesday, June 12th, 1938, the company started producing *The Mysterious Rider* by Zane Grey. Harry Sherman, producer of the Hopalong Cassidy pictures, would make the Paramount and Leslie Selander's movie, who will direct it. The location for a sizable amount of the movie is in the Cactus Forest just west of the Tucson Mountains. The site was later chosen for the location of Old Tucson.

The Saguaro Forest west of Tucson near the present
location of Old Tucson. 1939 (Bob's Collection)

CHAPTER TWO:
The Building and Filming of Arizona

What was to be later named Kinney Road was first developed as the Old Mile Wide Copper Company Road in November 1922. On December 30, the road was designated County Road #62.

In 1939, Pima County Supervisors leased Columbia Pictures County Road #62 running from Ajo Way to Tucson Mountain Park with a stipulation that no plants along the side of the right of way would be harmed.

A lot of wild horses roamed the hills and valleys adjacent to County Road #62. It is hard to tell where they all came from, but at least one rancher with a spread near the base of "A" Mountain would round them up occasionally to sell off for use as dog food.

Within the park, a Preventorium (Established in 1936 it could handle about 130 children. In the summer, the children were moved to a health camp in Oracle) continued to care for children taken from homes with members stricken by tuberculosis.

In 1943, unpaved County Road #62 was officially named Kinney Road on topographic maps, after J.C. Kinney, Chairman of the County

Board of Supervisors from 1931-1932. The unpaved road, later to be called Gates Pass Road, was named Saguaro Forest Road. Traveling this road was slow going but a scenic route to Tucson Mountain Park and the mining prospects that dot the mountainsides. It crossed over Gates Pass, named for a local miner, Thomas Gates.

Wesley Ruggles, the Academy Award-winning director of the western film classic, *Cimarron,* in 1930, was looking for another script when he ran across the story, "Arizona." The novel "Arizona" was first published in book form by Harper Brothers in1939 and promoted as the extraordinary story of the girl who made pies, money, and American history along with the promise of excitement, romance, and adventure. The book immediately found its way into the hands of an eager reading public. It was also serialized in the Saturday Evening Post.

Inspired by the book's strength, it gave the men of Columbia Pictures confidence to convince Harry Cohn (head of Columbia Pictures) to take a chance with over $2 million and consider filming the movie well outside the studio backlot boundaries.

"The walls, like the buildings inside, were of adobe. They formed a square enclosing a space equivalent to a modern city block. At the corners were towers. The general appearance was like some of the old American colonial frontiers' log stockades, and the original purpose was similar, protection from the Indians," as the book describes Tucson.

The "Arizona" story, by Clarence Buddington Kelland, told of Tubac and Tucson's early days.

The first chore was to locate a spot on which to reproduce the town of old Tucson as a replica of Tucson in the 1860s. Ten officials of Columbia Studio came to Tucson from Hollywood to look over southern Arizona for a possible location on which to shoot the movie. According to information from Hollywood, if "we find nothing suitable around Tucson for a location, we shall look around Phoenix. Should a spot around Tucson be deemed appropriate for filming a story about Tucson, then the company will be put on location, and shooting will start in early September".

Wesley Ruggles, an early time film actor, found his way to the director's chair in 1918 and learned his craft in the silent days. He successfully transitioned to sound films, as evidenced by his receiving an Academy Award for directing *Cimarron* (1931). Director Leslie Celander had most recently traveled to the Saguaro Forest west of Tucson by way of Gates Pass and down the long winding dirt road. He found inspiration to film *Mysterious Rider,* the screen version of the 1921 Zane Grey book that was filmed just to the north and east of what would later become Old Tucson Studios. They came to the intersection of County Road #62 and The Saguaro Forest Road and found the town site's ideal spot.

The first chore for the producers of *Arizona* was to come to Tucson and verify the story's accuracy to know from who to get permission to use the characters. Some months prior, the studio sent members of its research department to Tucson to work at the Arizona Pioneer Historical Society, securing photographs of the Tucson and Tubac pioneers who Kelland names in his novel. They also checked historical material and made photographs of significant quantities of old pictures of buildings in both cities.

Jim Pratt, the construction supervisor, oversaw the building. He said that it will require five or six weeks and that the shooting should start in September.

Columbia Pictures paid Kelland $52,000 in cash for the script, with $30,000 more to come on the movie's release date. The set's construction was the largest building project of adobe in the world, requiring an estimated 250,000 adobe bricks. Columbia's art director Lanell Banks, who designed the set, spent many months looking into the source material to create a scale model. Following the set design, Jim Pratt, Columbia's construction superintendent, was given a 40-day construction schedule to build the half-million-dollar background investment plan by Columbia. Blueprints that Pratt received weighed 36 pounds and covered 1600 ft.^{2} of plyboard.

On top of the 250,00 adobe bricks, they also needed a hundred thousand feet of sawed lumber, 2000 long poles of Spruce, 150 telephone poles for beamed ceilings, 3000 eucalyptus polls, 1,042 mesquite poles for tomatoes, 20,000 feet of Ocotillo branches for corral fences. Also, thousands of feet of water pipes, concrete for reservoirs, tons of gravel, tons of cement to lay the adobe bricks, pressure and storage tanks, gallons of paint, and tons of plaster. They needed dozens of trucks, tractors, graders, and buses to haul workers and prepare the building site.

The company built the town utilizing 300 union workers laboring under pressure to make the buildings complete inside and out. The set would be shot from every angle on the ground and above. A few buildings far away would only have three sides covered with plaster casts made from existing Adobe walls and rock houses. Some buildings would have movable roofs so interiors could be shot. In addition to finished interiors for dressing rooms for the cast, for equipment storage, mess halls, and mechanic quarters. There were no flimsy temporary wooden structures on the lot.

Work on the set, which besides calling for the construction of an entire city, also calls for drilling a well. Pratt said, "The set will be one of the six largest ever built outside of Hollywood, and the technical costs alone will be around $100,000".

Columbia leased the county-owned site for $10 and gave a check to the Pima County Preventorium for $600.

Contracts would be signed for grading of the site and possibly for the making of the adobes. Columbia sent Tucson a Technicolor cameraman to take sample shots of adobe buildings and the surrounding scenery (since money was tight, the movie would be shot in black and white).

Work on the church enclosure. 1939 (Bob's Collection)

They had two possible sites within 12 miles of Tucson, and on one or the other, the company would build Phoebe's house, barns, corrals, and other structures described in Kelland's story.

Workers laying bricks on one of the buildings. 1939 (Bob's collection)

The 82 buildings, all Spanish colonial style, were authentic duplicates of Tucson's town's original structures. They include a mission, civic offices, homes, stores, saloons, granaries, stables, stage depot, and corrals. Early maps of Tucson were followed closely to layout the walled city and the houses built outside the wall and along the Arroyo that ran through the town.

Jean Arthur was cast as Phoebe Titus, the central person of the Kelland story. Her character ran a freight line around Tucson and often did her own bull whacking and was strong-minded, fearless. Phoebe dominated even the bad men of Tucson. She meets and falls in love with Peter Muncy (William Holden), a Union Army soldier. She fights against Southern sympathizers and crooked businessmen.

Wesley Ruggles, producer and director of the picture, said he had invited Stephen Ochoa of Tucson to "play the part of his grandfather as he was in real life."

These "good citizens" of Tucson will include Stephen Ochoa, Solomon Warner, the Ouray Brothers, Charles Poston, and Pete kitchen. Mr. Jameson had the job of arranging for all of Pima, Tohono O'Odham, and Apaches, who would work in the picture and all the costumes.

Jamison had already arranged with the San Carlos Reservation Indian Agent for 100 Apaches to be transported to Tucson. He would go back to Fort Apache to cast more Indians. He had already arranged for 50 Tohono O'Odham and Pima Indian basket and pottery makers. A technical expert on Apaches will be on hand during the shooting to ensure every detail of costume, horsemanship, and appearance is accurate.

Approximately 500 extras would be used and paid three dollars per day. The extras were transportation to and from the set, and each given lunch while on location. Jean Anderson, unit manager, gave September 15th as a probable date for the beginning of the work in which the extras will be used. The company sought pioneer types, such as miners, ranchers, gamblers, and teamsters. They were also hiring Mexican, Tohono O'Odham, and Pima Indian families, including children of all ages.

Principally wanted were ox team drivers and other characters of old Tucson. The interviews were conducted in a store building at Fifth Avenue and Congress Street, rented by the studio.

The largest family ever hired to work in motion pictures was signed by producer/director Wesley Ruggles for Columbia's *Arizona*, which went into production the following week. The script contains a scene that calls for the presence of a large family group.

The Ochoa clan numbered Ochoa, his wife, and 20 children; however, two of his sons could not report for work in the picture because they had jobs. Each member would be paid prevailing extras wages whenever they worked, and the combined income would be $60 a day. The company would hire the main characters during the building of the town.

George Cole had been in and out of Tucson seeking the livestock and rolling equipment needed for the film, most of which he says has already been secured. Some of the freighting wagons Phoebe commanded were already on location in Tucson. Some of the ore wagons owned by the Tucson Rodeo Association were used and possibly other pieces of equipment, all of which Cole photographed for future reference. Livestock has already been moved into the extensive corrals a quarter of a mile beyond the Old Tucson set.

The livestock and rolling equipment department has bought 104 head of oxen and brought in from Gallegos, Chihuahua, Mexico. These have been broken and worked with yokes, but they must be broken to neck reining in the next three weeks. Six men each have been assigned to six pairs for teams to draw covered wagons, schooners, and freight wagons. Five old-time bull whackers, the oldest being 76 years old, have been hired. Cole finally obtained the 54 pieces of rolling equipment needed.

Also wrangled up by Cole were 300 head of horses and 500 cattle. They contracted for 10 tons of stock feed daily, and the daily feed bill ran $125. He lined up a score of Razorback hogs and enough goats but complained of the lack of buzzards for rent. Because old towns had many stray dogs, the movie paid a year's tax and license on all dogs in the dog pound and let them roam free. After the filming was complete, Ms. Arthur raffled the dogs off to Tucson kids, paying three years of the license fee and a year's food supply.

The studio paid labor scales, and negotiations gave stock wranglers a boost in wages.

Signs of impending labor trouble between the Studio Transportation Drivers' Union of Hollywood and the Columbia Pictures made the film *Arizona* better the working conditions stock wranglers and drivers. Wranglers received $.75 per hour for eight hours with time and a half for overtime, or wranglers received $7.50 a day, with no time allowance considered if the studio pays board and room as well. That union men (fully qualified) received preference for the wranglers and drivers' jobs. The construction of a commissary and dormitory to take care of from 70 to 100 men handling stock.

The County Board of Supervisors agreed to cooperate to solve the traffic problem created by the spectators. The county will establish "no parking" zones immediately passing the filming location, perhaps grading out a parking lot further down the road. Highway Patrol would patrol Kinney Road during congested times.

With all the personnel, livestock, and contracts are taken care of, it was time to get down to building the set. The 300 laborers, 180 carpenters, 120 adobe workers split into two shifts and working under art and construction superintendents from Columbia Studios were in place, and the clock started running. The construction job would proceed at top speed for six weeks, but construction would not be completed when Wesley Ruggles started shooting the spectacular epic. The building would continue right through the production of the movie. The picture covers four hectic years in Arizona's early story.

Well and water storage during construction. 1939 (Bob's collection)

The first job was to drill a well to have water available during construction and be on hand while filming. The well was put down at the cost of $12,000. The location needed to pump 1000 gallons of water per hour, and the well hit water at 210 feet. Pratt thought it might go down to at least 300 feet unless they find that there are some unusual geologic formations at the greater depth, which will give us an even larger flow of water.

Pratt said, "We're going to need a lot of water to keep the arroyo in constant flow during the shooting of the film. We will also have several artificial rain scenes, water about 100 head of cattle, and provide water for several hundred persons during the picture's filming. The following week, the film company moved between 7000 and 10,000 gallons of water hauling tanks to the location for construction work and workman. The company also had put-up temporary storage and pressure tanks until the well could be permanently counted upon. Pratt estimated that the daily requirements of the company were 20,000 gallons of water.

View of Calle Real showing cattle coming into Tucson. 1940
(Author's collection)

A 900-foot stretch of the Calle Real, the old Main Street of Tucson, was built entirely, with 11 or 12 haphazardly intersecting cross-streets. The old walled quarter of the original presidio built by Spanish soldiery in 1776 dominated one-quarter of the set. Its walls 12 feet high and 2 feet thick in a square 288 by 288 feet were constructed entirely of adobe brick, as were all the pueblo's 82 buildings. With 50 men working on a building, they went up at a rate of one house per 2 hours and 45 minutes.

None of the adobes made by the thousands and used in the set could be made on the site because of the water and soil type. They are being manufactured elsewhere and hauled to the location by truck and putting them into place at dizzy speed.

The workers cleared the area of underbrush and the streets laid out and graded. That entailed the moving of some giant saguaros and the elimination of many other species of cactus.

A river was constructed and then was watered by the most intricate series of dams and pumps imaginable. The company lined the riverbed, so there was no loss of water from the seepage. Out of sight beyond the town was the water tank with a water drop high enough to give the river water a good fall. The 35,000-gallon cement tank had a check dam with spillways. The water was pumped from the well the company dug and up into the dam where the water can flow down the river and then reused. As the water flowed along, it reflected trees and shrubs which seemed to naturally grow out of the bank that the green goods man planted. But after the water has traversed the river's length, it will run into a catch basin where pumps picked it up and sent it back uphill into the cement dam. Before the well supplying sufficient water, Columbia had been hauling some to 30,000 gallons a day from Tucson.

Summer storms were created by the hoses of the company's 52-year-old steam fire engine. Once used by the Los Angeles Fire Department, the fire engine was put in use on the outdoor set because it was less noisy than modern pumping equipment; and because smoking exhaust fumes might drift in front of the cameras, thus ruining the film. The antique red boiler anchored in desert sand supplied the steam pressure necessary to send the rain to all standpipes, which were placed out of camera range on each side of the location over which the rain was supposed to fall.

Costumers were already working on dressing hundreds of cast members into miners, gamblers, Tohono O'Odham, Mexicans, United States dragoons, Confederates and California volunteers, stagecoach drivers, merchants, and vaqueros.

Pratt delivered the set to Frank Tittle, head set dresser, who put in old furniture, dishes, Faro tables, dry goods, chili peppers for

Phoebe Titus's store and the thousands of items that tell by themselves whether the building would be a bedroom, store, saloon, commandant's quarters, or ranch living room.

The greens men planted trees and to see that gardens and fields flourish. The horticultural Department made sure the trees, shrubs, and plants grew adjacent to the 725-foot-long arroyo built through the city. Water from the 50,000-gallon tank and cement reservoir kept them alive during weeks of filming.

Also built was one of the biggest indoor cooling systems ever installed in southern Arizona. Al Franklin, head electrician for Columbia Pictures, designed and superintended its installation. Five huge fans were placed on the set and blew through water filters circulating moist air over the re-created set. The buildings were air-conditioned during the time needed to film *Arizona* and cool the special trailer and dressing room for Jean Arthur.

Construction of the old Tucson set was begun July 22nd, 1939, only to be stopped when war broke out in Europe on September 7th, 1939. The war greatly affected European film markets, making the proper exploitation of the proposed two-million-dollar production impossible, studio officials said. Columbia recalled the studio personnel in Tucson, except for a few men who remained here to take care of the storing of properties. Also, to safeguard the $150,000 copy of old Tucson erected in the Tucson Mountain Park area 15 miles west of town.

According to the announcement, the picture would go into production as soon as world conditions permit expending the vast sum of money needed to film the epic about the Old Pueblo.

George Cole, studio animal man, would remain here to see that the livestock purchased for the production were adequately cared for. The unused *Arizona* set built by Columbia Pictures Corporation for the filming of C.B. Kelland's historical romance of the same name was open to public inspection from 6 AM to 6 PM daily. People were welcomed to visit the movie locale. Three watchmen were maintained on the set.

The following March, the film was again on, and the motion picture company had returned to Arizona.

Old Tucson was officially dedicated in March, with a colorful ceremony in which Governor Jones and approximately 20 mayors of Arizona cities would participate. Set aside as "Ruggles Arizona Day," festivities began with a luncheon at which Nick Hall, "Mayor of Old Tucson," was still the host of the Santa Rita hotel opening with "The Star-Spangled Banner." At the luncheon, the highlight was to present a key to the city to Wesley Ruggles, producer-director of Columbia's *Arizona*, by Governor Jones. Following the luncheon, studio buses conveyed the guests through Gates Pass to tour the old Tucson set. At Lazarus Ward's saloon, Governor Jone's daughter cut a tape stretched across the quaint street.

The first scene in *Arizona* was filmed in Rattlesnake Canyon, 22 miles from Tucson in Saguaro National Forest. Peter Muncie (Holden) leading an oxen train to a pass when he sees Tucson in the valley below. The director set up a camera on a mountain ridge for a distance shot.

To communicate, director Ruggles resorted to smoke signals. Ruggles was able to send messages with the help of a 90-year-old Pima Indian.

In one scene, William Holden saved a Tohono O'Odham from a stampede. Holden was not permitted to participate in a planned stampede of cattle by Indians. He watched while a group of Indians started to stampede the herd (500 cows and 100 Indians). The Indians drove the cattle towards a camera mounted on top of a bus. The Indians charged into the cattle, firing rifles, causing the cattle to stampede. Three Indians were thrown from their horses. Two got up and ran, but the third was injured and could not get up. Holden rode thru the cattle and stood guard over the Indian, Juan Gomez. Gomez was treated at St. Mary's hospital for a fractured shoulder.

When Old Tucson's United States Post Office opened, it was the first to be granted to a movie location. The entire company took a half-day off for the grand pageant through Tucson's downtown streets depicting the state mail transportation history. A rider decked out as a cowboy delivered two big copper letters to the post office on horseback. Unique commemorative postcards were issued with a first-day postmark.

Envelope with Old Tucson postmark. 1940 (Author's collection)

Most every Saturday night, they had a big birthday party and dance for some member of the company, to which Ms. Arthur and her husband, Frank Ross, always came down from their desert ranch to share the fun.

After two weeks of rehearsals, the entire company staged a hilarious variety show for its entertainment.

On another evening, the entire company captured the Tucson ballpark to show the town how not to play baseball. Jean Arthur pitched, William Holden was the catcher, and 30 bearded actors played center field. Over two thousand Tucsonans showed up for the game.

Jean Arthur donated to just about every charity in Tucson, such as the undernourished children's milk fund, to which she gave $500.

"By mid-June, all filming at Old Tucson was completed, and the company moved to Sabino Canyon for work at the Phoebe Titus Hacienda, constructed at the Double U Guest Ranch."

For the week leading up to the movie's premiere showing, on November 15th, 1940, all of Tucson turned out to celebrate. It was somewhat roughly estimated that the Tucson population grew by ten thousand people. Nick Hall was in his element, hosting parties, consorting with big shots from the studio, and generally responsible for making sure everyone had a splendid time.

For the world premiere of *Arizona,* Tucson threw a Menudo party for the whole town. A Tohono O'Odham Indian village was constructed on Congress St. The Hollywood Studio sent a "cracker Jack" press agent. A second Menudo luncheon was set for the Pioneer Hotel. As a practical joke pulled on the press agent during luncheon, a cow eye was put into his bowl. He left in a hurry, not to return.

Pima County Sheriff Ed Echols was busy passing out fancy badges and certificates to who every looked important, including the very popular radio star, Kate Smith.

One of the events was a contest to see who was related most closely to Tucson pioneers. They received their awards on Wednesday. The ten descendants of early Tucsonans are named in the movie *Arizona*. Winners get an original copy of the book "Arizona" signed by Jean Arthur, C.B Kelland, and William Holden. They also received free tickets to the premiere courtesy of Columbia Studios.

The list:

H.S. Corbet – Grandson of Sam Hughes
Theodore Cooper Treat – Grandson of Sam Hughes
Solomon Warner – Grandson of Solomon Warner
Steven Ochoa – Grandson of Estevan Ochoa
Albert Warner – Grandson of Solomon Warner
Mrs. Nellie E. West – Granddaughter of Pete Kitchen
Mrs. Emma Brumbaugh – Granddaughter of Pete Kitchen
Josephine O. Warner – Granddaughter of Solomon Warner

Mail being delivered to Old Tucson Post Office. 1940 (Bob's collection)

The week passed quickly with all the celebrations, and Friday, November 15th, arrived soon enough. The premiere was held at the State Theatre. But due to demand, the film was also screened at the Lyric, Fox, Rialto, and Temple of Music.

The next day, all the glamour was gone. All the movie stars had fled back to Hollywood, and out of town guests headed home. Tucson was once again a quiet, sleepy little town. But this was only the first big-time brush with Hollywood. In the years to come, Tucson would host many films and movie stars.

Shortly after June 18th, 1940, Columbia packed its equipment in trucks and headed to the railroad. The livestock was auctioned off, and the stray dogs headed to their new homes.

Quiet descended on the ruins of Old Tucson. Because of World War II, the county did not have the funds to repair or maintain the set. Periodic visitors to the location found the roofs caved in and wood door frames missing. Kids had started to use the site for parties.

Phoebe Titus delivering cattle and supplies to Tucson. 1940
(Bob's collection)

CHAPTER THREE:
The Early Years of Old Tucson

From the end of filming *Arizona* in 1940 until 1946, there was little or no effort to preserve Old Tucson from the ravages of sun, wind, and rain. Old Tucson did have some support from the local community. Still, the Pima County Board of Supervisors stated, "there is insufficient money in the current budget to keep Old Tucson repaired.

The Civilian Conservation Corps (CCC) worked in the area and had trouble with washouts on the roads. By the end of 1941, Kinney road received paving.

Nick Hall was confirmed Mayor of Old Tucson by proclamation of the governor for what it was worth. The local Boy Scout Council started utilizing the ruined set for camping and training in pit cooking and first aid.

During this time, one movie was filmed, which had an impact on Old Tucson. On February 22nd, 1942, the movie *Apache Trail* began filming in Star Pass on the Tucson Mountains west side. The story was one in which Apache Indians attack a remote stage station. The Apaches found housing at Old Tucson during production.

The site of Old Tucson stood on state land. So, Arizona put the area up for sale at $3.00 per acre plus $135,000 in "improvements." There were no bidders, so the county bought the land for $1.25 per acre on September 24th, 1941. They already owned the buildings, so there was no improvement charged in the sale. By May of 1942, the county-owned the patent on the land. When Columbia's lease ran out in 1944 on the 320-acre site, they chose not to use their option and did not renew the contract. Control of the land was then passed back to the county.

In 1944, so the legend goes, Rainbow Productions came to the movie set to film a scene for *Bells of St. Mary's*. There is no mention of this in the local paper, nor does any extant film match Old Tucson. However, the tradition of the studios lists this film from the earliest film lists. Another clue is that Sister Benedict (Ingrid Bergman) contracts tuberculosis and transfers to Tucson, one of the popular locales, to send patients to get the "cure." If that is the case, cutting this scene would have shortened the movie. I leave it up to the reader to decide which scenario is correct.

By 1946, the movie set was in poor condition, with just about all roofs fallen in, and the weather had ravaged the adobe bricks. However, the public still showed up to see the ruins. Enough so that the Junior Chamber of Commerce noticed and thought this would be a good community project. "We needed something to do," Explained John Alexander, whose Jaycee organization had sponsored attractions at old Tucson during the premiere of *Arizona*.

They approached the Pima County Board of Supervisors with a plan to repair Old Tucson and open it up to visitors. They came up with an agreement for a lease at $1 per year on a five-year term. The provisions of the contract included the following items:

1. the lease is to be for five years

2. the property not sublet

3. no intoxicating liquor was to be consumed or sold

4. the property shall be maintained and operated for the benefit of the public at all times

5. Pima County reserves the right to supervise and control the said property's use for the entire term of the lease.

6. No admission fee to be charged. However, Old Tucson could place a donation box in a prominent spot. That all funds raised this way would be invested back into the set.

Junior Chamber of Commerce workers restoring one of the buildings in 1946.
(Bob Shelton collection)

The first thing the Jaycees did was to form committees and divide up the projects. The weekly work was mandatory, with everyone pitching in their abilities. "The work was continuous," said Herb Bloom, another J.C., "We'd do one building. Go on to the next."

They had their work cut out for them. Porches sagged, doors and window frames were missing, and walls were collapsing. They used several contractors who were members to put in thousands of dollars in underground wiring and put in pit toilets.

The J.C.'s needed to find a solution to reduce the dust kicked up by workers and visitors. At first, several gas stations saved up their crankcase oil for spreading on the streets. This amount of crankcase oil was not enough, so they asked every station in the city to save their oil.

On August 20th, 1946, the Preventorium closed, and the Jaycees salvaged building materials to use at Old Tucson.

Members felt that more attractions were needed to draw people to the set, so they planned several new activities. The Jaycettes (women's branch of the Jaycees) would dress up and perform can-can shows. The men formed the Tucson Vigilantes and performed gunfight shows. On Sunday evenings, they held square dances open to everyone. Also, a few concessions opened on the weekends.

The J.C.'s established a sign-in book, and considering only about half the visitors would sign the register, they still had about 3,000 people through the park in February alone.

Advertisement for the Annual "Old Tucson Fiesta" held in conjunction with the annual Tucson Rodeo. c.1950 (Az Daily Star)

The committee came up with an idea to hold an annual event and approached the Supervisors with the concept. They accepted, and a nominal entry fee could be charged. In the fall of 1947, the Jaycees threw the town-wide open with a fall fiesta called "Old Tucson Daze," complete with souvenir shops, refreshments, and entertainment. Among the latter: can-can girls who looked suspiciously like Jaycee wives and Dr. I. Killum, who looked suspiciously like John Alexander. Fixing the town up a little more and throwing another fiesta became the pattern for years to come. "The Jaycees did all the shows, the stunts, and made their costumes," says Alexander. Despite this, the Old Tucson site continued in a general state of disrepair caused by a lack of manpower and funds, which could not keep pace with the location's maintenance logistics.

On September 25th, 1946, the Junior Chamber of Commerce named Ted Capon as "Mayor of Old Tucson." Nick Hall was appointed as mayor by Gov. Robert Jones's direction and was upset by Capon's appointment. Declaring Hall as mayor caused a small controversy over the mayorship, which had a lot of tongue-in-the-cheek rivalry. Mayor Capon accused Nick hall of not doing anything to improve old Tucson.

Gene Autry severed his association with Republic pictures in 1947 and went over to Columbia. Using cattle stampede stock footage from the movie *Arizona*, a film crew came to Old Tucson for a few weeks in May and June 1947 to film *The Last Roundup*. The story focuses on Autry 's effort to keep the peace between the ranchers and the Indians. He was trying to strike a deal to provide a needed canal for the future growth of Bay City. There was a significant discontinuity during the stampede scene. The Indians appeared in the costumes from the movie *Arizona*. In contrast, the *Roundup* costumes were considerably different and were of another tribe. The film cost approximately $300,000.

Autry used four different horses, depending on the scene. Champion Junior was his favorite. Other sites used were Rattlesnake Pass and San Xavier Mission.

The Chapel Tower bell for *The Last Roundup* filming belonged to Rev. Victor Stoner of St. John the Evangelist Church. He allowed using the 100-pound bell in exchange for help putting the bell up in St. John's bell tower when filming finished.

The movie company was charged $60 a day for the use of the facility. The supervisors were upset about charging the movie company; they were afraid that charging the movie company would scare them away. Eventually, cooler heads prevailed, and the Board OK'd the same fee on any future movie companies. This fee was an infusion of money that was desperately needed to help maintain the town. By August 1947, one store, a "saloon," was open on the weekends (it served soda pop).

The J.C.'s built a dance platform, and other concessions were in the works. They decided to break down the fiesta into three parts: Indian fair, Mexican Fiesta, and cowboy entertainment. They scheduled a celebration for November 15th and 16th. The Hopi Indians were to dance, and the Tohono O'Odham and Yaquis planned to help.

As the Old Tucson Daze approached, the theme chosen would be Tucson in the 1860s. The Vigilantes would hold the gunfights and stunts while the Jaycees would run a bank and exchange money for Old Tucson Daze Bucks, which would be good at all concessions. The fiesta would end each day with a real wedding in the town's Mission.

The Jaycees gave the festival nationwide publicity by releasing a story and pictures to 144 leading newspapers.

Advertisement for Indian Dancing put on by the Boy Scouts at Old Tucson.
c.1950 (Az Daily Star)

The concessions in operation would include Mexican food, barbeque, and souvenirs. Herget's Indian Trading Post opened and was in service during the fiesta.

Capt. Rudy Black of the city fire department was the fiesta Fire Chief and had charge of all bonfires; he wore a fireman's uniform of the "roaring 60s."

Visitors could have themselves photographed in Western clothing and armed to the teeth at the picture concession.

The committee met at the Santa Rita Hotel to hold some conversations with the manager, Nick Hall, who was still the honorary mayor of Old Tucson. The Jaycees now recognized his title, which seems to have become rather generally known.

To make for less traffic and convenience for visitors, Tucson Rapid Transit and the Occidental Bus Line ran buses from downtown to Old Tucson on both days. The fare would be $.35 one way or $.50 for a round trip.

A cowboy swing band provided the music on Saturday, and a five-piece Mexican group provided entertainment on Sunday. It was encouraged that people who are attending to dress in costume.

The union, Local 415 A T SE, which included technicians who worked on *Arizona*, adopted the stage depot to fix up.

Another idea from the committee was to have a parade downtown to celebrate the fiesta. Women and children paraded before the estimated 15,000 persons jam-packed downtown Tucson streets on Saturday, the 15th. They were leading what was probably one of the city's shortest, but not dullest, parade.

Applause from the crowds which overflowed from Congress Street sidewalks and hovered over rooftops to get as close a look as possible at the line of horses and wagons. Behind the posse came a battered old stagecoach, bulging at the seams with bearded and armed vigilantes, looking, no doubt, for that "Wild Bunch," which rode up from Tombstone to "case the joint." Tombstonians, just as bearded and heavily armed as their Tucson rivals, were little further back where they could keep an eye peeled for trouble.

Girls from the square dance clubs strutted down the street, flashing bright smiles to match their riotous silk dresses as their horses followed the leaders. Amid assorted war whoops, beating drums, and jingling bells came a dancing troupe of Indians. Accompanying them was a high chief, who, between native dances, introduced himself as Chief Chiuhugha, better known as just plain old Ed Jones. The "Indians," said the sign carried by the boy in front, were from the Explorers Troupe of the Boy Scouts.

Of course, there were the covered wagons and the old family buggies, with the father carrying the six-shooter, mom holding the parasol, and Junior holding a wicked-looking popgun, just in case.

The festivities moved to Old Tucson, where everyone pitched in for the annual outdoor bonfire dance, a special event for the first night activities. Sunday's activities included a four-hour variety show in the outdoor arena. The program included an old-fashioned melodrama, Western music, and skits. At noon, the Vigilantes and Indians would fight it out with a baseball game, giving way to six-gun and hatchets before the ninth inning. The Jayceettes wound up the affair with a western dance. The only problems with the best-laid plans, the Sunday of the fiesta, was rained out. A successful attempt to restage the event occurred on November 23rd.

The 1946 "Old Tucson Daze" would be the first of 14 celebrations until 1960. Also, the Jaycees would sponsor the official opening of the visitor season, just after Christmas.

The Board of Supervisors gave the OK for the Jaycees to charge admission during Old Tucson Daze. Adults cost $.50, and children charged $.25.

A headcount of 2000 people attended on Saturday and twice that number on Sunday. Prof. I. Killum and his Medicine Show, square and round dancing, included the Jayceettes putting on pantomime plays and can-can shows. The big show was a mass shootout between the Tucson Vigilantes (Jaycees) and the Tombstone Vigilantes.

By 1959 the following concessions were open for business on "Four Flags Days" (renamed this from Old Tucson Daze, to signify the four different national flags which flew over Tucson):

A Can-Can show sponsored by Old Tucson. c.1948 (Bob's collection)

Western Arts and Skills (copper and tin gifts)
Ward's Saloon (cold drinks)
Phoebe's Pie Shop
Chuck Wagon
Stage Depot

Buggy Wheel Trading Post (silver novelties)

Film Is Busy Needle Shop

Old Tucson Cactus Craft

Border Pete's (popcorn and peanuts)

Kerrigan Western Novelties

Old Tucson Assay Office

New Shooting Gallery

Lagos Cotton Candy

E. Bruce Wood Artist

Old Tucson sponsored an old-time fiddler contest on March 20th, 1948, followed on March 30th by a square dance contest attended by 2000 people. Square dancing had become a weekly Sunday night activity. By October, the Jaycees put in a concrete pad for dancing. Most Saturday nights, the Jaycees had a round dance with country music presented by local bands.

The registration book count was 6,000 visitors in March 1948.

The Jaycees periodically put out a newsletter, announcing activities going on at Old Tucson. The newsletter was entitled "Old Tucson Bull" and sent to hotels and tourist businesses around town as a form of advertisement.

On November 10th, 1949, the Jaycees refused to join the national organization. The national charter says anyone over a certain age was ineligible for membership, and the Tucson Jaycees did not want to lose anyone. They also had nominations for director and board members. The election would be during the "Daze" festivities.

Round dancing put on by Old Tucson. c.1948 (Bob's collection)

The need for a bell in the church steeple was solved when L.W. "Cat" Klene donated an old school bell.

In February 1950, Universal Studios began preparation to lens the final reel of *Winchester 73* at Old Tucson. On February 5th, actors and production crew arrived.

Scheduled to be shot on location in Utah and Nevada, but when the director was switched to Anthony Mann, the shooting location changed, and they filmed the last reel at Old Tucson. An old building in the town square was renamed and dressed as the "Bank of Tascosa." It is in this desert town that Stewart and Shelley Winters are reunited. The story involves Stewart winning a gun and having it stolen. He pursues the thief, and it all comes down to a final shootout in Rattlesnake Pass at the north end of the Tucson Mountains.

The Board of Supervisors granted the Jaycees a ten-year lease on the Old Tucson Site on February 8th, 1950.

On April 30th, 1950, the Jayceettes held a "Kiddie Jamboree" at old Tucson. Children performed all the entertainment. Dancing and games topped the bill.

Shortly after filming *Winchester 73*, October 12th, the movie *The Last Outpost* was filmed at Old Tucson, starred Ronald Reagan, Rhonda Fleming, and Bruce Bennett. The working title for this film was *The Apache Outpost*. It was based on a David Lang story and was initially released in May 1951 as *The Last Outpost*. The name changed to *Cavalry Charge* upon its re-release. It is the story of two brothers, one fighting for the North and one fighting for the South during the Civil War. Rhonda Fleming, whose love interest and opportunistic husband, deals guns and liquors to the Apaches. The two brothers reunite with the immediate threat of an Indian attack. For this movie, the producers added a second story to the "Warner's Store" (Presently Hotel Del Toro), and a wooden façade. The film employed about 75 Tucson Cowboys. The film company cleared a lot of brush and weeds from the set and updated several buildings, saving the Jaycees a lot of work.

The year 1950 saw a considerable amount of work put into the rehabilitation of buildings, upgrading the underground electric cable and upgraded the sewer system, adding a second bathroom. They managed to build a new jail building complete with a jail cell. Because of a lack of funds, a lot of the funds came out of the Jaycees pockets. They changed all the signs to reflect a 19th-century look, and they added a new museum to the existing concessions. It contained guns, saddles, and other western accouterments.

Plans for the village included installing water fountains and modern restrooms, new parking facilities, wooden sidewalks, and added fire protection. The Jaycees Governing Board hoped that the county would improve the roads leading to the area. They pointed out that such a project would also be an asset to the Trailside Museum in the Tucson Mountains (this would become the Arizona Sonora Desert Museum).

Three concessions were open every day, the remainder operating just on weekends. Open daily were Wards Saloon (where soft drinks and curios were available), the new Wagon Wheel Café (which served sandwiches and coffee), and The Western Photography Corral, where visitors can get their pictures taken. Concessions that opened on the weekends included Phoebe's Pie Shop (run by the Jayceettes), the Copper Shop (which specialized in copper work), and Calamity Jane's Indians Novelties. The Cactus Trading Post also opened (which had cactus lamps and other objects made of cactus), Popcorn, Pizza, the Cotton Candy Shop, and the territorial printers. The Jaycees pointed out that more concessions were always welcome. Activities included square dances held each Sunday outdoors. A Boy Scout troop planned teepee encampments on the premises.

The Jaycees began participating in Tucson's annual Rodeo Days. Their first function was a BBQ competition with Don Eddie of the "American Magazine" as a judge.

Starting in February 1951, the church would host Catholic Mass for several weeks to benefit residents and visitors.

On September 4th, 1951, a small movie company came to Old Tucson to film a project illustrating early California under Spanish rule entitled *The Scarlet Hawk*.

As a promotion of "Old Tucson Daze" on December 1st, 1951, special beer bottle labels were put on bottles sent throughout the Southwest. About 10,000 copies of the Old Tucson Bull were printed and sent to hotels and tourist attractions throughout New Mexico, Texas, and California. In anticipation of a high number of people attending, they expanded parking for an additional 2500 vehicles. Boy Scouts helped with parking. The numbers were much higher than expected at about 20,000 for the weekend. Parking spread out over the desert and along Kinney and Saguaro Roads. Due to a shortage of parking, many people did not get in.

The annual "Old Tucson Fiesta," in conjunction with "Fiesta De Las Vaqueros," presented Tucson's annual rodeo week and rodeo contests. It kicked off festivities with activities at the park. On February 17th, 1952, Bob McKeown and his ranch hands provided music for a round dance.

Tom Bailey Productions resumed filming *Draw When Ready* after the strike was over (it is unknown which strike this was). Three of the 13 half-hour films utilized old Tucson. No copies are known to exist.

The Southwestern Motion Picture and Television Production Company shot a T.V. western series called *Rawhide Riley*. It went into production on May 15th, 1952, and utilized Old Tucson and local ranches. It starred Richard Arlen, with Wayne Morris playing Rawhide Riley. By August 2nd, they had filmed seven episodes at the cost of $15,000 per episode.

On August 19th, 1953, gusty winds tore the roofs off several buildings at Old Tucson, and $2000 in goods were exposed to the rain and ruined.

Old Tucson's custodians were Mr. and Mrs. Joe Carruthers, the only occupants of the town.

A burglary at the Old Tucson jewelry shop occurred on September 25th, 1953. The thief stole an unknown amount of jewelry.

By the start of "Old Tucson Daze" on November 28th and 29th, 1953, Kinney Road to Old Tucson was paved, making the trip more comfortable. Approximately 5,000 people attended the festival.

That year, 1953, the toilets were of the flushing type. These toilets lowered the water level of the well from 88 feet to 150 feet.

The first full year, Old Tucson was open, 1946, 40,000 persons registered, and in 1953 that increased to 100,000 people. This figure is about one-half of the actual visitors to the park.

In April 1954, the film *10 Wanted Men* started production by Columbia Studios, starring Randolph Scott, Jocelyn Brando, and Richard Boone. The film was made under the title *The Violent Men* and should not be confused with the Glenn Ford movie the *Violent Men*, which started filming around this same time. The movie is about John Stewart (Scott), who gives refuge to Wick Campbell (Boone). Campbell kills Stewart's Brother, steals his cattle, and brings in a group of hired killers. Stewart then gets angry, runs the gang out of town, kills Campbell, and wins the girl. The cast and crew of *Ten Wanted Men* stayed at the Santa Rita Hotel and would be transported to Old Tucson by bus each day.

The Violent Men filmed the last of April 1954 and starred Glenn Ford, Barbara Stanwyck, and Edward G. Robinson. The movie centered on Lee Wilkinson trying to buy up or steal all the ranch land in the area. He tries to run Ex-union officer John Parrish (Ford) out of the territory. After the murder of one of his hired men, Parish decides to fight back. It was filmed at Old Tucson, Sabino Canyon, and the Tanque Verde Ranch.

The next movie in the queue, *Strange Lady in Town,* by MGM, started filming at the beginning of June 1954 and was a $2 million production. Greer Garson, Dana Andrews, and Cameron Mitchell star in this picture about a new female doctor in town. She eventually tames the other doctor, but his brother turns out to be a bad seed.

Construction for this movie included a two-story jail and a livery stable built in the space next to it. Enlarging the Assay Office, they also added a new porch put on the old Palace building. Also, the movie company built a hospital, home, and an old fashion, Mexican laundry. The church received a bigger bell, and part of the original presidio wall was rebuilt.

Sunday night, square dancing was put on hold for five months due to movie company construction. On October 1st, square dancing resumed.

The film *Backlash* began filming on June 18th, 1955. Starring: Richard Widmark and Donna Reed. Richard Widmark is searching for the only survivor of a massacre that killed his father. The survivor went for help but disappeared along with a lot of gold. Widmark is, in turn, tracked by several men trying to stop him. An incident occurred during filming when the stagecoach overturned, slightly injuring three people. The movie also used Rattlesnake Pass and an area north of Nogales.

In November 1955, Audie Murphy walked the dusty streets of Old Tucson for the first time. He portrayed legendary John P. Clum in the movie *Walk the Proud Land* for Universal Pictures. The book "Apache Agent," written by Woodworth Clum, is a biography of his famous father. It was one of the first productions to examine the poor treatment given to the Indians by the U.S. government in the late 1800s. *Walk the Proud Land* was filmed in Technicolor and entirely on location at Old Tucson. The movie starts on Clum's appointment as an Indian agent for the San Carlos Apache Reservation. In the end, he must confront and capture Geronimo. It starred Audie Murphy, Anne Bancroft, and Pat Crowley.

The third movie to be filmed in 1955 was *Broken Star*, starring: Howard Duff, Lita Barron, and Bill Williams. As a Deputy Sheriff, Howard Duff shoots and kills a man he claims was rustling cattle and drew on him first. The Sheriff investigates and finds that Duff stole $8000 in gold from the victim and then killed him to cover up the crime.

Starting the new year of 1956 was the filming of *Reprisal* starring Guy Madison, Felicia Farr, and Kathryn Grant. Frank Madden, a half breed, buys a ranch in an area where the whites are persecuting the Indians. The whites accused Madden of killing a rancher grazing cattle on Madden's land and marked him for a lynching.

Collier's magazine serialized a version of "The Petticoat Brigade," a novel by C William Harrison. The screen rights were secured, and the film shot while the story was still fresh in the readers' minds. Audie Murphy appeared at Old Tucson with director George Marshall to start shooting *The Guns of Fort Petticoat*.

The Mission got a new room by filling the arches on the north side of the building. Audie Murphy's character returned to his home in Texas to warn people of Indian hostilities. He finds that all the able-bodied men were out in the field, leaving only the women behind. When an Irish American cowboy, played by Sean McClory, stayed in town, he and Murphy organized and trained the women as soldiers to defend the old Mission. They hastily convert the Mission into a fort. Indians did eventually attack the Mission and were driven off by the women.

The filming locations included Old Tucson, Amado, and Arivaca, and filming took approximately three weeks.

On March 13th, 1956, filming started on *Conflict at the OK Corral* (released under *Gunfight at the OK Corral*). Filming locations included Elgin and the Empire Ranch.

At the time of the filming of *The Guns of Fort Petticoat*, Hal B. Wallace was in production, at Paramount, with director John Sturges for the movie *Gunfight at the OK Corral*. The film examined the relationship between the Gunfighters and the Cowboys from a different angle. It starred Kirk Douglas and Burt Lancaster. For the final shoot out in this movie, the first half filmed in a Paramount backlot, and the second half filmed in the streets of Old Tucson. Stuntman Bill Williams broke his right wrist doing a horse fall.

That year, the Jaycees launched a beauty queen contest for the "Four-Color Days" festivities on November 24th and 25th, 1956. This parade was the first year to allow motorized floats, which drew 60 entries. Color film footage was shot and shown on KVOA-TV (this is the first time a color television program was broadcasted in Tucson). They hosted a banquet at the sports center at 700 W. Congress.

Glenn Ford arrived in Tucson for filming *3:10 to Yuma*, which filmed at Old Tucson, Wilcox, Elgin, and Benson. Directed by Delmer Davis, it starred Glenn Ford and Van Heflin. Ford was offered the hero role in the movie; however, he chose the psychologically complex outlaw, and Van Heflin assumed the part of a supporting actor. At the same time, Felicia Farr became a romantic interest of Glenn Ford. A poor dirt farmer (Van Heflin), under pressure to raise money to save his farm, escorts a killer (Ford) to the town of Contention to catch a train to prison. Trouble follows him in the form of the killer's gang. This production was the third collaboration between Frankie

Laine and Ned Washington for a catchy title song on vinyl records and had plenty of radio play.

In January 1957, Joel McCrea filmed *Gunsight Ridge*, the story of the mysterious stranger who arrives in the town on a secret mission revealed after the story is well underway. Joan Weldon, the local Sheriff's daughter, soon develops a romantic interest in McCrea when he finds out Mark Stevens was the target of his investigation. Following various crimes and violence McCrea went to chase down and capture Stevens and eventually had their showdown. While on Stephens's trail, Joel McCrea came upon a wedding ceremony with the groom, played by his real-life son Jordan McCrea.

Five years later, Jodi would return to Old Tucson to play the lead role in *Young Guns of Texas*. Also in the cast were James Mitchum (son of Robert Mitchum) and Alana Ladd (daughter of Alan Ladd). The company shot this film under the title of *Stranger at Soldier Springs*.

Playhouse 90 was a television program presenting short plays. At least four episodes filmed at Old Tucson:

Episode: *Lone Woman* April 25th, 1957; No record as to the plot of this episode.

Episode: *Without Incident* June 6th, 1957

Episode: *Invitation to a Gunfighter* March 1957

Episode: *Four Women in Black* April 25th, 1957

Without Incident Starred Errol Flynn, Julie London, and John Ireland and was filmed at Old Tucson, Box Canyon, and Twin Buttes. No plot summary could be found.

Invitation to a Gunfighter Starred: Richard Joy, Hugh O'Brian, and Anne Bancroft.

Town people pool their funds to hire a gunfighter to run the bad man out of town. They found out the gunfighter wants to take over the town, so they hire a bad man to run the gunfighter out of town.

Four Women in Black Starred: Richard Joy, Helen Hayes, and Janice Ruce. Four nuns, led by Sister Teresa, begin a treacherous trip through the Arizona desert on their way to Tucson to build a hospital.

The next film to shoot at Old Tucson was *The Lone Ranger and the Lost City of Gold*. Filming started on November 4th, 1957, and was also filmed at Sabino Canyon and San Xavier Mission. After 220, one half-hour films for television Clayton Moore and Jay Silverheels came to old Tucson and director Leslie Celander for the second big-screen adventure of the Lone Ranger. *The Lost City of Gold* was nowhere near the lavish million-dollar budget of the first feature.

As the opening titles and credits appear on the screen, a song retold the ambushed Rangers' classic tale. The Lone Ranger was the only one who was left alive, and with the kind help of Tonto, he becomes "The Lone Ranger".

The main intersection of Old Tucson became the town of San Dario. Located near the old Presidio sat Chief Jesus' village. Most of the action, including the final showdown, takes place near the village. The movie opens with the song "High Oh Silver." Each of the three murdered Indians were wearing a medallion. Together the medallions form a puzzle whose solution points to gold.

On November 10th, 1957, on NBC's Wide, Wide, Worlds: *Miracle in the Desert*, featured Old Tucson and the University of Arizona.

No information could be found on an Old Tucson production in December 1957, Starring Forrest Tucker and Gail Robbins.

Early February 1958, the movie *Buchanon Rides Alone* was filmed under the name of *The Names Buchanon*. It starred Randolph Scott, Craig Stevens, and Barry Kelly. Randolph Scott plays Tom Buchanan on his way home to Texas. He stops in the town of Agry and right into the middle of a family feud; and ends up with both factions trying to kill him.

On February 20th, 1958, even before *Buchanan Rides Alone* was finished filming, *The Badlanders* began shooting. Due to crowds, the set was close to the public except on Sundays. It starred Alan Ladd, Ernest Borgnine, and Katie Gerardo. Two inmates were released from the Yuma territorial prison in 1898. They decide to rob a small mining town of a gold shipment and get revenge on the town's people for having them imprisoned.

The television show *Wagon Train*, about a wagon train's adventures on the old west trail, was filmed in April 1958 at Old Tucson. The three episodes filmed were:

Cassie Tanner Story, Season 1, Episode 36. A trail hardened Cassie Tanner joins the train, which needs horses. She may be the only person who can get through Indian Territory and procure some horses.

The John Wilbet Story; Season 1 Episode 37. With tensions rising between the northerners on the train and the southern sympathizers, they accused a man who limps of being John Wilkes Booth, who many think is still alive.

The Monte Britton Story: Season1, Episode 38. The wagon train is low on water, and Flint leaves to scout the known water holes. He discovers all the water holes, either dried or poisoned. Now the only choice is to head to Fort Paiute, but first, he needs to find the train on foot with a possible deserter as his only company.

John Wayne and Ricky Nelson in a scene from Rio Bravo. 1958
(Bob Shelton collection)

Old Tucson gained 26 new buildings when *Rio Bravo's* producers came to Old Tucson in May 1958. A hundred thousand dollars went into the construction. The buildings were a land office, Sheriff's office, jail, gunsmithing shop, leather shop, stores, café, market, hotel, a Chinese laundry, newspaper office, barbershop, blacksmith, and stables.

The production company spent an additional $10,000 to build a warehouse, to blow up during filming. The company had to blow up the warehouse twice. The first-time the building exploded, the blast blew multicolored papers into the air spoiling the scene. The studio was closed to the public except on Sundays.

It starred John Wayne, Dean Martin, Ricky Nelson, Angie Dickinson, and Walter Brennan. John Wayne plays a small-town sheriff who must arrest an offender who is the brother of a wealthy and powerful cattleman and the gunmen he sent to free his brother. A drunken deputy (Martin) and a crippled jailer (Brennan) guard the jailed brother.

"It was Ricky Nelson's 18th birthday, and his mom and dad (Ozzie and Harriett) flew over for the celebration," Hoyt recalled. "The stars were all clowning around, and Dean Martin grabbed Ricky while John Wayne spanked his bottom with a pair of chaps. He dipped the chaps in a horse trough, so they were all wet, and you could hear them slap. Kitty Lenola (president of the Tucson Ricky Nelson fan club) and Kathy Stockwell (Secretary of the club) presented Ricky Nelson with a birthday cake.

Warner Brothers approached the Board of Supervisors to acquire 640 acres of land adjacent to Old Tucson to build a sound stage. The Board of Supervisors turned down the offer.

Horsing around on the Rio Bravo set, celebrating Ricky Nelson's birthday. 1958
(Bob Shelton Collection)

CHAPTER FOUR:
Bob Shelton Takes Charge

Robert Shelton, familiar with Tucson from his polo-playing days as a youth, was back in town in the late 1950s, looking around for something to replace his country club consulting business in Kansas City. Lunch with Arthur Pack, chairman of Pima County Parks and Recreation Commission, and cofounder of the Arizona Sonora Desert Museum, did the rest. Arthur Pack asked Bob, "why don't you take this place (Old Tucson) and fix it up?" So, Shelton went out for a quick gander at the town, which despite all the work of the Jaycees, he recalls the village looked like a bombed-out Berlin. The challenge of developing Old Tucson appealed to the 39-year-old Shelton.

Although he was born in Columbus, Ohio, he grew up in Kansas City, where he played on the high school basketball varsity team and graduated in 1938. He attended Kansas City Junior College and Kansas City University for three years, obtaining his Bachelor of Arts in Business Administration. He took postgraduate work at Hardin Simmons in Wichita Falls before entering the Air Force.

Upon his discharge, he returned to Kansas City in 1945 and was Assistant to the Vice President in charge of sales at the Aireon Manufacturing Company, which built jukeboxes.

In 1954 Shelton organized and headed Country Club Consultants, which built "golfless" country clubs and handled subdivisions for sale or lease. This work brought him to Arizona, where he saw the future in developing Old Tucson.

Next, a feasibility study meant counting the tourists' heads and the coins in the donation box. "It began to make some sense to me," said Shelton. "What I had in mind was not movie-oriented but more like a junior Knott's Berry Farm. But once I leased it, I was hit with a barrage of Western films."

The County Board of Supervisors unveiled plans to convert the Old Tucson movie set into a million-dollar "old west" attraction expected to draw a half-million visitors annually.

Under the proposal presented to the Supervisors, Old Tucson would add rides and concessions to turn the park into a Knott's Berry Farm type facility. All rides and concessions would stick to an old west theme. Bob Shelton states that the park would open by October or November 1959 and have a total of 175 employees, translating into a half-million-dollar payroll. They pointed out that about 200,000 people currently visit the Desert Museum annually.

Shelton further stated that the park would have about 80 usable building for concessions. The concessions would include a Ghost Mine Ride, Burro rides, a stagecoach, vintage cars, train rides, and a wild river ride operating on a small artificial mountain. Shelton estimated that it would require $250,000 and one year to complete the plans and open before all the rides were completed. His plans were well received by the Supervisors and the Parks and Recreation Department. After some hesitancy, the Junior Chamber of Commerce was brought on board and agreed to let their lease run out a year early.

The proposed lease included the following provisions: The lessees must assume all responsibility for liability insurance, telephone service, electric service, and getting natural gas into the area, and must spend a minimum of $75,000 on improvements, or promotion, or both, in the first year. It was previously proposed that $200,000 could be paid but over a more extended period. It was estimated that $75,000 would be spent in the first year to improve present buildings and add new facilities.

The new projects planned, including a stagecoach and train rides, to be ready by the opening date, Shelton said. The Pima County Supervisors must approve all development plans. Under the lease, the county would get $3,000 for the first two years. It then gets 5 percent of income with a guarantee of $7,500 per year for the remaining eight years of the agreement. The company would also remit 10% of admission receipts and 10 percent of all other income to the county. When this was accepted, in July 1959, Robert Shelton formed The Old Tucson Development Company, leased the site from Pima County, and began the park's restoration.

The next step was to ask the Superior Court for a declaratory judgment to clear the lease legally. Robert Shelton, president of the new corporation, said. "But we don't think this will hold up our progress; we can go ahead with the administrative details needed to get a project like this going while the suit is pending."

To cut down on the dust, Old Tucson had its streets covered in asphalt. 1961
(Bob Shelton collection)

In the development, Shelton and Tucsonans John H. Goodman,
the Santa Rita Hotel owner, George Masek, and Ralph Thompson, a
Kansas City contractor. The projected opening date of the Tucson
Mountain Park movie set under its new management was tentatively
scheduled for October 15th.

Under the lease, the Jaycees will have the park's free use twice a
year to hold their annual celebrations, and all Jaycees and their families would get free admission other times.

The Jaycees took over the Old Tucson property on March 1st for
the annual Old Tucson Fiesta to put on some plays entitled "Deadeye
Dick" and "The Gold Game." "Deadwood Dick was professionally
produced and took place in front of the mission building with 1600
people capacity bleachers.

The leases for the concessions were quickly parceled out. The
existing concessions were: The Red Dog Saloon, Western wear and

other specialty shops, a Mexican open market, and Golden Nugget Ice Cream Parlor.

One big amusement project, a track for a small gauge, diamond stack railroad train, was nearing completion by November. The specially built engine and tender and four 18-foot passenger cars were already built and located near the main entrance. Other rides that were available included an antique car ride, stagecoach, and burro rides. Shelton was excited, particularly over the Plaza antique car ride, just west of the church.

Nino Cochise planned a large Indian village at the northeast corner of the park. He is the grandson of the storied Apache chief of the same name and would be assisted by Chief Black Hawk, a Sioux tribal figure. Shelton said the Navaho Arts and Crafts Guild at Window Rock was also interested in having a sizeable Indian craft display adjacent to Cochise's village.

The company fixed the old mission building, and Shelton said he hopes the Tucson Council of Churches can take it over as a center for meditation and rest.

The correspondence of October 16th, 1959, from the National Amusement Device Company of Dayton, Ohio, had a good description of the recently purchased Locomotive. "This Locomotive was copied from the Union Pacific Locomotive featured in the Paramount Picture of the same name, and the Union Pacific Railroad says that this is the best duplication they have ever seen in the amusement field. The Locomotive and tender measure approximately twenty-five feet long and seven feet high. The cab is large enough for an engineer to sit inside as he runs the train." National Amusement Device built the locomotive in either twenty-four-, thirty-, or thirty-six-inch gauge, and any one of them is strong enough to pull from ten to fifteen cars without difficulty. "Up to this writing, our customers have elected to use our standard car with an old-fashioned paint job rather than to pay the cost of the special enclosed old-time enclosed cars, and the appearance seems to be quite satisfactory with this arrangement. Our standard car accommodates eight adults or twelve children, and in the older style, sells for $833.00 each. The price of this locomotive is $11,666.69. The total cost of the narrow-gauge railroad is approximately $50,000." The ¾ of a mile-long narrow-gauge railroad ride was among the featured attractions when the Old Tucson movie location reopened at the end of January. The railroad would take riders for a trip of more than ¾ of a mile around the park, through the desert, and over a wide wash. Regular train robberies were planned during the ride.

The General Crook engine pulled the small train ride. Built by
the National Amusement Device Company for about $50,000. c.1960
(Bob Shelton collection)

Another planned concession would be the Mystery Shack. A building where water runs uphill and other gravity-defying effects. The cost would be about $7,000 and should be very profitable since there is very little maintenance or overhead, and almost all the receipts are net except for the payroll.

As 1960 drew near, there was a lot of anticipation for the formal opening of Old Tucson. Almost a half-million dollars and nine months of labor made the old movie set into a modern theme park. The date set for the opening was January 29th, 30th, and 31st.

Many final touches needed to be made to complete the park. The narrow-gauge railroad had to be completed, and a lot of little details finished. With 35 stockholders, seven employees, and $96,000, Robert Shelton began adding new buildings and fixing up old ones they had to operate close to the vest, money-wise. Old Tucson Company operated as "Old Tucson" and was a privately held subchapter S corporation incorporated in the State of Arizona. The park opened its doors under the name "Old Tucson" ("studio" was not used at the time.)

The Little car ride was located on the west side of the Mission Plaza. 1952
(Bob Shelton collection)

On January 29th, Old Tucson reopened to record crowds even though Gates Pass Road was still dirt and the new Kinney road was narrow and twisting. "I got caught in a traffic jam 3 miles south of the old movie set, and I never did get there," Gilbert Ray, head of Pima County Parks and Recreation Department, said. We had 60,000 people over the weekend," said Shelton "we charged $.25." Admission prices have risen considerably since then. So has the county's share in what was once only ramshackle memory.

"A day or so after I signed the lease, we had a disaster. A rattle-snake hiding in one of the old buildings bit a little boy visiting with his mother. He nearly died. I thought we were finished before we'd begun. But the little boy pulled through. We paid the medical bills; the family was genuinely nice about it, and we survived."

Dale Robertson was made an honorary Deputy Sheriff upon his arrival here on the 28th of January 1960, by Sheriff Waldon Burr. He was also given a motor escort to the Santa Rita Hotel where he is staying. Robertson was the star of the *Wells Fargo* TV series.

The formal opening ceremonies began at 2 pm on Friday the 29th. Attending the ceremonies were Arizona and Mexican digni-taries, including Arthur N. Pack, president of the Tucson Chamber of Commerce. Following the dedication speeches, Dale Robertson "shot" the ribbon in half with his gun. After the dedication, a com-plete tour of the new Old Tucson for the dignitaries included a ride on the Old Tucson Railroad and a chance to pan for gold.

Flyer for events at Old Tucson. c.1955 (Az Daily Star)

On Saturday, Robertson also drove a copper spike to finish the miniature railroad. The ceremonies ended when Robertson raised the American flag. Also flying at full-mast were the Spanish, Confederate and Mexican flags — symbolizing the fact that each flag has flown over Tucson at one time.

Old Tucson at the time had 31 different types of western-styled stores and curio shops. Also included are snack bars, a blacksmith shop, a newspaper office, an old gun shop, and a rockhound store. The antique cars traveling on a monorail go through a long tunnel and finally end with a trip around a small "boot hill."

Three vintage biplanes of the Arizona chapter of the Antique Airplane Association flew over sprinkling champagne on the set.

A demonstration fast draw contest by the Tucson Thumbusters Club touched off Saturday's special performances. On the day's program were quick draw exhibits, gunfights, and visits to recent amusement additions to the park such as the stagecoach, old-fashioned auto rides, burro and donkey rides, Apache Indian Village, Indian trading post, antique shop, and firearms and blacksmith shop.

Nino Cochise, grandson of the famed Chief Cochise, and Black Hawk, a Sioux Chief, gave dance and song demonstrations, followed by an Indian dance by Chief Buck Eagle. A trick archery demonstration by the Tucson Bow Hunters Club, Indian dances and songs by Chief Black Hawk and Gray Squirrel in native costumes, and Buck Sharp, a veteran showman and owner of the mule and burro ride at Old Tucson; Sharp gave special shows with his trick trained burros, mules, and horses.

Bob Shelton and Dale Robertson on the day the little railroad
was dedicated in 1960. (Bob Shelton collection)

Buck's primary job at Old Tucson is handling the new "mule barn," which features a burro and mule ride around and through Old Tucson.

On Sunday, the festivities included a large-scale gun battle in the town's streets between the invading Tombstone Vigilantes and the Tucson Vigilantes totaling fifty gunfighters.

About the only old west feature missing was the dust. This was being controlled through street paving, which was completed just before the opening. The weekend ended with a square dance with music by "Dean Armstrong and his Arizona Dance Hands."

The traffic was still a problem, with 17,457 cars passing over traffic counters leading to the old movie set on the following weekend. The Parks Department planned to widen Kinney Road from Ajo Highway to Old Tucson and pave Gates Pass Road.

Buck Sharp's Mule ride. c.1961 (Bob Shelton collection)

Old Tucson, which drew an estimated 50,000 persons for its grand opening over the weekend, would be open seven days a week from 9 AM to 5 PM. Representatives of the amusement center estimated 30,000 attended the ceremonies Saturday and 20,000 Sunday, and 15,000 attended Friday.

As late as 4 PM Sunday, cars were bumper to bumper for 2 miles waiting to get into the frontier type village with its miniature railroad. The jam was so great that some persons reported it took 90 minutes to drive from Old Tucson to the Ajo Highway and more than two hours to get back into Tucson. Now that the grand opening is over, officials did not expect such traffic jams in the future. The following weekend saw about 10,000 visitors.

Opening day visitors. 1960 (Bob Shelton collection)

The train depot at old Tucson was originally in Amado, Arizona, built in 1900, then moved to Stockton, Arizona, in 1920 (where Prince Road crosses the railroad track). It was moved in 1959 to old Tucson when Southern Pacific put into effect the centralized traffic control system. The park's railroad was renamed "Southern Pacific of Old Tucson."

In telegraphy, a good operator could "bug" 50 words per minute. A "Prince Albert" can was used as an amplifier. A. B. Pinnell was a Southern Pacific train dispatcher and spent his time outfitting the station to the original state, including a standard railroad eight-day clock.

Inside is an old, polished wood counter, roll-top ticket case in service in 1900 at Bisbee Junction, an oil-burning lamp, and the tall, roll-front tariff rack, in which the operator could keep track of the changing figures for freight and baggage tariffs. The old safe in the depot was furnished by the Gila Bend Station and used from 1896 to 1958.

The park planned a wooden stockade fort to be built across Old Tucson's arroyo, with shops and a snack bar inside, but it was never made.

As of February 23rd, the average attendance was running about 10,000 per week. With visitors from 31 different states, more than 100,000 visitors have seen Old Tucson since its opening.

The Tucson Mountain Park had the most visitors, outdrawing Sabino Canyon and Mount Lemmon combined. Figures for March released by Gilbert Ray, head of the Pima County Parks and Recreation Department, showed that 23,745 cars passed through the park. Other statistics from John Walters, Catalina Ranger for the Coronado National Forest, showed 13,982 cars entered Sabino Canyon while 6,296 vehicles went up to Mount Lemmon.

The announcement coincided with the kickoff of a $200,000 stock sale to finance an expansion program at Old Tucson; it previously issued 80,000 shares at one dollar each. The stock offering price $2.50 on 180,000 shares at a par value of $2.50. Aggregate $450,000.

An Old Tucson development prospectus with projected earning shows:

Year	No. of people	Admission income
1963	176,000	$132,778
1964	200,000	$133,648
1965	205,000	$142,697
1966	210,000	$186,371

Adolph Zukor, a motion picture pioneer and father-in-law to Bob Shelton, kicked off the dedication of a new children's movie set at Old Tucson at 2:30 PM Sunday, May 13th, 1960. Called "Little Tucson," the set was built in one-half scale and included a saloon, general store, bank, jail, and livery stable in the first installment. The miniature set was located within Old Tucson and was the location for weekly movies, casting local amateur children actors and actresses, with a new cast each week. Scripts were written, and the Old Tucson staff did the filming for presentations on TV and at special showings.

The first film was shot Sunday, May 13th, 1960, by the world's youngest moviemaking company. Zukor's son, Eugene, Casting Director of Paramount Studios, also attended the dedication ceremony.

Tucson introduced a new television show entitled "Old Tucson Time." It was shown from 4:45 to 5:15, Fridays, on Channel 13, KOLD TV starred Carl Greene as master of ceremonies; Marshall Bert Oien and his sidekick, Buck Sharp, all of Old Tucson. M. C. Carl Greene was known as "Mayor Karl of Kid Town." The show featured Old Tucson personalities, interviews, Indian dancing, and weekly children's Western dramatic films. The producers shot the movies at Old Tucson's "Little Tucson" set. The program was dedicated to Tucson's children to enable them to relive the traditions and excitement of the colorful old west.

On May 19th, 1960, gale force winds hit Old Tucson and tore a 2-ton roof from the Castle and Import Shop about 7 PM, flipping in onto Richard Gushard, 22, of South Nogales Highway, an employee at the movie set. Gushard was walking past a one-story adobe building when the roof landed on him. He was taken to Tucson General Hospital in critical condition with a broken back and a fractured pelvis, a concussion, a broken arm, and multiple abrasions. Gushard survived and filed a lawsuit against the park.

The front gate in 1962. Bob Shelton on the left, Adolf Zucker in the middle, and an unknown deputy sheriff on the right. (Bob Shelton collection)

CHAPTER FIVE:
Coming of Age

The management decided in June to open the park at night-time and the regular programs during the day. Under old-fashioned kerosene streetlights, Old Tucson inaugurated a summer nighttime program starting June 17th. The evening program featured live music, round dancing (Saturday nights), and square dancing (Sunday nights). Other activities planned included live entertainment, art shows, talent contests, fashion shows, dramatic programs, and special activities for children, such as hobby shows and hayrides. Gunfights continued into the nighttime programming. All concessions, including the train ride, were also opened.

To celebrate the first night of performances, Old Tucson featured the original Banjo King, Eddie Peabody. Peabody was back in Tucson for a brief vacation before resuming the nightclub circuit. Bob Schmeling's "High Tones furnished music for dancing." Other entertainment included Chief Buck Eagle Sharp and his knife-throwing act; Buddy Byrum, "The Wandering Troubadour," and his folksongs; and several singing groups. Marshall Bert Oien of Old Tucson was the master of ceremonies.

To celebrate the park's first 4th of July, it hosted a quick draw contest. Tucson's Thumbuster Fast Draw Club hosted the first annual Western States Walk and Draw Championships, with four deputy sheriffs acting as judges.

The Old Tucson Development Company sponsored the event, with the Colt Patent Firearms Manufacturing Company, as a cosponsor. The competition would be in two divisions, open and women. The first prize to the open division will be a Single Action Colt revolver and draw a rig and $300 cash. Colt is donating three single-action revolvers and two derringers as prizes. The sponsors expected over 150 shooters.

Arnold Milton, the editor of fast draw guns magazine, acted as master of ceremonies and Colt representative. The championships' unique feature will be Ronald Echols and Ronald Echols II, a father-son trick shooting team from Tombstone. The Echols' have been billed as the nation's youngest father-son shooting team. Young Echols was five years old.

Paul Jenkins, a Phoenix gunslinger, has added the Western States Fast Draw Championship to his growing list of laurels. Jenkins, who already owns the state title, out-gunned nearly 100 competitors at Old Tucson at the two-day event. Mrs. Jerry Diffie won the title of the top gun of the week in the woman's division. Old Tucson Studios employs Mrs. Diffie.

Officials of the Old Tucson Development Company announced that nearly the entire town of Speed, Kansas, located near the Nebraska border, was purchased on September 8th, 1960, and would be shipped to the Old Tucson for reconstruction. Old Tucson did not move any of the buildings themselves. Interior furnishings, including those of an old theater, bank, apothecary shop, physician office, and a collection of relics from that era, would be packed and shipped here. The park would erect buildings to house the artifacts. Most important, historically, is a collection of early medical devices dating from 1860 to 1900, including a sweatbox machine for reducing fevers, a stomach pump, and a lung checking device. Much of the old medical equipment in the office was "modern" for such a Western community. The old town's restoration here was part of an expansion program.

Bob Shelton is sorting through items located
in Speed, Kansas. 1960 (Bob Shelton collection)

Dale Robertson, star of the television program "Tales of Wells Fargo," who was also an outstanding quarter horse race breeder, made his second appearance at the Western-style attraction since its grand opening last January. On September 17th, Robertson and his sleek thoroughbred riding horse, Jubilee, highlighted Old Tucson's activities on Saturday and Sunday.

The same weekend, Bozo the clown made his last appearance. Bozo, who made 36 motion pictures in the past decade, retired in Tucson following his weekend performances.

The park announced on November 26th that Old Tucson would receive all the props and wheeled vehicles from John Wayne's movie *Alamo*. Items included cannons, caissons, guidons, powder horns, saddles, and wagons. Up to this time, all the items were stored in a barn on Wayne's farm in Stanfield, Arizona.

Robert Shelton, President of Old Tucson, put a crew of men to recondition and assemble all the salvageable equipment. The items were on loan from Paramount Pictures under the agreement that the props could be used for free by any Paramount movie filmed and rented out to other companies. After eight years, ownership of the items would pass to Old Tucson. Shelton said that Old Tucson spent $15,000 to recondition the collection. The park placed the wagons and caissons on Old Tucson streets.

Contrary to a common belief that zebras could not be ridden, Old Tucson had a Zebra, Ribbons, which was broken to ride.

Old Tucson Announced on January 17th, 1961, it had obtained its first movie since opening as a theme park. The film, *Deadly Companions*, starred Maureen O'Hara, Bryan Keith, and Steve Cochran. The story tells of a woman who moves to a new western town with her young son. During a bank holdup, her son is killed, and the mother endures many hardships while transporting her son's body to another town for burial. Extras in the movie included tenants and employees of Old Tucson, plus other Tucson characters.

It took about three and a half weeks to film sequences at Old Tucson and surrounding areas made in Cinemascope and color by Pathe' Laboratories, Inc. and Pathe' American Co. The movie was produced by Charles Fitzsimmons, the brother of Maureen O'Hara, with a screenplay based on the novel "Yellow Leg" by Albert Sidney Fleishman.

One incident occurred when the stagecoach, driven by Chuck Hart Hayward, during a practice run, the horses spooked and stampeded. The driver could not control the stagecoach for quite some distance until he finally hit a tree and overturned, but Hayward emerged from the wreck unharmed.

Stagecoach ride. c.1962 (Bob Shelton collection)

All the cowboys utilized in the filming of the movie were actual cowboys from ranches located around Arizona. Bob Shelton made his second film appearance in this movie as a gambler. His first movie part was as a cavalry officer in *The Gal Who Took the West* in the early 1950s. The film company was charged $60 a day for the use of the facilities.

During a break in the action during the filming, Ms. O'Hara rested in the Red Dog Saloon when a man demanded some postcards. She said she did not work there. He then grabbed her and tried to kiss her. A bystander caught him and threw him out.

As of February 3rd, the Ghost Mine Ride attraction was nearing completion at the cost of $100,000. Also remaining to be finished was the car ride, Dr. H. D. Niblack's house of carvings, and the wax museum featuring movie gunfighters.

The Lost Dutchman Mine Ride was located on the north side of town. c.1961
(Bob Shelton collection)

The opening of the "Lost Dutchman Ghost Mine" on March 5th, 1961, gave the park another attraction. Thrill-seekers could view the "Lost Dutchman Ghost Mine" while "Spooks" haunt riders on old ore cars as they ride through the mine. Also open on this date was "The Dutchman Mine Mystery Cave" and the 1906 Horseless Carriage ride. The Mystery Cave, where, through visual effects, water runs uphill along with other mysterious apparitions.

The next movie up was A Thunder of Drums starring Richard Boone and George Hamilton. Richard Boone was already famous as the television character Paladin and his more recent appearance in the Alamo. George Hamilton played a young inexperienced lieutenant just in time to participate in a confrontation with hostile Apaches. Richard Chamberlain made his screen debut in this picture. Capt. Maddox (Boone) is an old veteran cavalry officer and Lieut. McQuaid (Hamilton) is a brand-new West pointer. Together they must deal with an outbreak of Indian violence.

Old Tucson built a wooden stockade fort for this film just north of Gates Pass Road, due north of Old Tucson.

A stockade was built to film *A Thunder of Guns* and used in *Custer's Massacre* and *The Long Ride Home.* It was located on the north side of Gates Pass Road and torn down when the Pima County Parks Department discovered it was not situated on Old Tucson property. c.1961 (Bob Shelton collection)

In March, Old Tucson started a new program, deputizing Tucson residents, allowing them to get in for $.25 throughout the season.

A documentary, *The Sounds of Arizona,* was shot in May. This documentary is a tour de force of the Tucson area. We see desert animals, Old Tucson Studios, Indians dancing, a square dance, a cowboy singing at a campfire, and a flight over the Grand Canyon.

As of December 31st, 1961, there was still no phone service at Old Tucson, and it published a public apology for the lack of phone service.

On December 31st, 1961, the company announced that the headcount for the first year of operation was 250,000 people.

Paul Newman made his first movie at Old Tucson, *The Outrage*, in January 1962. The film was based on a classic Japanese novel "Rashomon." In this movie, Newman plays a Mexican bandit, and his speech and his dress were entirely out of sync with his typical roles on the big screen. Laurence Harvey and Claire Bloom portray a traveling, upper-class couple victimized by Paul Newman. Edward G. Robinson narrated the film and examined the crime from each of the three participants' viewpoints.

As of January 1st, Indian dances were added as part of the regular schedule.

Native American dancing was introduced as a scheduled show in 1962.
(Bob Shelton collection)

The Rifleman in person: Chuck Connors made a personal appearance at Old Tucson to demonstrate his rifle skills. The forty-year-old actor played baseball with Seton Hall (majored in English) and played in the Brooklyn Dodgers and Chicago Cubs franchises. He batted .321 with 23 home runs with the Los Angeles AAA team. He started appearing on TV shows and got small movie parts before starring in *The Rifleman*.

The arroyo southeast of the main park was utilized when entertainment was expanded into an amphitheater seating 2,500 people. The first act at the new amphitheater was Dale Robertson.

Nick Adams of the television show *The Rebel* performed at Old Tucson on March 4th. Clint Walker visited old Tucson on April 8th and performed in the amphitheater.

In May of 1962, Richard Boone's *Have Gun, Will Travel*, the television series, running from 1957 to 1963, filmed at least seven episodes at Old Tucson. The series is about Paladin, a gunfighter who rents himself out to solve people's problems.

Summer hours began on May 25th, and Old Tucson was to be open from 10:00 am to 10:00 pm except Mondays. The summer program will include the melodrama "Deadwood Dick," which played each night. Dinner was served in the Red Dog Saloon.

Another improvement to the park were five different types of Indian homes. They were Navajo, Apache, O'Odham, Sioux, and Crow. Old Tucson planned to build a stockade to surround the buildings.

The county collected $12,089 from Old Tucson. This was the amount based on 5% of admission and 10% of all other sources. The county's first year got a flat $1000, the second year $2000, then the third year the percentage kicked in. As of September 1962, the 12-month gate count was 225,000.

August saw the filming of the movie *Young Guns Of Texas*, starring James Mitchum (son of Robert Mitchum), Alanna Ladd (daughter of Alan Ladd), and Jodi McCrea (son of Joel McCrea). A ranch foreman was heading a posse, looking for a stolen army payroll when the rancher's daughter elopes with a member of the posse. The rancher chases the group until Apaches attack the group. The rancher then joins the posse to fend off the attack.

The Mission Plaza, as seen from the west. c.1962 (Bob Shelton collection)

By the summer of 1962, Bob Shelton could look at Old Tucson and see success, but Shelton's big moment was still to come. Arriving late one morning in 1962, Shelton was greeted by his secretary, who said, "John Wayne is waiting for you," she blurted out. "I just thought it was a big joke," he reflected. "It was like an invitation from God. There he was, standing in the middle of our town. He was wearing a baseball cap and jumpsuit, and his hands were on his hips."

John Wayne during the filming of
El Dorado. 1965 (Bob Shelton collection)

"Hi! I'm John Wayne," Shelton said, recalling the meeting as if it were engraved in stone. "Shaking hands with him was like shaking hands with the Eiffel Tower." During the conversation, he reminded Bob that he had made another movie at that location a few years back, referring to *Rio Bravo.* Wayne was planning to shoot the film, *McClintock!,* starring himself and Maureen O'Hara in Old Tucson. He planned to construct some new buildings and wanted to know what Shelton would do in return. "I told him I had an old pocket-knife, a used Cadillac, and a wife who was a fair cook but a dynamite bridge player. You can have them all." Shelton said and laughed. "It was to be the start of a long friendship with the Duke and marked the coming of age of Old Tucson."

Aside from becoming a stockholder in the Old Tucson Development Co., Wayne also contributed to the town's construction. From *Rio Bravo* came a saloon, bank building, a doctor's office, and a hotel; "Rio Lobo" added a cantina, a granite-lined creek, a jail, and a ranch set; "El Dorado" left assorted buildings and improvements along Front Street.

John Wayne's one objection about Old Tucson was that the streets were paved and dangerous to horses and riders. Shelton had the pavement ripped out within a couple of days.

Batjac Productions (Wayne's production company) hired hundreds of workers to modify the movie set to the production company's specifications, including 13 new buildings. The anticipated starting date was October 25th. Old Tucson was closed for two weeks during the filming of *McLintock!* except for Sundays. The Board of Supervisors approved the improvements.

McLintock! starred John Wayne, Maureen O'Hara, Patrick Wayne, and Stephanie Powers. Cattle baron George Washington McLintock is at odds with land grabbing bad guys, his wife, and his daughter. A hilarious John Wayne movie.

The cast of McClintock! between takes. Seen are Patrick Wayne (left), Stephanie Powers (third from left), and Maurine O'Hara (fourth from left). 1962 (Bob Shelton collection)

The street names of Old Tucson were changed from the original Tucson names (i.e., Camino Real and Mission Road, etc.) to the names of movie companies (i.e., Warner Brothers and Paramount, etc.).

Clint Eastwood and Paul Brinegar from the TV show *Rawhide* appeared at old Tucson on the 10th and 11th of March 1963. Eastwood sang a solo act, while Brinegar performed a comedy routine.

Old Tucson was notified of a lawsuit from a female guest. She claimed she was hit by the train. Apparently, she did not hear the train whistle, horn, and bell, nor did she see the crossing signal flash, all of which were working at the time.

Dr. H.D. Niblack set up a display of hand-carved Western figures. They were mechanized by a system of pulleys and cables. The collection was on display during April before heading to Denver.

On April 7th, 1963, an article appeared about Jack Young. His motto was "thunder but no blood." He was the new Marshall of Old Tucson. He was 36 years old and born in Covington, Virginia. Jack had been a stuntman and gunfighter at various Western amusement centers and rodeos throughout the country. His gunfight concept is they should be bloodless, and it is essential that children see the gunfighters get up at the end of the show. He was a frogman in World War II, then an automobile salesman. He organized a small troop of gunfighters to put on gunfights at rodeos and country fairs. Before coming to old Tucson, he was Marshall and sometimes bad man at Apache Land Movie Ranch, where he directed street fights. At Old Tucson, Jack was put in charge of outside stunt shows.

Jack Young as "Blackjack," stunt coordinator and show organizer. c.1963
(Bob Shelton collection)

Stunt show at the Mission. c.1965
(Bob Shelton collection)

Gunfighters waiting for stunt show to start. 1965 (Bob Shelton collection)

Joseph Carruthers was run down and killed by his car at the back gate on July 15th, 1963. He was driving and got out to open the gate. As his wife slid into the driver's seat, she accidentally hit the gas pedal, striking Joe and dragging him 43 feet. He died at the hospital.

Old Tucson was finally connected to the rest of the world on July 15th, 1963, when telephone service was installed.

For Thanksgiving of 1963, Old Tucson presented a special deal. Admission was two dollars for adults and one dollar for kids, including dinner and a free ride. In the early days of Old Tucson, the admission only got the person into the park, and the rides cost extra.

To prevent overflow cars from parking in the desert, the county increased the parking lot's size to hold 2,000 vehicles.

By 1964, six gunfight shows were being performed each day. These were chosen from the list of prepared gunfights:

Squaw Man. A tale of Pauline Weaver, a mountain man, and scout for the army. He gets into a conflict with a couple of soldiers about his relationship with an Indian girl. Weaver shoots and kills both soldiers.

Gunfight at the O.K. Corral, which illustrates the circumstances leading up to the famous gunfight in Tombstone.

Violence is a Full Meal. Two acquaintances meet on the street, one is the sheriff, and one is a gunfighter. A stagecoach robbery is reported with a description of the robber. When the robber shows up, a fistfight and gunfight ensues, leaving the sheriff and the robber dead.

'Tis a Fine Day to Die. The sheriff and a miner, Jeb, are talking when Jeb's partner shows up. He is angry and accuses Jeb of stealing his money. Jeb tries to explain that the mine is unbelievably valuable in copper, but the partner will not listen. A fight ensues between Jeb and his partner. Guns are drawn, Jeb is shot and killed by the partner, and the sheriff shoots and kills the partner.

Day of the Hunter. A bounty hunter, Tanner, confronts the marshal. He tells the marshal that the storekeeper, Jeb, is wanted for murder, and he intends to take Jeb in dead or alive. The marshal disarms the hunter and tells him he can have his gun back when he is ready to leave town. Jeb comes out, and a fight takes place in which Tanner is beaten. Tanner goes to the marshal and says that he is leaving town and needs his gun back. Jeb faces Tanner and confesses that he is wanted. They each draw, and Jeb kills the hunter. The marshal arrives, and Jeb says he will not surrender, so the marshal kills him.

The Last Reunion. Jack Reese shows up in Tucson looking for long lost kinfolk. He is a well-known gunfighter and is confronted by

Brock, who is looking for notoriety. The sheriff, Larry Reese, shows up, and they recognize each other as brothers. Brock shoots Jack in the back, and the sheriff then shoots Brock.

Law of the Hip. After the Civil War, Jeremiah returns to Tucson, checks his horse at the stable, and proceeds to the sheriff to turn in his gun. When he comes back, he sees an individual walking on the street with Jeremiah's horse; the individual is identified as Concho. Jeremiah claimed that the horse is his. The horse has no brand, but Jeremiah does possess a receipt and demands the horse back. Concho refused to give him the horse back and stated that he got it on the open range and was his horse. Jeremiah, accused of being a horse thief, gets a gun and tries to stop Concho. The marshal shows up and confronts Concho. Marshal Eli tries to arrest Concho, and Concho points a gun at him. Conch states he knew Eli in prison, and he was no better than Concho. Eli admitted that he spent time in Yuma prison but that he had reformed and was now going straight. They determine to solve their problem by having a duel. Concho loses the gunfight.

Terror in a Small Town. Jack and Big Ed Callahan are the law in a lawless town. They started an extortion ring to shake downtown businesses for money. Jack goes into the Doc's office to collect extortion money and ends up beating Doc. Cassidy, of the Arizona Rangers, shows up and confronts Jack, who turns around, and a fight occurs. The marshal shows up and turns out to be Big Ed Callahan. The Ranger gives both 12 hours of leave town. A gunfight begins when they start shooting at the Ranger. Jack and Ed Callahan run into the bank as the ranger runs into the Doc's office for a shotgun, and he demands that Jack and Big Ed surrender. Big Ed sends Jack around the back to get behind the Ranger. Big Ed runs out of the bank and fires at the Ranger, who fires back and kills Big Ed. The Ranger then runs into the street, where Jack fires on him from the roof. The Ranger then shoots Jack off the roof.

Great Tucson Bank Robbery. The scene opens with the sheriff in the bank and two bank robbers, Frank and Kyle, come into town and try to figure out how to get the sheriff out of the bank. They decide to use the ruse called "steal my horse." While Kyle hides the robber horses, Frank starts yelling, "help someone stole my horse." At this time, the sheriff comes out of the bank and confronts Frank about the horse. While they discuss the horse theft, Kyle sneaks up on the sheriff and grabs him, and a fight ensues. The sheriff gets beat up by the two bank robbers, and they put him in the Doc's office to get him out of the way. They go into the bank with the dynamite and use it to blow up the safe. The sheriff comes out of Doc's office and corners the bad guys in the bank. Jack goes around the back of the bank to get behind him and climbs to the roof. The other bank robber lights a stick of dynamite and throws it into the street to draw the attention of the sheriff. The Sheriff chases it into the street and shoots Frank. He then confronts Kyle on the roof and shoots him.

The Old Tucson Gunfighters listed at this date were Grizzly Bob, Bob Wichita (Robert Baker), Kimo Owens, Johnny Concho (John Allen), and Ken Carlisle (Kevin Breslin).

When the *Judgment in the Sun* Company headed by Paul Newman left, it added to the Tucson Funds an estimated $250,000 in two weeks in addition to the salaries of the chief players.

When John Wayne's company was making *McLintock!*, they spent an estimated $1,000,000 in Tucson and its environs.

Clarence Kelland, the author of the book "Arizona, " died on February 18th, 1964, at his Phoenix's home.

March 20th, 1964, the Today Show's cast and crew came to the park, with Hugh Downs as the host. The Today Show has a daily audience of 13,000,000 viewers. The program was shown from 7 a.m. to 9 a.m. on KVOA-TV.

Pima County began building a by-pass around Old Tucson to relieve traffic congestion. The by-pass started at Kinney and Gates Pass Road and went southwestward to Triple C Ranch Road, allowing for the parking lot's expansion.

Old Tucson had an impressive summer offering every weekend between June and Labor Day, complete with roping contests, silent films, and new amusements. The program of silent films, complete with the appropriate piano background music, features greats like Tom Mix, Franklyn Farnum, Buck Jones, Blanche Sweet, Fatty Arbuckle, and Mabel Normand in four-period films, were shown in the Front St. Saloon.

The entire park, including rides, shops, and movies, was open Friday, Saturday, and Sunday nights. Visitors have their choice of a studio tour, horseless carriage ride, train, and stagecoach rides, or trying their luck in the Shooters' Gallery in the soon-to-be-completed Silverlake Park. Old Tucson's moved the 1909 carousel to the new complex.

On June 10th, 1964, the 20th Century Fox Movie *The Reward* started lensing. This film adds several buildings, including a fountain, a gas station, cantina, and the old adobe church's remodeling. Old Tucson remained open during the shoot. *The Reward* Stars: Max von Sydow, Yvette Mimieux, Efram Zimbalist Jr., and Gilbert

Roland. An airplane pilot and a sickly Mexican cop put together a ragtag posse to pursue a wanted killer. The posse ends up turning against each other for a larger share of the reward.

On October 4th, The Old Pueblo Chapter of the National Railway Historical Society persuaded amateur "Gandy Dancers" (railroad track layers) to lay track at Old Tucson. Southern Pacific Caboose No. 633 was the first piece of rolling stock to use the rails. The antique caboose made one more run from Benson to a place of honor at Old Tucson.

Gandy Dancers lay track to put caboose on display. 1964
(Bob Shelton collection)

The Old Tucson Development Co. provided the railroad museum's land, and Southern Pacific has donated track, ties, tie-plates, and spikes. Plans called for acquiring a stock car, combination coach, and possibly an operating steam engine.

The McLintock station, built by the movie company for the *McLintock* film, was moved to a track-side location and outfitted like a typical small-town passenger station. Equipment included a ticket cage, telegraph desk and key (with Prince Albert can for an amplifier), waiting room bench, stoves, tables, and chairs.

Custer's Massacre started filming on November 2nd, 1964 and was released under the *Great Sioux Massacre* starred: Joseph Cotten, Darren McGavin, and Philip Carey. The movie shows the actions leading up to the Massacre at the Little Bighorn.

One incident occurred during the set preparation. One construction crewman managed to shoot himself in the leg when he reached for an unloaded gun.

Portions of this film were filmed near Vail, Arizona.

Westerns would live again in Old Tucson for the second annual Old Tucson Night. The event, which started the previous year, was such a success it would become a yearly affair. Students will be entitled to ride the train, putt around in the Antique car, the old stagecoach, and tour through the Lost Dutchman gold mine as often as they wished, providing they have paid the admission price of $1.50 per person or $2.50 per couple. Dancing began at 9:30 with music supplied by the Phantoms. Gunfights and staged battles were featured throughout the entire evening. The affair is open to all high school students in the city, and tickets were available from any Tucson High School Hi-Y member.

The production company scheduled the next Audie Murphy movie to start filming on November 30th, 1964, at Old Tucson Studios. *Arizona Raiders* starred: Audie Murphy, Michael Dante, and Ben Cooper. Audie Murphy plays a Quantrill Raider who was let out of jail and was deputized as an Arizona Ranger to hunt down his former gang's remnants. Murphy finds that the gang is hiding out in an old mission and pretends to join the group. With the help of an Indian chief and some of his Rangers, the gang is captured. The writers borrowed several plot elements from the 1951 movie *Texas Rangers* based on a Zane Grey novel.

Arizona Raiders, starring Audrey Murphy seen in the middle of the picture. Bob Shelton had a significant role in the movie and can be seen on the left. 1964 (Bob Shelton collection)

At Old Tucson, the many buildings housed concessions such as Depot Lunch, Last Chance Casino, Ward's Trading Post, House of Carvings, Golden Nugget Ice Cream Parlor, Red Dog Palace, Cactus Corners, Wagon Wheel Snack Bar, Newspaper Office, Rock Shop, Candle Shop, Basket Shop, and the Casa Linda Gift Shop.

After two years of being used for storage, the mission was cleaned up, fixed up, and became available for religious services. The Interior was reconstructed from old lumber by Victor Boehnlein and A.B. Pinell. Boehnlein hand-carved profiles of monks and angels on the end panels of the pews. It Seated 68 people. The front wall was wood, and the altar was made from saguaro ribs, with the Candlestick made from Cholla stems. The main cross of the alter was made from one piece of Cholla wood. The benches were of plain wood.

On January 31st, 1965, the church held its first church service of the new era. The clergymen dedicated it as a nondenominational church. For the service, Rev. Richard Rowley spoke, and Rev. Rupert McCann played his accordion. The park charged no admission to persons going to the church service.

Interior of the Mission set during a church service. 1962
(Bob Shelton collection)

On March 26th, 1965, Mrs. Ruth Madson and Richard Kellett were the first couple to be married in the newly renovated church.

A talking bunny greeted visitors to Old Tucson as they roamed the streets on Easter. The bunny, which stands 10-feet tall, talked to children visiting the park. The Old Tucson management conducted a contest to get a name for the talkative hare. Unfortunately, the name was not published.

Jackie Coogan and Ted Cassidy (Uncle Fenster and Lerch) from the TV program *The Addams Family* visited Old Tucson on May 22nd and 23rd. They signed autographs and put on shows each day.

Filming started on September 18th on *And Should We Die*, Starring: Nathan Hale, Claire Bybee, and Dana Rosado. The movie, set during the Mexican revolution, tells the story of two Mormons arrested and charged with supporting Poncho Villa's opponents and following the wrong religion. They must warn a small Mormon community of the planned attack by Villista forces. The Latter-day Saints produced it at Old Tucson.

John Wayne returned to Old Tucson for his third film *El Dorado* alongside Robert Mitchum and Arthur Honeycut, with the production beginning in October 1965. This movie was about a sheriff with a drunken deputy and an old character actor as a sidekick. The production company added several set changes to Old Tucson, including a porch around the adobe stage depot and a few modifications made to the adobe mission. The church figured in a vital scene of a gunfight both from the exterior and the interior.

The movie starred James Caan in one of his first movie roles. John Wayne was not happy with the dapple horse given him for the film and stated that Howard Hawks is a poor judge of horseflesh in an interview. He said that Hawks showed that he was more concerned about how the horse looked on camera than how easy it might be to ride.

For this movie, a small store and porch were built on the front of the barn located on Front Street. In this building, James Caan was sold the sawed-off shotgun by Swede Larson, played by Olag Wieghorst.

Robert Mitchem (on crutches) and Bob Shelton take a break between scenes of *El Dorado*. 1964 (Bob Shelton collection)

By November 21st, 1965, there were 65 stockholders of the company, but Shelton and his wife, Jane, held 40% of the stock. In the beginning, the company leased concessions but bought up all except two. With the clerks and service people, the bank robbers, O.K. Corral gunfighters, who worked from scripts, and the miniature railway crew, there was a staff of 42.

A chapter of the Screen Extras Guild (SEG) was being formed in Tucson, with Robert Ketaily, the guild acting executive director.

Ketaily said he expects membership of approximately 500, adding that some 200 persons joined this week. The goal of the guild, he explained, is to raise extra wages from $10-a-day paid in Tucson to $29.15 as paid in California. This effort failed.

The county's annual income figures show that Old Tucson rendered to the county $12,089 for 1966. This money represents 5% of the admission price and 10% of all Old Tucson Development Company's gross business. The attendance was more than 250,000 people.

The movie-making business in 1966 showered an estimated $2 million on the county. That figure is from Robert Shelton, president of Old Tucson, the filming location of scenes for five major movies and eight television episodes during 1966. A lot of the money went into the pockets of locally hired extras and bit players. More Hollywood cash was spent for motel rooms, food, materials, and rent at Old Tucson and other locations. No telling how much money the free-spending show people-shelled out of their own pockets for dinners and entertainment.

On March 16th, 1967, Gov. Jack Williams signed a bill relaxing industrial insurance requirements for film companies. For years, movie company officials had to pay into Arizona Industrial insurance and their home state's insurance and protested that industrial insurance requirements were prohibitive.

In an accompanying action, Robert Shelton, Pres. of Old Tucson Development Company, announced a long-sought soundstage was to be constructed soon. For many years, both the new law and the soundstage have been considered keys to Tucson's future expansion as a filmmaking center. This has been even more true since television had shown such an insatiable appetite for Western series. The new law lowered the production cost, and a new soundstage would make it possible for a complete movie to be produced here.

As per law, Pima County had to put the lease availability out for bids. The old lease was up in three years, and Old Tucson was seeking a new 10-year lease. The new contract stipulated a minimum payment of $7,500 per year or 5% of gross receipts, 7.5% of revenue from motion pictures, 10% gross from all business, rides, and concessions. Old Tucson was the only company to bid on the lease.

Old Tucson Development Company had decided to make a stock offering to raise capital. They offered 180,000 shares of stock at $2.50 per. There were at the time 247 stockholders.

Death Valley Days began to film episodes on June 20th, 1967, for the new season. They started at Sabino Canyon and then moved to Old Tucson.

Lensing for a new pilot project began on June 25th for *Dundee and the Culhane*. The pilot will be a two-part movie entitled *To Catch a Thief Brief*. The pilot starred John Mills and Sean Garrison as two defense attorneys who must defend a juvenile against murder charges. The pilot was successful, and a total of 13 episodes were filmed in Tucson, Scottsdale, and Flagstaff. Filmways Corporation produced the series.

After years of needing one, the ground was broken on Old Tucson's $190,000 soundstage on July 13th, 1967. Mrs. Robert Shelton turned over the first shovel full of dirt after many speeches. The bulldozers immediately began leveling the land to hold the 2,800 square foot building. They planned that construction would be complete by October 1st.

The sound stage (Stage 1) is seen from the west. Kansas Street is on the north end of the soundstage to the left. 1968 (Bob Shelton collection)

A major monsoon rainstorm hit Old Tucson on August 8th. What may have been a small tornado caused considerable damage to the studio, including tearing down the whole hospital from *Strange Lady in Town* and tore the roofs off several buildings. Damage exceeded $10,000. The bell in the tower of the mission was knocked down. The south wing of the chapel was also heavily damaged. Water ran boardwalk deep in the Park. Pounding rains crashed through the "town." Buildings walls collapsed, whole sets went down, and mud ran six inches deep through many buildings.

On October 3rd, 1967, another rainstorm crashed into Old Tucson. For the first time in six months of production, filming was halted for about a half a day on the Old Tucson set of NBC's *The High Chaparral*, a western adventure television series. More than150 extras sat beneath leaky fake porches (on NBC's budget) as the rain ran in rivulets down the main street, which was being used in the present episode for a July Fourth horse race and celebration.

The annual report showed that gross receipts from the year 1967/68 were $424,740 compared to $389,695 for the previous year. Net income for the 1st quarter of fiscal 1967/68 was $15,000 versus $7,000 for the prior year. There were 55 employees.

Old Tucson got a new main street. To camouflage the new sound stage, false fronted buildings were erected on the sound stage's north side. These false fronts were in the form of two-story buildings, including a hotel. The design allows each section to be pulled out, and production companies could change the appearance of the set by inserting false fronts, called "plugs" or "wind walls."

Initially, the sound stage looked like a large barn, but adding the facades created a new street, called Kansas Street, for filming. The new fronts had an 1890s look and gave a counterpart to the rest of the studio. The new sound stage is 12,800 square feet, or 160 by 86, feet and is two stories high.

The new sound stage seats 3,000 people and is the largest banquet facility in Tucson.

The grandson of the famous Indian Chief, Cochise, was a prime mover in developing the enlarged Indian village. Indian dances occurred at scheduled times, and Indians worked there on various phases of their tribal life

A $700,000 expansion of the movie location was completed in January 1968. It was an amusement area reminiscent of Silverlake Park, a recreation spot along the Santa Cruz River a century ago. The new park area included the Iron Door Mine, an arcade shooting gallery, and a waterway. The existing river was extended to wind through the park and trees planted on its banks. Several bridges spanned the stream at various points, and Old Tucson's 1909 carousel was rebuilt. In addition to this project, the park spent $27,000 to create a new entrance, gatehouse, and a tourist patio.

The drive-in teen exploitation movie *Mini Skirt Mob* began 2 ½ weeks of filming in the area. It starred: Jeremy Slate, Diane McBain, and Sherry Jackson. This movie centers on a pack of females known as "The Miniskirts" and the "Roughriders" in mountainous desert terrain looking for trouble against an innocent trailer couple. It was filmed at the sound stage after outside filming was complete.

Death Valley Days began filming three episodes, including *Pieces of the Puzzle*, which is mostly an interior shoot and was the first to use the sound stage. The film started 2 ½ weeks filming on January 22nd, 1968. *Death Valley Days*, Scene 6-B Madison Production #810 *Pieces of a Puzzle* is about the Riavas land fraud case. Robert Taylor, Russ Johnson, and Garry Walberg star. The set designers created an interior marshal's office and courtroom for this shoot.

Andy Warhol contracted with the studio to use the facilities for a short film entitled *Lonesome Cowboy*, beginning January 26th. It was to star Julian Burrough, Joe Dalessandro, and Eric Emerson. The plot was complicated: In the wild wild west, Ramona Alvarez, a perpetually stoned nurse, ran into five gay cowboys. The seven members of the party desired a handsome male drifter. The cowboys' rape Ramona, who subsequently had sex with the drifter. The drifter rejects her and rides off into the sunset with another man. Due to the subject matter and the amount of nudity, Old Tucson stepped in and threw them off the property.

The crew and cast went to Oracle to complete the film.

On February 12th, 1968, a burglar stole $15-$20,000 worth of guns from the gun collection at Old Tucson Studios.

The Old Tucson Stagecoach was operating normally, driven by Kenneth Lee when it hit an embankment and overturned. Neither of the passengers was injured.

An accounting report showed that Old Tucson earned $5,561 in February 1968, with a yearly total admission of about 300,000 people.

The "Kansas Street" facade of the sound stage was completed on April 16th. With the addition of these buildings, old Tucson became a full-fledged movie studio capable of handling films from the early 1800s through the 1910s. The construction of Kansas Street cost around $200,000 plus $60,000 for new equipment, including lighting, editing, and other soundstage items.

Bob Shelton is standing in front of the new façade screening the sound stage and named Kansas Street. 1968 (Bob Shelton collection)

At the same time, the front gate was made larger and represented an early Arizona stockade. Another new addition to the town was the Chapman drugstore building with items obtained when Bob Shelton bought the small town of Speed, Kansas.

On May 29th, 1968 the movie, *Heaven with a Gun* began filming at Old Tucson Studios. This movie was an MGM film and starred Glenn Ford, John Anderson, David Carradine, and Barbara Hershey. Anderson and Carradine play a father-son team of ruthless bullies that rule over the town during a range war. A stranger comes to the town to build a church and spread the message of the Lord, and elevated what might have been just another Western movie to one with a message and with an authentic historical background. During one fight scene, Glenn miss-swung a punch and hit Carradine in the mouth.

In the summer of 1968, Old Tucson Studios picked up its first full television series, *The High Chaparral*. The park built the sound stage to support this production. Until the sound stage was built, the *High Chaparral* interior shots were filmed in Hollywood. After the soundstage was made, the filming occurred at Old Tucson. A new set was constructed just to the east of Old Tucson as a ranch house and barn used as the High Chaparral Ranch headquarters. It also acted as an ongoing example of what Old Tucson looked like to millions of viewers for the next four years.

Riders approach the High Chaparral Ranch set built just east of town. c.1968
(Bob Shelton collection)

The film *Young Billy Young* Starring: Robert Mitchum, Angie Dickinson, Robert Walker Junior, and David Carradine, began filming in June 1968. A man named Ben Kane (Mitchum) takes a job as Deputy Marshal of the small town of Lords. He is not a lawman but accepts the badge because he has an old score to settle with the town's chief troublemaker (Anderson). Once on the job, Kane must also deal with a young sharpshooter named Young (Walker Junior) and a sharp and sassy saloon owner, Lily (Dickinson). *Young Billy Young* was the first motion picture filmed entirely at old Tucson utilizing the sound stage.

The area's population was mighty small, but enough visitors were going through Old Tucson to warrant postal services, postal officials said. The post office quarters opened to the public on December

2nd, 1968, were inside the movie studio's gates. The next month, new quarters were built outside the gates so nearby residents and visitors to the park may use it. Tucson Postmaster Arnold R. Elias, who had jurisdiction over the new contract branch station, said about 300 letters were on hand for the first-day cancellation. Old Tucson's earliest post office was in operation in 1940 for the filming of *Arizona*. That post office lasted only a few months, and the new one was expected to be more permanent.

The year ended on a down note when on December 4th, 1968, a burglar stole $5,343 from the personnel office.

Burt Sugarman of Los Angeles and Gabriel Alarcon Junior from Mexico City agreed to buy one million shares of common stock for $2.5 million in the Old Tucson Development Company. At a special meeting of the Board of Directors of Old Tucson reached an agreement on February 6th, 1979. It also called for granting Alarcon and Sugarman an option to acquire an additional 500,000 shares for 1.25 million.

The Old West Corporation, which owned and operated the Old Vegas theme park in Henderson, Nevada, also became a wholly-owned subsidiary of Old Tucson. Old Tucson then owned 80% of Old West's outstanding stock from a stock transfer in September. Principal Old Tucson shareholder Johnny Mitchell also agreed to transfer more than 100,000 shares of stock to Alarcon and Sugarman and establish a voting trust for the two given voting control of more than half of the outstanding Old Tucson stock.

On February 10th, the film *The Mountain Men* began shooting. The film starred John Strong and James Michaels. They needed 6 to 10 dogs. No further information could be found on this film, and it probably did not get released.

For an unknown reason (possibly rocks on the track), the little train derailed on March 1st, and two of the cars overturned. Five people were injured badly enough to be transported to the hospital. The most severe injury was a broken leg of a 14-year-old boy.

A new "old" town was built near the railroad stop of Mescal in May 1969, for the use on the movie *Monte Walsh*. The location is about 15 miles west of Benson, Arizona. The town, known as Harmony, was built on the Wheeler Ranch for $200,000. Early negotiations were completed, and permission was given for the erection of a fence. Old Tucson would be responsible for putting the area back to its original state whenever the set is dismantled. This consideration will be 50 – 50 share of rental received by any movie company.

Aerial view of Mescal. c.1970 (Bob Shelton collection)

The movie starred Lee Marvin, Jack Palance, and Jeanne Moreau. Monte Walsh (Marvin) is an aging cowboy facing the last days of the Wild West era. As barbed wire and railways steadily eliminated the cowboy's need, Monte and his friends had fewer and fewer options. New work opportunities are available to them, but the open prairie's freedom is what they wanted. Eventually, they say goodbye to the lives they knew and try to make a new start.

Also built for this movie was a ranch set known as the "Slash Y," located on the Empire Ranch near Sonoita, Arizona. At one point during the building of the ranch house, the director did not like the exact location, so a group of cowboys watching the construction picked up the house and moved it.

Slash Y Ranch set near Sonoita, Arizona. It was built in 1968.
(Bob Shelton collection)

The production company planned to dispose of the town at the completion of the film. Instead, Old Tucson bought the town and about 320 acres of land and made it a permanent part of Old Tucson Studios. The company changed the name to Mescal, and it became the second favorite place to film outside Old Tucson. Unfortunately, 30 minutes after signing the deal, a storm hit Mescal and blew down 18 of the 20 buildings then in existence.

On June 7th, 1969, a fire occurred on the north end of Old Tucson. It started in a teepee in the Indian village and spread to Haunted Mine Ride and Mystery Cave and destroyed a false front set from 1962 built to screen the Haunted Mine Ride building. The fire started at 1:30 pm and was fought initially by the crew and cast with garden hoses. Then by 2:00 pm, Rural Metro and South Tucson Fire Departments arrived and put the rest of the fire out before it spread to the Red Dog Saloon. Also lost in the fire was caboose #633 donated to Old Tucson by the Old Pueblo Chapter of the National Railway Society. About 300 guests were in the park at the time. No one was injured. And the park lost the Indian wiki ups and offices belonging to the mayor, Sheriff, and dentist office of Old Tucson. The total loss due to the fire was $100,000.

A French film was lensed in July. *Un Homme Qui Me Plait* starred Jean Paul Belmondo and Annie Giradot. Henri (Belmondo) and Francoise (Giradot) film a movie in the United States and fall in love. The director was Claude Lelouch, who filmed a couple of other productions at Old Tucson. The American name of the movie was *Another Love Story*.

Death Valley Days returned to Old Tucson to film three episodes in July 1969. Dale Robertson replaced Robert Taylor as host. *The Great White Hope* shot at Old Tucson, Globe, and Spain, and the episode, *Valdes Is Coming,* was filmed in Tucson.

Old Tucson Studios opened a fine arts gallery and Indian trading post in the former photographic gallery. The trading post had for sale blankets, pottery, Kachina dolls, and Zuni and Hopi silver and turquoise jewelry. The first Displays at Old Tucson were four western artists who shared a group showing at the studio's first art exhibition: S. W. Shafer, Robert Wagoner, Boris Bogdanovich, and the late George Phippen. Oil and watercolor landscapes by Shafer and Wagoner were on display; the oil paintings by Bogdanovich were brilliant abstracts representing western scenic impressions, and bronze works represented Phippen.

According to a financial report, Old Tucson grossed $893,000 in 1969 versus $643,000 in 1968.

CHAPTER SIX:
The Movie Factory

The Tucson Boys Chorus was the subject of a United States Information Agency movie when Don Cuozzo produced the film on January 16, 1970. The company shot additional scenes at San Xavier Mission and the Capitol Building in Washington, D.C. The producers distributed the film internationally.

The new post office, which straddled the front gate, was finished on January 18. It was made from an original train car and made to look like an old express railroad car. It was situated so customers could enter from the outside or inside the park.

An M.G.M. feature film starring Frank Sinatra and George Kennedy began shooting on February 9. It was called *The Ballad of Dingus Magee* and is based on a western comic novel by David Markson. The previous summer, M.G.M. used the western town built near Benson for *Monte Walsh*.

Frank Sinatra plays Dirty Dingus Magee, a criminal who would steal anything from anybody. He robs a friend and heads to Yerkes Hole, a small backwater town. Here he finds that Bell Knobs, the mayor, and owner of the local bordello, has appointed Hoke (Kennedy) as town Sheriff. Belle wants to start Indian trouble so that the local cavalry garrison will stay in the area. Spending $70,000 to build a three-story brothel, it also added five new buildings at $20,000. The production company released the movie under the title of *Dirty Dingus Magee*.

The new post office was established next to the front gate
and made to look like a railroad mail car.

John Wayne and director Howard Hawks returned to Tucson in April 1970 to film *Rio Lobo*, a full-length C.B.S. feature motion picture. The set construction started for the movie on February 14. Old Tucson added a cantina, Philip's Ranch, a river, and a new front street look. In addition, they dressed Front Street to look like two different towns depending on whether the perspective is from the north or the south. The front of the mission church also got a new exterior look by adding a barn-looking front facade.

Dirty Dingus Magee (Frank Sintra) was upset
at the small reward on his head.

Filming started in April. *Rio Lobo* starred John Wayne, George Rivero, Jennifer O'Neil, and Jack Elam. Col. Cord McNally, an Ex-union officer, teams up with a couple of ex-confederate soldiers to search for the trader who sold information to the south during the Civil War. Their quest brings them to Rio Lobo, where they help recover the little Texas town from ruthless outlaws led by the trader they sought.

The director is setting up a scene for *Rio Lobo*.
John Wayne can be seen in the center of the photo.

During a break in the filming, John Wayne went to Hollywood to accept an Oscar for his part in *True Grit*. When he returned to Old Tucson, he noticed that no one would look at him. So back on the set, at a given signal, everyone turned around, and each person was wearing an eyepatch to honor Wayne's role, Rooster Cogburn, in *True Grit*. His character wore an eye patch. The crew also unveiled a 16-foot statue of the Oscar as a gift.

The Rio Lobo River appeared to be a rushing torrent while shooting the film. Scuba divers flapping their fins beneath the water made it look like a rushing river.

The giant "Oscar" the Art Department made to celebrate
John Wayne for his Oscar win.

During the filming of *Rio Lobo*, John Wayne and writer-adven-
turer George Plimpton filmed a short movie, *Shoot Out at the Rio
Lobo*. Plimpton is supposed to be shot down by John Wayne. Plimpton
had one line "This here's your warrant, mister." He rehearsed it for
a week. But when it came time to shoot the scene, they changed it
to read: "I've got your warrant right here, sheriff." Wayne belts him
across the mouth with a rifle and shoots him in the chest. Throughout
Plimpton's involvement with the picture, Wayne called him Plankton.
Plimpton was unamused. "I had hoped to do a dramatic death scene,
you know. Staggering all over the place, and perhaps muttering a line,"
he said. "Instead, they put a harness on me with two wires attached to
the back. When Wayne shot me, two men off-screen jerked the wires
to enhance the appearance of being shot."

In March 1970, Amy Snell of the art department noticed that
hair on the two stuffed dummy Indians sitting on the train station
bench were starting to lose their hair. Train driver, Danny Wash,

was told to watch for the culprits. Instead, he found that two Gila Woodpeckers were taking the hair to build a nest.

A new gunfight show, "The Lucky Cuss," highlighted Easter weekend activities at the park. The new show, a story of prospecting and claim-jumping, was the first in a complete cycle of recent gunfights performed by Old Tucson actors and stunt performers.

Visitors could take exciting rides on the stagecoach or train, see museums, and outdoor motion picture sets. In addition, they could take a personally guided tour in Old Tucson's air-conditioned Sound Stage. This tour included explaining how sets are built and used and other interesting facts about the motion picture industry.

Tourists could have lunch at the Red Dog Saloon and Restaurant and an ice cream sundae at the Golden Nugget Ice Cream Parlor. They could buy rock candy, jellybeans, licorice, root beer, and sarsaparilla with its reminiscent taste. Souvenirs and gifts could be purchased at the General Store, the Western Store, the Hospitality House, and the Candle Shop. Old Tucson featured paintings by famous western artists in its "Indian Trading Post and Western Art Gallery."

The Golden Nugget as seen in the production of a movie.

On May 1, 1970, Walter V. Murphy, supervisor of the Arizona State Land Department's leasing division, reported that the Profit Corporation was issued a mineral lease on a half-section of land just east of the *High Chaparral* set at Old Tucson. The lease was the first sign of an attempted takeover of Old Tucson (explained in October 1970).

Shelton said earnings per share for 308,047 shares outstanding as of March 21 were 16.92 cents, and book value was $2.10 a share compared with $1.87 a year. On May 2, 1970, old Tucson declared a six-cent dividend.

A new pilot was shot on May 3, called Petrocelli, which starred Barry Newman, Susan Howard, and Albert Salmi. The pilot episode was entitled *Night Games*. Tony Petrocelli is a lawyer in Tucson, Arizona. The television series centered on the various cases he handled as a defense attorney. Barry was nominated for the Outstanding Lead Actor in a Drama Series for his title role in Petrocelli's Tucson-based N.B.C. series.

The interior set for The High Chaparral was moved from its previous location in Paramount Studios to the sound stage at Old Tucson.

Powderkeg's pilot was shot on May 20 and starred Rod Taylor, Dennis Cole, and Fernando Lamas. Taylor and Cole play a team of mercenaries that drive around the old west in their Stutz Bearcat sports car, looking for adventure. They took on challenging rescues and political problems for a "blank check," which they will fill in after each job. *Powderkeg* was the title of the pilot film, and *Bearcats* was the series's title. Filmways filmed it for C.B.S. In the filming of an episode in November, the Reno was used in an Old Tucson production for the first time.

Powder Keg is the only movie in which a tank is seen.

June of 1970 saw the filming of the movie, *The Animals*, starring Michele Carey, Henry Silva, and Keenan Wynn. A pretty schoolmarm is raped during the holdup of the stagecoach she is riding. She then proceeds to track down the men responsible with the help of an Apache Indian. X.Y.Z. Productions produced *The Animals*, which also featured Tucsonan Francesca Jarvis. she previously played a nun in *Lilies of the Field*.

Filming at the same time as *The Animals* was *Again a Love Story*. Directed by Claude Lelouch, it starred Jean-Paul Belmondo, Annie Girardot, and Kaz Garas. The French film told the story of a French composer working in the United States. He meets and falls in love with a married actress. The film was a sequel to *Another Love Story*.

A new "antique" car ride went into operation in June 1970 at the park and installed a $35,000 track nearly half a mile long to accommodate it. In addition, a fleet of new cars, three-quarter scale replicas of circa 1908 Stutz Bearcats, were purchased for an additional

$30,000. The vehicles came equipped with a single-pedal control for the accelerator and the brake. The pedal control simplified the operation of the cars.

In June, the *Bonanza* NBC-TV series company came to Old Tucson to make several segments for its 1971-72 season. It starred: Lorne Greene, Parnell Roberts, Michael Landon, and Dan Blocker. This production was to begin the 12th season.

Bonanza was a long-running television show about Ben Cartwright and his three sons. They owned a large ranch in Nevada's Lake Tahoe area. The episodes were primarily filmed in that area, but the following episodes were filmed at Old Tucson and Mescal.

Episode: *Power of Life and Death* 1970

Episode: *Top Hand* 1970

Episode: *The Desperados* 1970

Lorne Green on horseback during the filming of *Bonanza* at Old Tucson.

Old Tucson requested a 25-year lease from the County to expand its tourist attractions and moviemaking facilities to attract more film contracts. County Supervisor Jim Murphy said on May

20, a 25-year lease "could conceivably raise county income from Old Tucson because it has grown since the last lease was signed." "The present 10-year lease had six years to run. An amount of time that didn't allow Old Tucson to finance any important expansions," said Robert Shelton, company president. He prepared the longer lease for the October stockholders' meeting. Under the old lease, Old Tucson paid the County ten percent of the gross gate and five percent from concessions. The income rose from $12,000 in 1962 to $39,000 in 1968. The 1969 receipts topped $50,000. Inflation and a $750,000 planned expansion prompted Old Tucson officials to seek county approval on a proposed increase of adult admission rates from $2 to $2.50.

M.G.M.'s future looked bleak in the early 1970s, and it sold off props and costumes for extra income. Shelton bought a semi-truck load of costumes in a New York auction. Old Tucson kept all Western apparel but sold such items as the non-Western wardrobe to the general public. Costumes for sale were displayed in the Old Tucson jail. Over one weekend, they sold $2,500 worth of costumes. First, old Tucson's wardrobe department took all the Western costumes. The studio then received a second truck of outfits, including glamorous grubbies worn by the stars. Also included were Fantastic hats and sandals, jackets, uniforms of all descriptions, fringed shirts and pants, vests, beaded necklaces, German belts, and a treasure trove of movie relics and wild apparel. Deciding to move the sale of costumes in the University of Arizona area, the store moved to the orchid fronted Lothlorien Building at 923 East University Blvd near the University of Arizona.

The two-story Wardrobe Department housed the most extensive collection of western costumes globally.

Tucson financier Allan J. Norville on October 10, 1970, launched a proxy fight to gain control of Old Tucson. "Norville's attempt to buy 180,000 shares of Old Tucson Development Company's 308,000 shares outstanding is a raid," said Robert Shelton, the largest stockholder. Norville, president of Financial Associates Inc., offered 5 cents a share for the option to purchase before June 30, 1971, each claim for $2.50. "The last time stock sold, it went for $1.50 a share," he said. Old Tucson shares were sold through First Pacific Investment Company, which quoted the price as "between $1.50 and $2" per share. Old Tucson, in 1969, had gross revenues of $898,000. "It came as a surprise to us, and the management of Old Tucson will give the information on this takeover move to the company's more than 1,200 stockholders," he said. In reply to Norville's claim that earnings per share had declined, Shelton said. On the contrary, old Tucson's gross revenues increased over the past five years. "Old Tucson was never in better shape, and its future never looked brighter.

Naturally, earnings per share will decrease when the stock issued and outstanding increases from 66,000 shares to 308,000." Norville once headed a Chicago company barred from the stock market for deceptive and manipulative practices. Allan J. Norville acquired proxies representing 34,000 shares of Old Tucson Development Company stock and sought a seat on the Board of Directors on October 20. Norville, who the previous spring attempted to gain control of the company, criticized its management, declaring that earnings per share had declined over the past three years. He offered to buy options on 180,000 shares of the company's 308,000 shares but failed. When the election dust settled at Old Tucson's sound stage, Norville claimed to have 5000 proxy votes illegally taken from him. He said he filed approximately 34,100 proxies with the company on October 9 and lost his takeover of Old Tucson.

Walt Disney's *Scandalous John* came to Old Tucson to film. The movie starred Brian Keith, Alfonso Arau, Michele Corey, and Rick Lenz. Robert Butler directed. John McCandless (Keith) is an old feisty ranch owner who does not want to follow the new West's rules. He and his helper, Paco (Arau), must take his only cow to town and sell it to save his ranch. *Scandalous John* started filming on October 14.

Aaron Spelling was filming *Yuma,* a 90-minute movie for ABC TV. *Yuma* in September 1970. Clint Walker, Barry Sullivan, Kathryn Hays, and Edgar Buchanan starred. Dave Harmon (Walker) is a United States Marshal assigned to Yuma, where the life expectancy of a lawman was short. Upon arrival, he kills the brother of a local rich and powerful man, Arch King (Woodward), in a gunfight. Framing him for killing another of King's brothers, he must prove his innocence. George Duning, on Jan. 18th and 19th, 1971, recorded the score for *Yuma.*

Engine No. 11 of the Virginia & Truckee Railroad, nicknamed "Reno," was acquired by Old Tucson in September 1970. The Reno was the first of five 4-4-0 engines on the Virginia & Truckee Railroad and accumulated 73 years of active service with the short line, six years more than any other V&T locomotive. The number eleven was turned out on May 22, 1872, by I.A. Baird & Company at the Baldwin Locomotive Works of Philadelphia as shop No. 2816, the 300th Baldwin 4-4-0 specification.

On September 15, 1872, the "Brass Betsy," as the highly polished No. 11, was affectionately nicknamed, headed the first train the 52.2 miles between Reno and Virginia City amidst considerable publicity. For the next half a century, the classic 4-4-0 hauled the V&T's through express between Virginia City and the transcontinental railroad junction, which had Reno connections. In its boom days, the wood-burning Reno hauled down some of the $600 million in silver and gold produced by the Comstock Lode.

Orphaned at the famed Virginia & Truckee demise, it was rescued from a junkyard by M.G.M. Converted to diesel fuel, and it starred in many films. For $500, Paramount Pictures obtained in 1938 an option to lease or purchase Engine No. 11, Reno. Rented between August 1938 and March 1939, to Paramount Pictures for their epic *Union Pacific*, No. 11 finally headed for Hollywood after being sold to Metro-Goldwyn-Mayer Incorporated on March 1, 1945, for $5,000.

In 1969, due to financial difficulties, M.G.M. sold the engine to the David Weisz Company. This auction house auctioned off the engine on May 14, 1970, for $65,000 to a man who said he represented an anonymous client. When the successful bidder defaulted, Weisz quickly resold the locomotive to Robert Shelton, President of Old Tucson. Shelton bid $50,000 but insisted on the addition of another railway car.

The Reno, under full power in the movie
The Life and Times of Judge Roy Bean.

After filming the T.V. movie *Powderkeg* in December 1970, Twentieth Century Fox sold a Central Pacific six-axle coach to Old Tucson. The coach was built circa 1880 and acquired by the Fox Film Corporation before its merger in 1935 with Twentieth Century Pictures. The Paramount Pictures rolling stock was moved from a spur of the Union Pacific Railroad in Los Angeles and sold in October 1971. Robert Shelton purchased all 27 cars, kept 5, and sold the remaining 22 cars to Short Line Enterprises. The five cars held by Old Tucson were: an 1872 Kimball baggage car no. 1, an 1874 Detroit Car Co. combine no. 15, a Central Pacific boxcar no. 1001, a Central Pacific boxcar no. 1007, and an 1875 Wells, French & Co. derrick no. 50.

Insuring the engine for $100,000 before shipping, the 98-year-old, 65,000 lb. the movie star took up permanent residence at Old Tucson. Arriving by reverse piggyback, the famous and historic "Reno" steam locomotive and a tender and a passenger car were

The Reno arriving at Old Tucson and being
offloaded at the front gate.

delivered by three trucks of Contractor's Cargo, Southgate, California. Giant cranes lifted the behemoth from the truck beds to newly laid railroad tracks at the movie studio's main entrance.

Jack Young specified the Train's rental would be $1,000.00 per day for the first two days, $750.00 per day for the next two days, and $500.00 per day after that.

Reno's first film was *Courage of the West,* shot on location on the Virginia & Truckee Railroad in 1937 before the line's abandonment. Its first use in a full-length motion picture was in the Cecil B. DeMille picture *Union Pacific.* This film was Paramount's only use of the train. At the same time, it retained ownership of the engine.

Old Tucson Studios bought 30 historical pieces from M.G.M. and used them in *The Life and Times of Judge Roy Bean* on November 20, 1970.

The engine appeared in over 100 productions, including movies, commercials, and television productions. The following is a small list of its productions.

Abe Lincoln in Illinois (1946), *Again a Love Story* (1969), *Ambush at Dark Canyon* (2012), *Annie Get Your Gun* (1950), *Backtrack* (1974), *Bless All the Dear Children* (1983), *Calamity Jane* (1983), *Cheyenne Autumn* (1964), *Cheyenne Social Club* (1970), Cimarron (1969), *Four Eyes and Six Guns* (1991), *Gambler* (1979), *Gunsmoke* (1977), *Hard Bounty* (1994), *Harvey Girls* (1945), *How the West Was Won* (1962), *Joe Kidd* (1972), *Last Hard Men* (1976), *Life and Times of Judge Roy Bean* (1971), *Lightning Jack* (1994), *Little House on the Prairie* (1977/1979), *Man Who Loved Cat Dancing* (1973), *More Wild Wild West* (1979), *New Maverick* (1978), *Poker Alice* (1987), *Posse* (1975), *Scandalous John* (1970), *Shootist* (1976), *Stay Tuned* (1992), *Support Your Local Gunfighter* (1971), *Support Your Local Sheriff* (1971), *Tombstone* (1993), *Twilight Zone* (1962), *Union Pacific* (1939), *Villain* (1978), *Wild Wild West* (1999), *Wild Wild West revisited* (1979).

Celebrities who rode behind the Reno on business to Virginia City include President Grant, General Sherman, George Pullman, and the entourage of Baron Rothschild.

The locomotive appeared in many M.G.M. Films and was occasionally leased to television producers and other Hollywood movie studios. In the 1969 Centennial celebrating the completion of the first Transcontinental Railroad, the company dressed the Reno to look like the Union Pacific Locomotive at the driving of the Golden Spike at Promontory Point, Utah.

If a movie company shot a western and needed the Reno, they turned to Gene Smith, the engineer. Old Tucson made him the caretaker of the 106-year-old steam locomotive, one of four operating in the country at that time. He kept it running like a top. He knew every bolt, screw, needle, gauge, and hydrostatic lubricator on the Reno. He could play the whistle like a musician, change smokestacks in a flash, get the ancient train chugging up to 35 mph, and stop it on a dime. Of course, he never hit a star. But what he did best was grip the throttle, tug his cap down over his eyes, lean out the Reno's window, and look just like an old-time steam locomotive engineer.

Gene Smith, piloting the Reno, spoke with Charleton Heston and Michael Parks in "The Last Hard Man."

On December 6, 1970, *Wild Rovers* began filming at Old Tucson (Philips Ranch). It would also shoot at Mescal, Sonoita, and Nogales. It starred William Holden, Ryan O'Neal, and Karl Malden. Ross Bodine (Holden) and Frank Post (O'Neil) have big plans. They hope to get themselves a small ranch somewhere in Mexico. Unfortunately, they are broke and decide to rob a local Montana bank and head south towards Mexico.

The brisk wind, un-warmed by the famous Tucson sun, chilled the crowd watching the filming at Old Tucson's Mexican Plaza. "Cut," yelled the director. The spectators immediately converged on the center of the attraction. The people who braved the freezing weather to see was country music giant, Johnny Cash, making a television special, *Ballad of the Old West*. The show's stars included Roy Rogers and Dale Evans, Chill Wills, Walter Brennan, Kirk Douglas, and Andy Devine. Screen Gems aired the one-hour special on A.B.C. – T.V. on February 3, 1971. Cash had to sing "Streets of Laredo" for his special *Ballad of the West*. As he began the song standing next to the Reno, he said: "I hate trains, I'm supposed to like them, but I hate them." Other acts for the special included June Carter, the Carter Family, the Tennessee three, Statler Brothers, and Carl Perkins.

More than a quarter of a million people visited Old Tucson during 1970. Robert Shelton, president, and executive director of the company, reported to stockholders. In his annual report, Shelton said: "Our past year was a highly successful one. More than 250,000 persons from all sections of the country visited the amusement park".

An enthusiastic crowd is watching a stunt show
being performed on Front Street.

As of April 1971, the gunfight shows at old Tucson were "Terror in a Small Town" and "Lucky Cuss." Stunt performers knew about eighteen 15 to 30-minute presentations, and they were to introduce 12 to 16 new shows within the following year. Jack Young said it cost about $1000 per show to produce. Six stuntmen performed what Old Tucson movie production coordinator Jack Young called "our biggest attraction."

After a script was approved, Young found suitable music or a recorded soundtrack and then blocked out and timed Main Street's action. Next, the dialogue was tape-recorded at a local radio station. Then came two weeks of rehearsal, generally at 6:30 a.m. before the movie set opened until the show was ready for the public.

The television show, *The High Chaparral,* announced its cancellation on March 10. This cancelation was a $200,000 loss to Tucson per week.

A new movie was filmed at Mescal and began lensing on April 2, 1971. The new film was entitled *Dirty Little Billy* and starred: Michael J Pollard, Richard Evans, and Lee Purcell. This production was the story of Billy the Kid when he first arrived in New Mexico from New York. He befriends Goldie, who teaches him the outlaw way. Not the typical "kid" movie, Billy is a short, fat kid with a "no care in the world" attitude.

During June, the new Powder Keg series, filmed by Filmways for C.B.S. and starring Rod Taylor, also arrived at Old Tucson to shoot several segments. The name had been changed to *Bearcats* when CBS-TV picked it up. They used a 1917 Standard J-1 biplane in filming *Bearcats,* which landed at the High Chaparral set. CBS-TV axed the series that proved tame in the Nielsons' ratings)

The *Bonanza* NBC-TV Series Production Company was at the movie site at Old Tucson in June to make several segments for its 1971-72 season.

Old Tucson Development Company owned the restaurant at Ryan Airfield, which lost $1100-$1200 a month. They terminated their lease on December 1, 1971.

An advertisement for July 4, 1971, celebration stated: "4th of July weekend fun at Old Tucson, Visit Chief Geronimo in our new Apache Village, and Special weekend guest Lloyd O'Dell and his beautiful horse "Hombrecito." Plus, all the tremendous Old Tucson fun, live-action gunfights, stagecoach, and train rides. Buy or bring your lunch in our air-conditioned ramada with ice-cold watermelon on tap".

Paul Newman was at the Old Tucson's Mescal site where *The Life and Times of Judge Roy Bean* was filmed by First Artists starting on October 30. Judge Roy Bean was "the law west of the Pecos." The story centers on the eccentricities of Judge Bean and his brand of justice.

Paul Newman on the set of "The Life and Times of Judge Roy Bean."

The Oscar-winning Wardrobe mistress, Edith Head, was the head costumer for this film. Newman worked in Bean's old saloon's replica inside the Old Tucson sound stage for weeks. By December 15, 1971, except for a few days filming indoor scenes at Old Tucson, most of the movie about the fabled "Hangin' Judge" and his law west of the Pecos was made at Mescal. The production company burned the tall oil derricks and some parts of town as the film ended. As the script stated, starting in 1885, the town belongs to Bean. He leaves for a long while and returns to find an oil boom and that a man named Gass owns everything.

Old Tucson filmed a documentary about the park narrated by Lorne Greene named *Classic Westerns: The Movies and Old Tucson*. The film was shown to guests and illustrated the history of Old Tucson.

A troupe from Universal Studios was at Old Tucson on October 10 to start producing the motion picture, *Joe Kidd*. It starred Clint Eastwood in the title role and was filmed under Sinolaand. The company used the antique railroad engine and several cars from the movie set and expected completion in three weeks. New construction or remodeling existing buildings by a production company are routine at a filming location and studio, such as Old Tucson. The results are mutually beneficial to both the studio and the production company. Universal built a new movie set for Sinola. Construction was adjacent to Old Tucson. The town included new buildings, relocated old buildings, a depot, cattle pens, and 700 feet of railroad track. Universal technicians were busy one day, ripping into the saloon before putting balsa wood to cover the building's side. Eastwood, as the engineer, runs number 11 through the saloon walls. That's what you'd call a $40,000 shot.

Joe Kidd, Clint Eastwood drove the engine (Reno)
through the Railroad Saloon.

The construction extended Kansas Street from the sound stage building three-quarters of a mile eastward toward the "High Chaparral" set. According to the usual contract with the studio, they had to put everything back the way it was before leaving old Tucson.

Joe Kidd, 1971, starred: Clint Eastwood, Robert Duvall, and John Saxon. When a corrupt and wealthy Landowner tries to steal the land from a group of Mexicans, they fight back with the formidable revolutionary, Chama. Unfortunately, the landowner hires a bunch of gunfighters to battle the Mexicans. Joe Kidd first stays out of the middle of the conflict, but eventually, Chama's sides.

Old Tucson became one of the most significant railroad operations in Arizona. They purchased Paramount Studio's collection of 30 historic railroad pieces. The average age of the equipment was 80 years, with many pushing 100. The equipment was placed into service immediately in the filming of *The Life and Times of Judge Roy Bean*. Of some 30 cars purchased, Old Tucson kept the best for the motion picture railroad. The rest were sold to a California railroad museum.

C. Lyles produced M.G.M's *Rabbits,* a science fiction drama from Russell Brodden with Hal Dresner's screenplay. Gene Kearney started filming on January 31, 1972. It starred: Stuart Whitman, Janet Leigh, and Roy Calhoun. Cute little bunny rabbits injected with a hormone to control their population turn them into 10-foot man-eating killer rabbits that terrorized the town. The bulk of the film was shot in the Sonoita area, but a small-scale model of Ajo, Arizona, was built on Old Tucson's backlot. The rabbits attack the town and are fired upon by the National Guard. Betty Schumacher spent two and a half months training rabbits to run as a herd. The release name of the movie was *Night of the Lepus.*

Special effects men build a miniature town on the north end
of Old Tucson for the rabbits to attack.

Appointment with Destiny was a television program that chronicled various incidents in American history. The segment filmed on February 28, 1972, at Old Tucson centered on the *Gunfight at the O.K. Corral.* David Vowell, Robert Tyndall, Tim James, and Lorne Greene starred.

On April 30, 1972, the Santa Rita Hotel was demolished. Its place in Tucson film history goes back to the early days of the talkies.

Gunsmoke, the long-running television western, came to Old Tucson to film several episodes beginning May 18. The following are episodes filmed at Old Tucson, including two made for television movies.

Episode: *Valley of Tears* 1973

Episode: *Comanche's of Cibola Blanca* 1974

Episode: *The Stringer* 1974

Episode: *Gunsmoke III:* 1991

Episode: *Gunsmoke V:* 1993

Marshall Dillon (James Arness) leads a stagecoach into town.

After 12 years of service, the little engine of the Old Tucson narrow gauge railroad, General Crook, was retired and replaced by the engine C.P. Huntington, bought from Chance Manufacturing Company in June 1972.

July 1, 1972, saw the introduction of a new live-action gunfight called "Too Late for Killing." Jack and Silas ride into town to rob the bank. A man and his wife are in the bank, who get caught in the middle. After they blow the safe, the town drunk confronts the bad guys, and an old friend faces them. A lot of shooting occurs, and the man from the bank and both robbers are dead.

This date also saw the opening of "The Hole in the Wall Arcade," Old Tucson's new shooting gallery.

The growing number of visitors to Old Tucson has forced the County to expand parking facilities at the studio location. Today the Board of Supervisors awarded a $79,000 contract to the Ashton Construction Company to add 293 parking spaces and rebuild a small section of Kinney road that fronts Old Tucson. Gilbert Ray, County Parks and Recreation Director, said the road's southbound lane would be moved westward and constructed the new lot at its present location.

The Herschell-Spillman Company built the carousel in 1909. It has a 40-foot canvas top, and it is referred to as a side curtain merry-go-round. It is electric driven and has 33 "Jumping" Animals and two chariots. It was used initially in Slippery Rock, Pennsylvania, then moved to the Mall in Washington, D.C.

The carousel at its location near the front gate.

Metro-Goldwyn-Mayer moved into Gila Bend on January 22 and began filming the Burt Reynolds project, *The Man Who Loves Cat Dancing*. The crew filmed in Ajo, Rio Rico, and Mescal and starred Bert Reynolds, Sarah Miles, Lee J. Cobb, and Jack Warden. A defiant woman leaves home and her husband to ride along with a gang of outlaws. The 100. year-old locomotive, the Reno, was the star to the local residents. Shooting on the M.G.M. picture began filming after a week of preparation. Still, the big crowds were drawn to the Tucson, Cornelia & Gila Bend Railroad station in Ajo to watch the venerable engine's unloading and cars.

ABC TV/20th Century Fox filmed a pilot, *The Boomtown Band and Cattle Co.*, which started filming January 17 at the Mescal facility. The movie was an unsold pilot starring Ramon St. Jacques, a former slave who travels in the old West. He adopts three orphaned children and creates a troupe of minstrels.

At certain hours throughout the day, a 25-minute film telling the story of moviemaking in Southern Arizona was shown in the town's "First Electric Theater." The film, narrated by Lorne Greene, included clips of many westerns made at Old Tucson.

Old Tucson Studio acquired the costume inventory from *Death Valley Days's* television series. The facility purchased the wardrobes from *Bonanza* and *High Chaparral*, bringing the total stock to more than 14,000 pieces of period apparel.

Gunsmoke went to Old Tucson's Western Street at Mescal and other southern Arizona locations on April 21, 1973. They filmed segments of several episodes for the 1973–1974 season. The project included a two-parter, *Valley of Tears*, directed by Vince McEveety.

The cast of the show "Diamond Studs"
performed in the sound stage.

Diamond Studs premiered on June 14 at Old Tucson and was performed by Arizona Civic Theatre. The musical was scheduled for a 10-week run and centered on the life of Jesse James.

The U.S. Borax company came to Tucson to film a commercial under our bright sunshine, but rain canceled it.

Replicas of 1910 Buicks, built 10½ scale, were made by East Coast Amusements and put in use by July 1973 on the Little Car Ride on the new 1200-foot track.

Lensing began on June 26, 1973, for the murder mystery, *A Knife for the Ladies,* starring Jack Elam, Ruth Roman, and Jeff Cooper. In the small Southwest town of Mescal, someone is killing prostitutes with a knife. After killing the mayor's daughter, he brings in a private investigator William J. Burns, founder of the Burns Detective Agency, to solve the case. The film was a Western version of Jack the

Ripper. The script for the movie *A Knife for the Ladies* was written by Bob Shelton and produced by Larry Spangler and Stan Jolley.

Shelton wrote a fight scene into the script, which was key to the movie. Co-producer Spangler, also the film director, worked with Kimo Owens, head actor-stuntman at Old Tucson, in choreographing the battle. Every lunge, blow, dodge, kick, and punch was carefully blocked out. Then the two Old Tucson stuntmen, who doubted the principles in the fight, had to be "taught" the fight sequence. In a long blond wig, Jerry Richards doubled Elam, and John Pearce doubled Cooper.

When the film was ready for its premiere, the airlines lost the Knife for the Ladies' final copy. They had to rush the printing of another copy.

The Old Tucson Development Company Board of Directors declared a 5 percent stock dividend to be paid on October 1 to stockholders of record on August 15. Robert Shelton, president and chairman of the Board, said the dividend is the equivalent of 12.1 cents per share on a share valuation basis of $2.50.

A crew from A.B.C. was in the Tucson area filming on October 24 for a "Movie of the Week," starring Andy Griffith, William Shatner, Robert Reed, and Marjoe Gortner. Old Tucson dressed the High Chaparral Ranch to look like a cantina and decorated the town to look like a Mexican town. *Pray for the Wildcats* is about Sam Farragut (Griffith), a prominent businessman who hires an ad agency to buy into a sales campaign in the lower Baja. However, he insisted that they scout the area on motorcycles. The trip is full of adventure and danger, threatening their families, marriage, and lives. They filmed at Old Tucson, Gates Pass, and Rio Rico.

William Shatner, Marjo Gortner, and Andy Griffith wait on
their motorcycles on the set of *Pray for the Wildcats.*

The University of Arizona Rodeo team hosted the Grand Canyon Region's fourth intercollegiate rodeo of the season on November 13th and 14th at Old Tucson Studios. The Grand Canyon Region is one of 11 regions that make up the National Intercollegiate Rodeo Association (NIRA). Old Tucson held this annual rodeo until 1994.

Other rodeos held at Old Tucson were the annual Pima County Community College Rodeo and the Turquoise Circuit yearly rodeo. In addition, special rodeos were performed, such as the Law Enforcement Rodeo Association's annual rodeo and the Professional Bull Riders Association's bull riding competitions.

The corporation, Old Tucson Delaware, was incorporated in 1973. The original Old Tucson Development Company was formed in 1959 in Arizona. These two entities were incorporated in Arizona as a single corporation on December 10, 1973.

Old Tucson also had plans to begin serving liquor in its main restaurant in 1974. It required separate approval by the supervisors (which they gave).

The University of Arizona hosted its
annual rodeo at Old Tucson.

As of December 22, the newest attraction, horseback riding, was included in admission.

A Dino DeLaurentis production starring Charles Bronson was filmed on old Tucson's Main Street on January 21, 1974. The feature film, titled *Death Wish*, utilized a regular gunfight, "The Great Tucson Bank Robbery," for the background action during the Old Tucson portion of the movie. Paul Kersey (Bronson) is a New York architect whose wife was murdered by a street punk gang. On a trip to an old western movie set, he saw a staged gunfight and got the idea of becoming a one-person vigilante. A "mugger" in New York attempts to rob him, and Kersey shoots him. Regular guests at Old Tucson, who were in the audience for the filming, actually ended up on the screen.

An ABC-TV "Movie of the Week" starring Steve Forrest, Cameron Mitchell, and Arthur O'Connell filmed at Old Tucson January 22 through January 26. *The Hanged Man* was produced by

Andrew J. Kennedy for Bing Crosby Productions and directed by Mike Kathy. This film was intended to be a pilot but was not picked up by the network. A gunfighter survives a hanging and then finds that he can read minds and use it to help people. He assists a young widow in keeping her land from the land baron trying to steal it.

Stuntmen perform a gunfight for the filming of *Death Wish*.
Charles Bronson can be seen watching the show in the distance right.

Another ABC-TV "Movie of the Week" began filming at Old Tucson on February 5 through February 22. *The Gun and The Pulpit* starred: Marjo Gortner, Slim Pickens, and David Huddleston. A gunslinger on the run from the law finds the body of a dead minister. He assumes the dead minister's identity to evade lawman tracking them.

On February 8, 1974, Gray Line Tours started running four buses a day to Old Tucson and the Arizona-Sonora Desert Museum. The round-trip costs $2. The two businesses agreed with the bus line because attendance figures were lagging. Spokesmen said there was little doubt that the slowdown was related to the scarcity of gasoline. The buses to Old Tucson and the museum departed El Con shopping center. They stopped at various other points in the city before winding into the Tucson Mountain Recreation Area. A tape recording described the scenic area. The bus company discontinued the service in April.

The studio site owners rejected an offer of oil and gas lease rights on land next to Old Tucson to prevent mineral prospecting was denied on February 28 by the studio site owners as attempted blackmail. Bob Shelton, president of Old Tucson, said that this offer had no merit, and he would not pay for the mineral rights, which he doubted existed. A Signo Vinces spokesman said the intended proposal would give Old Tucson a chance to prevent drilling and control the mineral rights or enter the mining business.

Dick Clark's Action 74 ABC-TV series group presented three concerts at Old Tucson on April 14, and Bo Donaldson and the Heywood's performed in the Desert Theatre outdoor arena. The group's varied style includes hard rock, country-western, and progressive brass.

On April 5, 1974, Gunsmoke started shooting a two-part episode, *Comancheros of Cibola Blanca*, to open its 20th season. Harold Gould wrote the film, *Cibola Blanca*. The episode revolves around Doc capturing a woman friend while traveling from Santa Fe to Dodge and holding prisoners in an outlaw's hideaway deep in the desert. The film company shot *Comancheros* and 12 partial episodes at Mescal and the Slash Y Ranch set.

Members of Tucson's Explorer Post 377, with 17 teenagers, delighted in learning how to beat up and kill each other painlessly. The 12 boys and five girls, primarily high school sophomores and juniors, spent about eight hours each Saturday sharpening their skills in delivering the "chin drop," "gut shot," and 18 other moves with similar names. The post specialized in learning and performing stunts. In recent years, the national scouting program has included girls in its Explorer-level activities. The first girl joined Post 377 in 1971.

On June 8, 1974, Old Tucson added the country-western singing of Lynne Bruce to the movie set's new Front Street Beer Garden. Food was also available at the air-conditioned saloon.

Fast Eddy and the Rodeo Kings inaugurated Old Tucson's summer program of evening entertainment events starting June 16. As part of Old Tucson's summer programming, "Sebe Stewart and his Group" performed at Old Tucson's new Front Street beer garden.

Gruff-voiced Neville Brand was in town June 17, 1974, to make a television commercial and a sales film for Ray-O-Vac batteries. Old Tucson's Mescal Western set near Benson was the locale for the three days of filming.

Petrocelli started filming its first season in Tucson on July 8 for 13 weeks. The sound stage at Old Tucson Studios was used as Petrocelli's office, as were the Courtroom scenes. The pilot, *Night Games,* was filmed in December 1973, and the new show premiered on November 11, 1974. Petrocelli is a defense attorney who defends wrongfully accused defendants.

Ricky Nelson enters the office of Petrocelli (Barry Newman).

The University of Arizona Band presented a concert at Old Tucson on July 6, 1974, as part of its post-Fourth of July celebration that included a fireworks presentation.

"Johnny Duncan's Country Western Show" was featured on July 10 in two performances at Old Tucson's outdoor Desert Theater. Country music singer and composer Don Gibson was featured in two shows Saturday, August 10, at Old Tucson's outdoor Desert Theatre.

Country entertainer Ferlin Husky also performed Friday, August 23, at Old Tucson's Desert Theatre. Husky, who used three different names to sell more than 20 million records, included his popular "Simon Crum" character in the musical shows. There was no increase in the admission price for the special shows at the famous movie location. All rides and shops were open throughout the evening. Cocktails and food were available at the Front Street Beer Garden, where the Lewallen Brothers western musical group held additional entertainment.

The picturesque San Xavier Mission was one of the locations for Twentieth Century-Fox's *Mark of Zorro* feature film, which began shooting on August 19 starring Frank Langella, Ricardo Montalban, Robert Middleton, and Yvonne DeCarlo. The action-adventure film wrapped up shooting at Old Tucson on August 24. The swishing fop Diego de la Vega becomes the swashbuckling masked hero Zorro when tyranny threatens his people in 19th-century California. During a scene for the *Mark of Zorro,* stuntman Alan Pinson doubled for Frank Langella. He was supposed to jump from the roof of the building onto the back of a horse. As he jumped, the horse moved. Pinson broke his wrist.

The Paramount film *Posse* began filming on October 12 at the Southern Pacific Railroad spur in Florence, Arizona. The Reno was moved there for a train chase. Kirk Douglas putting the Reno through fast chase sequences, developed six hot boxes on the antique engine in one day. Quick changes of wheels and axles kept the production (and the train) rolling on schedule. The film was produced by Howard Koch for Paramount and directed by Kirk Douglas. The movie starred Kirk Douglas, Bruce Dern, and Bo Hopkins. A politically ambitious Marshall (Douglas) decides to capture a notorious outlaw. It will give him a leg up on his Texas Senate run. Unfortunately, his posse turns against him when his political career takes over his dedication to the law.

Bruce Dern holds Kirk Douglas at gunpoint when the pursued becomes the pursuer in the 1975 movie *"Posse."*

BackTrack, ABC-TV "Movie of the Week" started filming at Old Tucson on October 4, 1974. The movie starred Jack Palance, Jack Warden, and Keith Carradine. Three union P.O.W.s try to cross the desert to escape their Confederate pursuers and rampaging Apaches. Instead, they find a dying woman and her infant child. They promise a woman that they will take care of the child and get it safely across the desert, even though none of them knows anything about children or babies. The movie was a remake of the John Wayne film *The Three*

Godfathers. The action-adventure yarn was filmed at Old Tucson and Ajo, where much of the action took place on the old "Reno" train consisting of a locomotive, coal car, and two unique cars.

Producers Leon Mirell and Sal Grasso spent three days at Old Tucson to film the studio's history. They used still photographs, newspaper articles, publications, and live-action films and clips from features made here over the years to tell the story. The 20-minute production traced the evolution of Old Tucson from the first appearance of Clarence Budington Kelland's novel *Arizona* in the Saturday Evening Post, the construction of the movie set by Columbia Studios in 1939, and its restoration from 1959 to 1974. Old Tucson's visitors could view the film in the "First Electric Theater."

Jack Young, the executive production manager of Old Tucson, announced his own company's formation on November 7. Jack Young Film Services had offices in the Desert Inn, 1 North Freeway. Young's company motto, "Finders of Everything a Filmmaker Needs," tells you exactly what the business did.

The Quinn Martin Production entitled, *The Abduction of Saint Anne* was produced by John Wilier and directed by Harry Palk. The film utilized Old Tucson's Mexican plaza on November 10 and December 2. It starred Robert Wagner, Kathleen Quinlan, and EG Marshall. A detective and a Roman Catholic Bishop begin to investigate the supposed power of a living saint (Quinlan). She was being held captive by her father. The Bishop wanted to rescue her and place her in a convent.

Old Tucson's held the corporation's annual meeting at 10 a.m. on December 17.

Kathleen Quinlan and Robert Wagner run lines on the
mission set during "The Abduction of Saint Anne."

The revenue for 1974 was $1,629,209 compared to $1,569,896 for fiscal 1973. An alcohol beverage license issued to the company in April will contribute considerably to expanding food and beverage operations. Old Tucson Corporation purchased 32,865 shares of its common stock in November (approximately 8 ½ percent of the outstanding shares). This purchase changed the number of outstanding shares to 351,961. According to an announcement by Robert Shelton, the transaction had the net effect of increasing the book value of each share, then outstanding from $2.21 to $2.41, Shelton reported. "The purchase was authorized by the Board of Directors when the block of stock became available from a large Florida investor.

The tag line "Twelve miles and a hundred years from town" was used for the first time in a news release on January 20, 1975.

Admission was $2.50 and each attraction was paid for separately, or buy a bonus book for $3.95, which included admission to sound stage which was normally $.40, First Electric Street movie normally $.50, French fries $.40, burger with fries $1.75, miniature railroad $.65, stage coach ride $.80, carousal $.35, car rides $.65, horse rides $3.50, and Shetland ponies $.50.

The longtime T.V. series Gunsmoke's cast and crew started shooting for their record-breaking 20th season at Old Tucson on April 5, 1974. The company had completed an episode at the Mescal set near Benson and the "Slash Y" ranch set at Sonoita. With James Arness in his familiar U.S. Marshal Matt Dillon role. It also starred Milburn Stone as Doc Adams, Ken Curtis, and Buck Taylor. The company was at Old Tucson through April 23.

A.B.C. "Movie of the Week," *Katherine, an American Terrorist,* filmed starting June 15, 1975, starred Art Carney, Sissy Spacek, and Henry Winkler. The tale of a woman in the late 1960s disillusioned by American society. After trying to teach illiterate Mexican immigrants to read, she turns into a radical bomber

Old Tucson's wardrobe department, headed by capable Pat Wareing, was in stitches and patches and ready for 300-pound local actor and stuntman Tiny Wells. And his britches-bustin' stunts in a breakfast cereal commercial for TDF Films, Toronto, Canada, and shot on Kansas Street July 19, 1975. Unfortunately, tiny toppled from a second-story window onto a porch roof and bounced onto the street, splitting his britches.

An N.B.C. television crew from New York arrived at Old Tucson on Tuesday, July 19, to prepare for videotaping an episode of the children's program, *Go U.S.A.* They videotaped in Old Tucson's Mexican plaza from Thursday, July 31, through Sunday, August 3. The program's full name was *Go U.S.A., The Deed of Jose Diaz.*

Fox started to build the sound stage set for *The Last Hard Men.* Based on the book "Gun Down' by Brian Garfield. Old Tucson's antique railroad equipment will be taken to the San Manuel Railroad and used there. So grab hold of the old girl's 65,000 lbs., pop them off the tracks at Old Tucson and onto the back of a big flatbed truck, drive the flatbed on Oracle Rd. to San Manuel, and then just plop that thing back onto some railroad tracks up there. Cost? At least $310.00 each way. The movie starred Charlton Heston, James Coburn, and Barbara Hershey was about Zach Provo, a convicted prisoner escaping from a chain gang with six other convicts. He sets off to exact revenge on the lawman who sent him to prison and who he blames for the death of his wife. He kidnaps a lawman's (Heston) daughter; the lawman strapped on his guns and went after him.

Charleton Heston and Micael Parks
walking north on Front Street.

Old Tucson's sister set at Mescal was activated November 21, when the shooting began on *Josey Wales, Rebel Outlaw,* starring Clint Eastwood. Shooting time for Mescal was 6 ½ weeks and then it moved to Patagonia. The company scheduled four weeks of construction at Old Tucson's Mescal western street. Outlaw Josey Wales, the movie's release name, starred Clint Eastwood, Chief Dan George, and Sondra Locke. After Union soldiers burned his home and murdered his family, Josey Wales (Eastwood) turns into a hardened Union hater. He seeks vengeance for the wrongs done him by the Union Army. Josie heads west pursued by a U.S. Cavalry unit out to kill him. As he travels west, he picks up a band of people looking to him for help. Eventually settling down with these people and starting a ranch, he has one final run-in with his pursuers.

Some 250 carolers from local chorus groups participated in Old Tucson's first annual Christmas tree lighting ceremony Saturday, December 6. A 30-ft. tree, decorated with old-fashioned ornaments and candles, were lit at sunset during the program at the High Chaparral Ranch set at Old Tucson.

Young Pioneers, a two-hour pilot film for a projected television series, filmed at Old Tucson from Thursday, December 11, thru Tuesday, December 16. The company filmed in the courthouse square and train depot area and starred Linda Purl, Roger Kern, and Robert Hayes. This show was a short-lived (three episodes) series about Molly and David Beaton, two teenage newlyweds, in the Dakota Territory in the early 1870s.

Mulberry Square Productions descended on Old Tucson with a star-studded cast and 13 camels on November 24. They began production on *Hawmps,* a western comedy about camels in the cavalry during the late 1850s. Joe Camp produced and directed the movie. The story, based on the real-life episode of the mid-19th century when the U.S. Army imported camels to the Arizona desert to work as pack animals. *Hawmps* used sixteen grown camels, and one young camel named Valentine (9 months old). The all-star cast included: James Hampton, Christopher Connelly, Slim Pickens, Denver Pyle, Gino

Conforti, and Jack Elam. Several out of ordinary things occurred during filming.

Chris Connelly, former star of T.V.'s *Paper Moon* series, was unaware that his mount was a camera hog. He and other actors on camelback were galloping along the landscape when they approached the camera. Chris's camel promptly stopped, blowing the whole scene. It took two or three repeat performances before the trainers realized what the problem was. Then they have Chris another *Hawmps* to ride.

"Some of these camels were rounded up in Australia's Outback," explained Camp, "and never before heard the likes of generators, chainsaws, and helicopters." They just jumped the curbs on Old Tucson's streets. The camels streaked across the surrounding Arizona-Sonora desert with anyone precariously atop hanging on for dear life.

The Camel, Tanya, was being led to the corral by her trainer-rider Paul "Sled" Reynolds Monday evening when a young man bolted in front of them with two security guards in pursuit. "The guards yelled for me to chase him," said Reynolds, 25, who hopped on and took off. "It's usually hard to guide a camel, but she took off right after him." Reynolds and Tanya pursued the youth, accused of shoplifting jewelry from the Hospitality Shop, south across the parking lot, and into the desert. "Probably nothing would have happened," Reynolds said, "but the guy picked up a rock and started to throw it at us, then Tanya got mad and hello, ran at him." He dropped the rock and threw up his hands and said: "I give up, don't run that camel over me!" The 17-year-old was taken into custody by the security guards and transported to the Pima County Juvenile Center.

During the filming of *Hawmps*, Rillito Race sponsored a camel race. Sweet Lips Tanya won.

As Mimi's stand-in, Stacy was often required to do the "dirty work" involved in different scenes. One such scene was when Mimi fell into a mud puddle and then had molasses poured on her. She says that it was water with water thickener and coloring added to it. Mimi did the scene using a mud puddle. Then, the wardrobe department carefully wrapped the mud splotched dress in plastic so it would not dry overnight. The next day, Stacy traded places with Mimi. She put on the damp, muddy dress (she had a plastic wrap to protect her from feeling the dampness) and proceeded with the scene. In the middle of one of the streets at Old Tucson, two crew members dumped a concoction that looked like molasses all over Stacy. The film shows the molasses covered Stacy, who is walking up the middle of the street with her back to the camera, not Mimi.

A report put out at the beginning of January 1976 gave the following information: "The front gate can handle 800-900 guests per hour, and admissions raised $77,750. The hospitality house expanded from 400 feet to 2,000 feet, and Merchandize sales were $546,816, up from $129,533. The remodeled Front Street Saloon (formerly the Beer Garden) and the completion of the expansion of the "A" car ride, six Arrow Flyer Autos, added $30,000".

A one-hour television pilot shot on location in Tucson started in early January. *Royce* used Mescal Street near Benson and some places in the Sonoita area. This pilot which was not picked up as a series, starred Robert Forster, Terry Lynn Wood, and Mary Beth Hurt. Royce (Forster), a westerner raised by Comanche's, tries to help a woman and two kids go west to find their husband and father who abandoned them in Kansas.

In February, a radio tower was built on the Bushmaster peak in the Tucson Mountains, overlooking Old Tucson. The tower was painted brown and blue to camouflage it for filming. A beacon was put on the towers with a light installed, which can only be seen from the air.

An NBC-TV World Premiere movie and pilot, *The Quest,* was scheduled for 14 days of filming at Old Tucson starting January 30. *The Quest* tells the story of 2 brothers searching through Wyoming for their sister, captured by Cheyenne Indians. One of the brothers had also been captured and adjusted to the Indian way of life when white men recaptured him. He is conflicted between the two conflicting cultures.

Main Street was a thoroughly watered down and muddy street representing Cheyenne, Wyoming, in 1890. The company altered the facades on its buildings to give it a new look. A blacksmith shop was added, along with smoke pots along the wooden sidewalks where the pioneers could warm their cold hands. Mexican Plaza became a fort, and they built a Chinese alley along the east side of the sound stage.

The Chinese Alley made for *The Quest* needed a population. The producers recruited many Asian college students and Vietnamese refugees as extras.

The Quest involved 100 head of cattle driven through the streets. It took three takes to get the animals to stampede. One stuntman had to fall off a ladder into the mud for the scene, which he had to do three times.

The script called for a race between a camel and a horse. During which the driver of the camel was to lose control and let the camel get into the saloon where it was to tear up all the furniture and exit through a large plate glass window. With three cameras in position, five unsuccessful attempts were made to get the camel to go through the window. Finally, the primary camera ran out of film. Just as the cameraman removed the film cartridge, you guessed it, the camel crashed through the windowpane. *The Quest* starred Kurt Russell, Tim Matheson, Brian Keith, and Keenan Wynn.

Old Tucson's sale was final March 16. Controlling interest in Old Tucson Corporation transferred to television production company owner Burt Sugarman and Gabriel Alarcon Jr., a Mexico City industrialist. The agreement was signed on March 10, 1976, by Old Tucson's Board of directors and Burt Sugarman and Calhoun Nevada, a corporation controlled by Alarcon. Under it, Sugarman, Calhoun, and others were to purchase 1 million shares of Old Tucson Corporation common stock for $2.5 million. The agreement also allows the group to acquire an additional 500,000 shares of common stock for $2.50 a share.

A condition of the sale was a pending voting trust agreement with Johnny Mitchell. He was a principal shareholder of Old Tucson Corporation, which would give Sugarman and Alarcon voting control of more than 50 percent of the outstanding stock. Old Tucson operated the Western theme park and movie location west of Tucson. Old West Corporation operated the Old Vegas theme park in Henderson, Nevada. Upon completing the agreement, Sugarman, president of Burt Sugarman Inc., a television program production company, would be chairman of the Board and chief executive officer. Remaining on the Board as president was Robert E. Shelton. Joining them was Alarcon, vice chairman, David Gotterer, director, and Jerry E. Blackwell, director.

Due to the excellent cooperation of the Anamax Mining Co. in allowing the use of its Empire Ranch property, Barbara Streisand's company, Barwood Films, Ltd., built an $80,000 motion picture set on a plateau overlooking the vast expanse of the Empire Ranch. This project included the tearing down of the Slash Y Ranch set.

First Artists began filming in the Phoenix and Tucson area on March 15, 1976. The movie, *A Star is Born,* starred Barbra Streisand, Kris Kristofferson, and Gary Busey. Rock star John Norman had seen his popularity dwindle, and he had difficulties keeping promises to use an agent and journalist. He met the younger singer Esther and helped her get a contract with the record company. She had a breakthrough; Norman becomes more and more depressed. This movie is not the same as the 1954 version with Judy Garland and James Mason.

Moonshine and Sassafras, a tent musical comedy based on the saga of an old-time medicine pitchman, was featured as a part of Old Tucson's summer program for 1976. The main street of Old Tucson featured an old-fashioned street carnival complete with pitch games and other entertainment. The summer program and new summer hours began with the gala world premiere performance of *Moonshine and Sassafras* on Wednesday, June 23, and continue through Labor Day. This musical and amusing play details the trials and tribulations of Dr. Claybourne W. Pepper in his efforts to peddle his Egyptian Elixir, "the secret formula from the Pharaohs' tomb." He brings his traveling medicine show to a rough, tough small town in Arizona in the late 1800s.

Beginning on Thursday, July 18, Twentieth Century-Fox Studios filmed for eight days at Old Tucson on a two-hour film for ABC-TV, titled *The Most Wanted Woman.* This movie was a sequel to *Butch Cassidy and the Sundance Kid.* It starred Katherine Ross, Steve Forrest, and Hector Elizondo. The Sundance Kid's widow, Etta Place, joins Pancho Villa and portrays the conflict between the Yaquis

Indians and Mexico. The film highlighted the revolution's hostilities and was released under the name *Wanted: The Sundance Woman.*

One of the principal players had some bad luck. He accidentally shot his wrangler with a blank, then accidentally shot himself, and then banged his head as he got into the car to go to the hospital.

John Wayne fans enjoyed a visit to the Alamo Museum, where memorabilia from that film was displayed. The interior of the old train depot was complete even to the antique roll-front tariff rack. Another building housed a replica of Tucson's first schoolroom. Quality western wear from boots to Stetsons were for sale in the Western Emporium. And Old Tucson's Hospitality House contained a large selection of western and movie-themed souvenirs.

One of the fascinating interiors was that of the sound stage itself. If a film production company was not using it at the time, guides explained some of the secret tricks and motion picture production techniques.

Even after watching a live-action gunfight show and taking a trip on the miniature train, a ride on the 1909 carousel, a bumpy journey on the stagecoach, a gallop along desert trails on horseback, and a chugging circuit of the miniature antique car track – there were lots still left to do at Old Tucson. Its frontier buildings were a browser's or bargain hunter's bonanza. Inside the "Greer Carson House" next to the Mexican mission, they could peruse a collection of still photographs taken during the filming of movies and television shows. Inside the Arizona Theater, they could see a selection of memorabilia from Arizona, the film for which Old Tucson was built, and a 20-minute movie, *Hollywood in the Desert.*

Teamsters Local 310 tried to organize Arizona movie extras and represent them bargaining with producers for better wages and working conditions. William McCollum, president of the local, said 216 people who worked as extras in productions filmed at Old Tucson signed cards authorizing the Teamsters local to represent them. They were getting $17 per day to pay for extra work, but McCallum believed they should get at least $26.25 plus overtime. Arizona is a right to work state, and labor does not have to organize. McCallum was trying to rile them up and join the union. He was having a close race for the union president and tried getting people to join the union to get him more votes. The union did not garner enough signatures to complete the attempt.

Old Tucson's first annual Bluegrass Music Festival kicked off a full weekend of "Fingerpickin' good" old-time music with a sundown concert on Friday, October 22, 1976. This music festival would continue up to the present under different auspices.

Kidnappers took Geronimo, the wooden Indian, which stood in front of the Old Tucson Trading Post for 15 years. Old Tucson officials discovered the wooden antique missing Sunday morning after a dance sponsored by the University of Arizona's Intercollegiate Rodeo. The Geronimo kidnappers released the wooden statute to a local television station about 3:30 p.m. The kidnappers asked for "ransom," of 100 passes for the Centers for Youth Development and Achievement residents, a rehabilitation program for Indian teenagers. Bruce Subeck, marketing director for Old Tucson, said: "We are thrilled he is back. It has been with us so long that it would not be the same without him." He said that he was not interested in pressing theft charges against the kidnappers and that Old Tucson was more than glad to agree to the "ransom" terms. The kidnappers left a message taped to Geronimo's chest, warning officials of another strike: "We're wanted men, we'll strike again! (But first we'll have another beer") from the W.I.L.M. (Wooden Indian Liberation Movement)."

Visitors to Old Tucson were startled to see a red and white checkered covered chuck wagon galloping up Old Tucson's streets. It was the crew from Parker Studios who were shooting a Ralston Puppy Chow commercial for the Ralston Purina Company.

Bert Sugarman made many hasty and unpopular decisions concerning the development and future of Old Tucson. He closed Old Vegas, tried to sell Mescal, and ordered the dismantling of several projects at Old Tucson. The Board felt that they needed to restructure the organization, so through the influence of Johnny Mitchell of Mitchell Energy in Houston, Texas, they bought Sugarman out and got rid of him.

In August 1976, Production Manager Hal Klein and Art Director Bob Clatworthy were starting preparations for Claude Lelouch's western for United Artists, *James and Jane.* (Released under the name of *A Man and A Woman*). A crew of approximately 25 painters and carpenters headed by Wayne Conard were constructing new sets. Also refurbishing old ones and giving Old Tucson's Kansas Street and railroad corral area a new look.

In January 1977, *Another Man, Another Chance,* a sequel of *A Man and A Woman*, lensed at Old Tucson. It starred James Caan and Genevieve Bujold. Bujold's character immigrates to the United States to escape the war between Prussia and France. She moved to the wild west to open a photo business and falls in love with a lonely widower, James Caan, whose wife had been raped and killed by outlaws. A new location for the big race scene in Claude Lelouch's *Another Man, Another Chance* had to be found in a hurry during their last days of filming here. With 600 extras and many horses and wagons, the scene was scheduled for the dry lake at Willcox. The only trouble was when it was time to do the scene, the "dry" lake contained two feet of water.

The cast and crew of N.B.C.'s *Little House on the Prairie* arrived in town on January 22 for two weeks of filming on a two-hour special. The episode involved the Ingalls family moving from Walnut Grove during a depression. Pa (Michael Landon) decided to head west with the whole family in search of gold. They filmed at Sonoita Creek near Patagonia and Old Tucson's Mescal western street near Benson and Old Tucson.

But there had been a small recurring problem — Arizona saguaros tended to pop up in the Dakota landscape. So, the question was: How do you dress a saguaro to look like it's not a saguaro? The burden was placed on film editors to scrutinize the scenes to avoid showing a cactus. In some cases, the prop department had to "mask" the cacti to blend in with the Dakota landscape.

The cast of *Little House on the Prairie* and KVOA-TV and K.T.K.T. radio held a charity softball game. The proceeds went to the Community Organization for Drug Abuse Control.

Columbia Pictures T.V. started filming March 3 for the ABC-TV movie *Go West, Young Girl,* which starred Karen Valentine and Sandra Will. A female New England reporter and the widow of a cavalry officer team up to go out west and wind up trying to evade outlaws, gamblers, and the law.

The movie, *The New Maverick,* started filming on April 17, 1978 and starred: James Garner, Charles Frank, Jack Kelly, and Susan Blanchard. Charles Frank played the nephew of Brett and Bart

Maverick. The three Mavericks' set out to capture some train robbers for the reward. The Reno, a 65,000-pound steam locomotive built in 1872, was hoisted off her home track at Old Tucson onto a flatbed truck for a short journey to San Manuel for a role in the movie.

Dale Robertson fired a shot in the air to officially open Silverlake, a $700,000 capital improvement. An old-time band played Oom-Pa music. Since the soundstage, Silverlake Park, the most substantial addition, opened in June 1976 and became home to the antique carousel and the new depot for the C.P. Huntington narrow gauge train and antique car ride. The new park area had the Iron Door Mine ride, the shooters gallery, and the Indian Maze. Silverlake Park area also included a snack shop, a ride ticket booth, and an arcade with both antique and modern coin-operated machines and games. The plans turned the southwest quadrant of the park into an amusement area. Reminiscent of the old Silverlake Park, which existed along the Santa Cruz River near the foot of Sentinel Peak (now "A" Mountain) before the turn of the 20th century.

They added an air-conditioned prop storage facility to the west side of the sound stage. Architecture One designed the facility to be approximately 35 by 55 feet. The addition's interior was double-tiered storage for motion picture props and set dressing similar to that used by major Hollywood studios.

The capital improvement program also called for expanding and remodeling the Golden Nugget Ice Cream Parlor on Old Tucson's main street. When completed, it seated 132 in a decor of early-day ice-cream emporiums, with stained glass windows and paddle fans.

Old Tucson Studios began a summer program on weekend evenings on June 24, 1977. Jackpot roping, old-time movies in Front Street Saloon, and dancing to Becky Rose and the Country Set's music were all planned activities. The entire park, including rides, shops, and movies, were open. Visitors had their choice of studio tours, horseless carriage, train, and stagecoach rides.

Eleven persons were taken to the hospital with minor injuries after a horse-drawn stagecoach overturned at Old Tucson on August 28, 1977. According to the stagecoach driver, Roxanne Bute, something "spooked" the horses, causing them to bolt. The coach then rolled onto its right side, she said. Witnesses said the stagecoach was traveling at a slow, average speed on level ground when the horses suddenly bolted. Ramona Hartman, 28, and her 4-year-old daughter, Tanya, both of Phoenix, were held overnight at Saint Mary's Hospital for observation. None of the injuries were severe, hospital authorities said. The other eight passengers were treated for minor cuts and bruises and released from St. Mary's a few hours after the 5 p.m. accident. A spokesman for Old Tucson said this was the first accident of the ride in its 15 years of operation.

The next film to be shot was *The Incredible Rocky Mountain Race,* filmed from September 26 through October 8. It starred Christopher Connelly, Forrest Tucker, and Larry Storch. After an old man watches a boy bully another boy, he tells them a morality tale. It was a story about a legendary race to the Rocky Mountains between Mark Twain and his adversary Mike Fink.

The Tucson Advertising Club sponsored what they called "Octoberwest." The event included an art show all three days in the movie soundstage and a film festival featuring three movies, filmed at Old Tucson. Tucson Advertising Club held this festivity for three years.

Old Tucson Corporation directors declared a 2-for-1 stock split to stockholders on November 1. The Corporation announced a net income of $120,738 or $.34 a share for the fiscal year ended June 30. And revenue increased from $57,295 or $.15 a share from the year before. Robert Shelton, the president of Old Tucson, said the western theme park and motion picture location had its best year ever. The gross income increased by $2.58 million compared with $2.4 million in the previous year.

How the West Was Won, scheduled to shoot at Old Tucson's Phillips Ranch set, had to move inside to film scenes due to rain. The episode, which started filming November 5, 1977, was called *Cattle Drive*, and guest-starred Slim Pickens. Regulars in the cast included James Arness, Bruce Boxleitner, Kathryn Holcomb, Vicki Schradt, William Kirby, and Cullen Flanagan. They filmed at least two episodes at Old Tucson. The main story centered on the Macahan family, heading west from Virginia to Oregon. After the murder of their parents, Zeb Macahan takes charge of the children. With the help of Aunt Molly, Culhane continues the voyage.

On December 17, 1977, the cast and crew arrived to make a two-hour ABC-TV movie entitled *Wild and Wooly*. It starred Christiane Delisle, Susan Bigelow, Elyssa Davalos, and Doug McClure. This period feature is about three escaped female prisoners (unjustly jailed). Their historical-fiction antics included the attempted assassination of Teddy Roosevelt. A group of "Charlie's Angels" on horseback must clear their names by stopping a killer trying to kill the United States president.

An advertisement for Old Tucson on December 17 used a proto-gunfighter logo, which was a crude outline of a gunfighter pointing his weapon slightly to the right. This advertisement was the first time the park used this classic logo.

Josephine Tussaud opened the Old Tucson Movie-land Wax Museum near the front gate, which is now known as "The Last Outpost." The Actual construction of the wax museum started in November 1977. Costumes were supplied by Old Tucson, with wardrobe mistress Pat Wareing supervising their selection and getting them ready to be placed on the wax fixtures.

Gems Wax Models made all the wax figures for the Tussaud Museums of London. The hair was imported from Italy and placed one strand at a time with an electric needle. Each figure required 60,000 to 90,000 hairs — this includes beards and chest hair. The chin stubble was created by using a full beard inserted in the face and then partially shaved. Standard beeswax was used for the face and hands with a chemical mix to make them heat resistant. The eyes were made of medical glass by an optical company in Germany, and the teeth were genuine dentures. It took three to six months to make a figure from scratch, and when finished, each was worth about $18,000.

The figures included the cast of *Rio Bravo* and *Arizona*. Also included were: Gene Autry, James Arness, Sidney Poitier, Audie Murphy, Frank Sinatra, Clint Eastwood, Paul Newman, Charles Bronson, Jack Palance, and Charlton Heston, The Earps, Holliday, Bill Clanton, and the McLowerys. Shelley Winters, Kirk Douglas, Frank Sinatra, Bert Lancaster, William Holden, Jean Arthur, and Bonanza's actors Lorne Green, Michael Landon, and the late Dan Blocker.

Old Tucson held its first annual Can-Can contest April 29th -30th with free admission, lunch, and a souvenir newspaper. The April 21 "Dandy Dime" newspaper contained an official entry form. Cash prizes ($100 plus a trophy) were given to the five winners. Old Tucson actors served as judges.

Old Tucson's 1978 summer show theme was "The Great '78 All-American Hoedown Showdown," which began June 9. Going into effect that day was a new "one for all" admission policy embracing unlimited rides on the 1909 carousel, Old Tucson Stage Line, the scenic train ride, the antique Stutz Bearcat cars, and the Iron Door Mine dark ride.

Numerous Tucson top bands and performers made music Fridays, Saturdays, and Sundays through September 4. Th contest culminated in a "Battle of the Bands" over Labor Day weekend, the most popular acts determined by visitors' votes.

An extensive collection of Hopi Indian Kachina dolls went on permanent display at Old Tucson, on June 29. Located in the Indian Trading Post, the Kachina Doll Museum was another example of Old Tucson's continuing effort to preserve our Western heritage.

A new feature in the Silverlake area was the Indian maze made from saguaro ribs. The labyrinth was in the shape of the O'Odham "man in the maze."

Old Tucson Corporation acquired the personal films of Elvis Presley from his wife, Priscilla. The films were shown at the theme parks in Tucson and Henderson, Nevada, during the month of August. The Presley footage, most of it shot by Priscilla, was edited into a one-hour film. She introduced and narrated the film. Scenes include Elvis with his daughter, Lisa; Elvis in Hawaii surfing and playing on the beach; Elvis in Aspen snowmobiling; Elvis at his mansion, Graceland, horseback riding; and Elvis at his wedding in Palm Springs.

A two-part T.V. adaptation of the third novel of Louis L'Amour's *The Sackets* was filmed at Mescal and Old Tucson. It starred Sam Elliott, Tom Selleck, Glenn Ford, and Ben Johnson. The story follows the three Sackett Brothers as they travel out west from their Tennessee home. Along the way, the oldest, Tell, prospects for gold. Simultaneously, the two younger brothers, Orin and Tye, herd cattle, and later helped bring order to a racially divided Santa Fe.

A spoof of the western genre, *The Villain,* was produced. Kirk Douglas in the title role and muscleman Arnold Schwarzenegger as the romantic lead, and Anne Margaret as the fem Fatale. Hal Needham, a former stunt man, directed the film. They divided the shooting between Old Tucson, Rio Rico, and the Flying V Ranch. Charming Jones (Margaret) must travel to her ancestral homeland to claim an inheritance. Handsome Stranger (Schwarzenegger) escorts her. Avery Simpson (Elam) wants the money for himself and hires Cactus Jack (Douglas) to stop Jones and Stranger. Cactus Jack is not particularly good at his task. *The Villain* shot October 16 to December 1, 1978, at the cost of $920,000.

The gunfighter logo was a drawing of a cowboy holding a pistol with the words "Old Tucson," written in the background, was first used in 1978.

Filmed in December 1978, Mescal was home for the movie *Frisco Kid* with Gene Wilder and Harrison Ford. On his way to San Francisco, a Polish rabbi saves an outlaw, protecting them from being burned alive by the Indians.

February 5, 1979, saw the filming of a C.B.S. "Movie of the Week," *Wild Wild West Revisited,* which starred Robert Conrad, Ross Martin, Paul Williams, and Harry Morgan. Once more, agents, West and Gordon, are called out of retirement to stop the plans of the villain, Loveless. He has replaced the crown heads of Europe with clones and holds the real ones captive. His next plan is to kidnap President Cleveland. West and Gordon, riding their private train, have to stop him from exploding his atomic bomb. *Wild, Wild West Revisited* filmed February 1 to February 12 at the cost of $187,000.

The next movie up was *Hunter's Moon*. Set in Wyoming, this 20th Century Fox story was about activities during the range wars between cattlemen and sheepmen around the beginning of the 20th century.

On the same date, March 9, as *Hunter's Moon* was filming at Old Tucson, the film *Tom Horn* was being shot at the Mescal set. It starred Steve McQueen, Linda Evans, and Richard Farnsworth. A renowned former Army Scout is hired by ranchers to hunt down rustlers. Getting caught in the middle of local politics, he finds himself on trial for the murder of a boy when he carries out his job too well.

The 1979 Summer live show was "Billy the Kid," a mini-musical melodrama about a kid who was shunned by society when he suspected his parents' deaths.

June 21, 1979 Veteran tough-guy actor John Wayne, who symbolized the strong American in hundreds of movies, died of cancer that he had fought for the last months of his life. He was 72. Wayne had been in a coma for 24 hours before his death at 5:30 p.m. at U.C.L.A. Medical Center, said hospital administrator Bernard Strohm. Wayne's seven children, a nurse, and a doctor were with him when he died.

The Japanese have a weird sense of humor, as was seen in the *Ultra Quiz Game Show* shot at Old Tucson on September 10, 1979. Contestants traveled around the U.S. and at each stop, are subjected to some indignity. At each round, they eliminated more contestants. Seven survivors made it to Old Tucson. The seven contestants were sent into the desert to retrieve an envelope with a question. The first six to answer right, advanced, and the seventh, a woman, was sent home. After standing in the Arizona heat for an hour, they used a stagecoach to kidnap the loser taken by horseback to a roofless jail. Her legs shackled and told she would be left there overnight. Half-hour later, she was released, given a bulletproof vest, then shot (with blanks), taken to the airport, and sent home.

Little House on the Prairie wrapped up filming and went back to California but left a controversy behind. More than 100 local Indians and 20 elderly Tohono O'Odham in Sells were angry at not being hired as extras. According to Merle Ross, director of the Tucson Indian Center, Frank Kennedy, under contract to the show to provide extras. He indicated he would hire 24 elderly Indians and 30 Indian riders as extras, among others. Ross, who is also co-director of the Southwest Indian Actors Workshop, said he had provided Kennedy with a list of more than 200 Indians who were willing to work. Kennedy says the figure is exaggerated and adds he interviewed more than 150 Indians. "As we understand it now, he hired only six of the riders and only five of the elderly. Old Tucson feared that this controversy would cause Little House to leave Tucson. The producer was upset by a news article which criticized Little House for not hiring Indians. They stated this was a big lie. Old Tucson was supposed to hire 50 Indians. But the casting company used Mexicans. *Little House on the Prairie* had nothing to do with the selection. The newspaper reported the resolution of the problem.

To help celebrate Old Tucson Studios' fortieth anniversary, the Fifth Cavalry Memorial Regiment had an encampment, with demonstrations and mock battles.

Old Tucson selected as the site for the traditional "chiliheads" cookoff presented by the "Chiliheads of Arizona." On October 13,

Arizona chili cooks participated in the state championship Chili Cook-off. The top three winners would automatically compete in the World Championship Cook-off at Terlingua, Texas, November 3. This cookoff would become a yearly tradition until about 2007.

The Retail Clerks Union Local 727 filed four labor complaints against Old Tucson. The union alleged that Old Tucson fired an employee for engaging in union activities, not allowing employees to wear union buttons on their work clothes, and without notification, changed certain work regulations. The union is attempting to unionize about half of the Old Tucson labor force, 160 full-time and part-time workers. The association only got 25 votes out of 160 employees to unionize. At a meeting, the employees voted not to let the union organize.

Based on "The Gambler," the hit recording by Kenny Rogers was slated for the filming of a television movie of the same name. Rogers, who starred in the production, started filming on the streets and in the Old Tucson sound stage on November 26. The movie company shot some sequences at Mescal, Old Tucson's western auxiliary set near Benson, Arizona. Besides Rogers, it also starred Christine Belford and Bruce Boxleitner. Brady Hawks (Rogers) is a gambler on his way to help his son. He meets Billy Montana (Boxleitner), a not so skilled gambler. Hawks teaches Montana the ins and outs of gambling. The Gambler won the 1979 Grammy best country song; it went platinum and was on top of the charts for 25 weeks.

CHAPTER SEVEN:
Hollywood in the Desert

Hart to Hart, a popular television series that starred Robert Wagner and Stephanie Powers, who play private investigators, shot parts of one episode at Old Tucson. The production company utilized various sets around the famous movie location and was on the lot January 23rd, 29th, and 30th. In this episode, the private investigators' friend is kidnapped and held for a ransom of $1 million in diamonds. Jonathan and Jennifer head to South America to ransom their friend.

On February 9th and 10th, 1980, Old Tucson celebrated its 20th anniversary by reuniting the *High Chaparral* cast. They appeared in the arena to meet fans, pose for pictures, and sign autographs. A mariachi band graced the Mexican Plaza each day with songs and colorful costumes of Old Mexico. The 5th Cavalry Memorial Regiment, and "A" Troop, demonstrated 19th-century military tactics and uniforms on Saturday. The Tucson Mountain Men set up a typical frontier campsite and demonstrations of that long-ago lifestyle on Sunday. The Tribal Dancers, 20 performers, dedicated to preserving the culture and heritage of the Tohono O'Odham nation, performed traditional dances Saturday and Sunday. Members of the High Chaparral television series cast and production team will be the first to be inducted into the Old Tucson Western Film Hall of Fame during ceremonies this weekend.

Construction began at Old Tucson for an NBC-TV feature movie, *The Buffalo Soldiers.* The production crew built a fort in the Mexican Plaza area for the filming, which began on March 20th. The film was about the Ninth Cavalry (Buffalo Soldiers) in the Southwest and their efforts to subdue a renegade band of Apaches led by Victorio. It starred John Beck, Stan Shaw, and Richard Lawson.

A second film sequel to the TV series *Wild Wild West* began filming on May 12th, 1980. *More Wild Wild West* starred Robert Conrad, Ross Martin, Jonathan Winters, and Harry Morgan. Agents West and Gordon are called out of retirement to stop another mad scientist, this time Albert Paradine, who can become invisible at will, and now plans to take over the world.

High Noon Plateau filmed at Old Tucson using the train, sound stage, and streets from Monday, June 16th, 1980, through Saturday, June 28th, 1980. It starred Lee Majors, David Carradine, and J. A. Preston and is a sequel to *High Noon.* After a long absence, Will Kane returns to Hadleyville to find the town marshal, and two deputies have terrorized the town. They are trying to kill a drifter for a crime he did not do. The drifter asks for help, and Kane takes his side, leading to a final shoot out. The film was released under the name of *High Noon Part II.*

The Fifth Cavalry Memorial Regiment held their semiannual get together at Old Tucson Studios on September 11th. They hosted several other units, the 5th Cavalry Memorial Regiment; "H" Battery, 4th Memorial Artillery; "E" Troop, 6th Memorial Cavalry; and the 8th

Memorial Infantry fife and drum corps. They entertained visitors with staged battles, horse and foot drills, and a booming cannon.

A writer's strike occurred in the summer of 1980, and it put a crimp on filming activity. However, a lot of the routine filming carried on at Old Tucson because commercials and documentaries were not affected by the strike.

ASCAP sued old Tucson for $10,000 for infringing copyrighted songs during open hours as background music. There were five songs that they claimed were infringed on. The park believed that their payment to BMI covered the music. After negotiations with ASCAP, the parties settled the case out of court.

A movie for HBO, produced by Los Angeles based Wizan Properties, Inc., began production of *El Diablo* on December 12th. It starred Paul Le Mat, Catherine Hicks, Stephan McHattie, and Wilford Brimley. This film was a contemporary tale about a divorced mother, her young son, and her new boyfriend who starts on a road trip through Death Valley and runs afoul of a serial killer.

Santa arrived in a horse-drawn wagon on December 20th, 1980. Old Tucson Studios decorated the town with old fashioned bunting and decorations for Christmas.

Set to start filming at Old Tucson on March 9th was *Father Murphy*. It was a two-hour NBC-TV movie starring Merlin Olsen, Moses Gunn, and Katherine Cannon. They were regulars on the NBC- TV series *Little House on the Prairie*. Michael Landon was the director and executive producer of this pilot film. This show was a spin-off, and Merlin Olsen pretends to be a priest to help orphans.

Osmond Studios began filming an NBC TV Movie titled *I Married Wyatt Earp* at Old Tucson's Mescal Street near Benson in

March. The company moved to Old Tucson from Mescal and wrapped up around the first of April. The movie starred Marie Osmond, Bruce Boxleitner, John Bennett Perry, Martin Cast, and Ross Martin. The film is based on a book by the same name, penned by Josephine Marcus Earp, and chronicles Wyatt Earp's adventures as seen through her not so unbiased eyes.

The Doctor Wheezer's Medicine Show was introduced at Old Tucson as an on-going entertainment attraction and has played to many Old Tucson visitors' delight. The somewhat eccentric Doctor is trying to sell a miraculous potion to guests.

The W.W. Wheezer Medicine Show. 1981 (Bob Shelton collection)

Old Tucson presented a musical melodrama, "Turmoil in Tucson or Just Desserts in the Desert," from August 22nd through September 7th, 1981.

Over 6000 people visited Old Tucson on July 4th, and the park had to turn 2500 people away. The park can hold approximately 5000 people and 4000 People parked in the desert, crushing plants. They fired off individual fireworks and became a fire hazard. The Board of Supervisors passed a traffic ordinance to allow the county to shutdown Kinney Road and Gates Pass Road when the Old Tucson Studio parking lot is full.

On March 9th, 1983, the county gave a rent rebate of $100,000 to Old Tucson to repair the facilities. The rent payments averaged $250,000 per year.

The film *September Gun* began shooting on April 18th. It starred Robert Preston and Patty Duke. Sister Dulcina (Duke) hires a gunfighter (Preston) to guide her group of Apache children to Colorado's new mission church. When they get there, they find that the church is now a bar and retreat to a barn until they can figure out what to do.

Old Tucson converted Kansas Street to look like Deadwood, South Dakota, complete with mud and tall pine trees for the CBS feature film *Calamity Jane* starring Jane Alexander, Frederick Forrest, and Ken Kercheval. Jane Alexander is Calamity Jane, a bigger than life frontier woman who knows more four-letter words than most mule skinners. Filming started on May 27th, 1983.

Kansas Street during the filming of *Calamity Jane*. Street decorated to look like Deadwood, South Dakota. 1983 (Bob Shelton collection)

The Fourth of July fireworks were canceled due to problems the previous year with large crowds.

At the end of 1982, construction began on Old Tucson's Plaza to convert it to the Pinto Ranch, a mythical Nevada bordello, in preparation for the July 1983 filming of *Cannonball Run II* starring Burt Reynolds, Frank Sinatra, Dom DeLuise, Sammy Davis, Jr., Dean Martin, and many others. The sequel to the original *Cannon Ball Run* is about a group of eccentric characters racing across the United States in a contest to see who can be the first to reach California. A real tour de force of Tucson from the 1980s. The Board of Supervisors okayed the use of fireworks for Harvest Films for *Cannonball Run II*. The set was closed during the scene and would not repeat the problems from July 4th, 1982.

Mission plaza decorated to be Las Vegas for *Cannonball Run II*. 1982. (Bob Shelton collection)

Little House on the Prairie filmed a two-hour made-for-TV movie entitled *All the Dear Children* starting on August 24th, 1983.

The Reno starred in its 111th birthday jubilee at Old Tucson on October 26th, 1984. Mayor Lewis Murphy presided at a cake cutting at 2 p.m. Saturday, and No. 11 steamed along 700 to 800 feet of private track pulling a restored Virginia & Truckee coach. W.O. Zelnicker built the coach around 1890 for the Virginia &Truckee Railroad, and MGM sold it in 1947. Although the interior has been refurbished, the outside, trucks (wheels and their carriages), and some interior furnishings were original.

The Reno under steam during the filming of an unknown movie. 1984
(Bob Shelton collection)

Pat Wareing, Old Tucson spokeswoman, said the celebration drew history buffs, tourists, and railroad enthusiasts. Festivities included performances by a barbershop quartet, drum and bugle corps, and a fine-arts exhibit by the Society of Steam' Artists of America, including works of well-known railroad artist Howard Fogg. His works grace the dust jackets bought by many rail buffs.

The Don Simmons Gun Museum opened on January 21st, 1984, and displayed his 50 years of collecting. There was a demonstration by the 4th Texas Confederate unit and the Mountain Men to celebrate the opening. On Sunday, the 6th U.S. Cavalry presented a mounted display.

An NBC pilot for *Highway to Heaven*, a television production, was shot starting on March 12th, 1984. It starred Michael Landon and Victor French. A probationary angel is sent back to earth, and with the help of an ex-cop, he goes around helping people. At least two episodes were filmed at Old Tucson.

A segment of *Ripley's Believe it or Not* was filmed in a one-day shoot, Saturday, June 2nd, c.1984. Starring Jack Palance, this episode was about eccentric Justice of the Peace Judge Roy Bean's life, who billed himself as the law west of the Pecos.

The July 4th music jamboree had nonstop music in the soundstage from 11 am to 7 pm. It featured the "Titan Valley Warheads" bluegrass band and "The Saddle City Band." The jamboree begins Summerfest featuring numerous local bands such as the "Dana Wagner Group," "Doug McLeod Band," "Titan Valley warheads," and "Westbound" on August 18th. On August 25th, big band sounds in the soundstage with "Cliff Juergens Orchestra," August 26th, the "Steven Levy Quartet," and Friday the 31st "Los Lasers."

The new inside show was "Front Street Follies," a song and dance show, every Friday, Saturday, and Sunday in the Front Street Saloon.

The DRD Ventures Corporation started negotiations to buy Old Tucson Studios from Westworld Incorporated. The three prospective buyers are Donald Diamond, Donald Pitt, and Richard Bloch. The three also owned the Phoenix Suns, basketball team. Their offer was $3.5 million. At that time, the Westworld Corporation was the sole owner of Old Tucson Studios.

Westworld wanted to use the proceeds to explore for oil and gold. Old Tucson had 145 full-time and 40 part-time employees. The Mescal Corporation, 125 acres west of Benson with the movie set, was part of the Old Tucson sale to DRD Ventures Corporation. The deal was an effort to keep Old Tucson under local ownership. It must have the approval of the Board of Supervisors and the county parks board (which they did on December 9) because the Old Tucson site was leased from the county, and money was deposited in escrow with a formal written contract. In a prepared statement, Shelton said the principles of DRD have expressed their intention was not to change the operations performed at Old Tucson and did not anticipate that there would be personnel changes.

One of the new inside shows for the spring season was "Miss Jubilee Jones and The Red Dog Review," held in the newly refurbished Red Dog Saloon. The other spring show was "Raise a Ruckus," AKA: "Rompin' at the Red Dog."

Exterior view of the Red Dog Saloon located at the north end of Main Street. (Bob Shelton collection)

The Ringling Brothers and Barnum and Bailey Circus presented a unique reading program with the Ringling Reading Clown on June 13th, 1985.

Summer hours began on June 15th, with the Park opened at night on Wednesday through Sunday, and the saloon show, "Jubilee Jones Jamboree," happening in the later hours.

A pair of half-hour television programs, *The Ascension* and *The Descent of the Holy Spirit*, were filmed in June 1985. Presented by the Father Peyton Family Theater, they starred Stuart Whitman and Joe Campanula. These were part of a series entitled Mysteries of the Rosary.

Classic Pictures of Los Angeles spent ten days at Old Tucson in November 1985 filming a mini-series, *Dream West*, for CBS Entertainment. It was about John Charles Fremont, a 19th Century frontiersman, first U. S. governor of California, and first Republican candidate for U.S. President. Richard Chamberlain stars in the seven-hour drama as Fremont, Rip Torn plays Kit Carson, and Rene Enriquez (of *Hill Street Blues*) is General Castro. *Dream West* also filmed scenes in northern Arizona, Wyoming, Colorado, and Richmond, VA. At Old Tucson, principal photography revolved around The Reno steam engine and station, Mexican Plaza, Front Street, and the sound stage.

The Southwest Cross Country Carriage Driving Championship was held Saturday, December 7th. There was excitement as the best horse and buggy drivers competed on an 8.4-mile marathon obstacle course in the rodeo arena.

Moving West, a Celebration, which was a multimedia extravaganza, was presented in the soundstage during Christmas week.

Old Tucson was open at noon on Christmas Day, beginning its 25th Jubilee anniversary celebration. The yearlong celebration introduces a rousing musical revue in the Red Dog Saloon.

The CBS telefilm, *Stagecoach*, wrapped production on February 6th, after three weeks of shooting in and around Tucson. The story followed a stagecoach ride through old west Apache territory and starred Johnny Cash, Kris Kristofferson, Waylon Jennings, John Schneider, and Willie Nelson. This film is a remake of the classic John Ford movie originally starring John Wayne. On board the stagecoach is a cavalry officer's pregnant wife, a prostitute with a broken heart, a Marshal taking his prisoner, Johnny Ringo to prison, a crooked gambler, and the infamous Doc Holiday.

The *Three Amigos* began to film early in February. Old Tucson's Main Street and the Mexican Plaza received a facelift to resemble a small Mexican town in 1919, and an entire Mexican Mission set was built just north of Old Tucson. This new construction was the most extensive remodel since *Cannonball Run II*.

"Bad Guys" leaving the El Guapo castle, in a scene from
The Three Amigos filmed in 1986. (Bob Shelton collection)

The company filmed in Old Tucson and on the El Guapo set until March 8th. It starred Chevy Chase, Steve Martin, Martin Short, and Patrice Martinez. The Three Amigos, stars of the silent films, go to Mexico thinking they will film a movie. They find that they have just stepped into the middle of a real battle between a local bandit gang and a small Mexican town.

J. C. Productions of Los Angeles spent half of March and most of April making the western feature film, *Buckeye and Blue,* at Old Tucson, Mescal, and Sabino Canyon. Principal photography at Old Tucson, including Kansas Street, sound stage, and the Reno engine. Robyn Lively, Jeff Osterage, Rick Gibbs, Patrick Johnson, and Kenneth Jensen headed the *Buckeye and Blue* cast. Buckeye (Lively) falls for Blue Duck Harris, and after the Civil War, she joins the McCoy gang and sets out trying to find Blue Duck and ends up a bank robber.

Old Tucson celebrated Memorial Day 1986 with the Dixieland band, "The Olive Street Stompers," May 24th; the country-western group, "Horsefeathers," May 25th; and the dance band "Pepper," a variety/pop band performed on Memorial Day, May 26th. All bands presented their music in Old Tucson's Red Dog Saloon from noon to 5 p.m.

On May 29th, U.S. Marshal's Service filmed a documentary about its history to celebrate the service's 200th anniversary hosted by James Arness.

The lease on Old Tucson was the largest revenue producer for Pima County Parks Department. Old Tucson planned to make $4 million in improvements. However, members of the County Parks and Recreation commission said that the proposal from old Tucson Company would amount to a significant change in the lease and the County Attorney's office researched as to whether the lease should go out for bid. The company had been unable to get the $5 million liability insurance required by the lease. A state fire marshal said that Old Tucson could not use the soundstage for banquets.

The next film in the can was *Here a Thief/There a Thief*, filmed in the Mexican plaza. It starred Audrey Hepburn and Robert Wagner. The Baroness (Hepburn) steals three Faberge eggs from a museum. She takes them to Mexico to pay a ransom. There she meets Mike Chambers (Wagner), and Mexican bandits kidnap them. The producers released the movie under the name of *Love Among Thieves*.

The Labor Day weekend special ran from August 30th through September 1st and included the "Saddle City Band" and laughs with Hugo the Cowboy Clown, who juggled, stilt walked, and rode a unicycle. Also presented was Fred Rhodes, the "Sadsack" cartoon artist.

Columbia Pictures came to Old Tucson around September 1986 to use the sound stage for *Desert Bloom*, a story about family dynamics in the early 1950s. It starred Jon Voight, JoBeth Williams, and Annabeth Gish.

The sound stage was modified and redone to accommodate 1,800 people instead of the 1,050 before the improvement in October.

In Old Tucson's first experience with animation, Lee Mendelson Production Company utilized Old Tucson's backlot for filming a scene from *It's the Girl in the Red Truck, Charlie Brown*, on October 25th, 1986. It starred Jill Schulz, Molly Boice, and Greg Deason. Principal photography took place in and around the large railroad trestle on the tracks of the small train. The story was based on the Charlie Brown comic strip and features Spike, Snoopy's brother. Spike takes off for an adventure with Jenny in her red truck. This picture is a live-action/ animated movie.

The world-famous Old Tucson professional actors and stunt-men re-created the historic "Shoot-Out at the O.K. Corral" at Old Tucson on Saturday, October 25th, and Sunday, October 26th, 1986. This re-enactment of the infamous Tombstone show-down between the "Earps" and the "Clantons" took place on the 106th anniversary of the actual event.

From December 26th through the 30th, Joan Embry presented her show, "Vanishing Wildlife," a show where she explains various exotic animals. During her time at Old Tucson, she entertained an estimated 10,000 guests in the sound stage.

The Old Tucson Company film department and construction crews started to arrive for the *Duell McCall* motion picture, filmed at Mescal and Old Tucson.

Construction commenced on Monday, November 24th, and continued throughout December at Mescal and was the first of several films featuring Duell McCall, an outlaw who is really not bad. Principal filming began January 12th, 1987, and starred Alex McArthur, David Warner, Yaphet Kooto, and Ronald Moffat. McCall gets into different adventures that show off his good side. The film was released under the name of *Desperado*.

The new spring Red Dog Show was "Stagecoach Swing." It was held four times daily, on Wednesday through Sunday.

Song and dance show on the stage of the Red Dog Saloon. c.1987
(Bob Shelton collection)

Bob Manning, production manager of New World Television, announced that their next film *Poker Alice* starring Elizabeth Taylor had been given an approximate start date of January 26th. Construction and pre-production started at Old Tucson in early January. The movie starred Elizabeth Taylor, Tom Skerritt, and George Hamilton. Alice Moffat, "Poker Alice," has been disowned by her Boston family because of her incurable penchant for gambling. She was traveling with her cousin, John, when she wins a house in a train's poker game. The house turns out to be a bordello, which Alice decides to run until she can sell it. She falls for a bounty Hunter, Jeremy Collins, who is about to settle down in California. This conflict ended the lifelong relationship between the two cousins.

Elizabeth Taylor and George Hamilton had to cross picket lines to get to the set of *Poker Alice*. The pickets were protesting the movie for not using union labor.

Elizabeth Taylor got a gift every day when she filmed *Poker Alice* at old Tucson. Everything from a mink coat to jewelry, of course, and southwestern art.

From February 25th, 1987 through April 5th, old Tucson hosted Encyclopedia Britannica's traveling exhibit "Tribute to the Great American Indian Leaders."

"Alvin and the Chipmunks" performed in the soundstage from April 15th to the 21st. The proceeds went to benefit the Children's Miracle Network.

At a wardrobe auction on August 7th, 1987, Old Tucson sold 3000 pieces of costumes and memorabilia and a chariot from *The Ten Commandments*. There were guest appearances by Henry Darrow and Don Collier. The money went to upgrade the wardrobe department.

Old Tucson Company changed their pet policy and began allowing pets if they were on a leash.

On September 7th, Old Tucson presented the Royal Lipizzaner stallion show in the rodeo arena.

A celebration occurred for Mexican Independence Day on September 20th, traditional dances were performed, along with strolling mariachi bands.

An American couple moves to the little town of Ibarra in Mexico. They help the villagers reopen an old mine, bringing prosperity to the town and peace of mind to the couple. This was the storyline for the Old Tucson shot *Stones for Ibarra* starring Glenn Close, Keith Carradine, and Alphonso Arau. The movie used the studio's Mexican set for filming. Hantett Doerr, the 78-year-old author of *Stones for Ibarra*, nearly came undone when she visited the Tucson filming site of the Titus Productions telepic based on her award-winning first novel. The villa, set in a remote Mexican village, "looked exactly as I'd conjured it in my head," she said.

The studios presented a Christmas special with a program entitled "A Storybook Christmas," a 45-minute program with favorite songs and Christmas stories.

January of 1988 saw the premiere of Old Tucson's new inside show, entitled Cactus Can-Can, "Dan Wiles one-man circus" (Rides unicycle on a tight rope), and the Old Tucson Mariachis.

Unusual filming took place from January 7th through the 9th, when a soap opera from New York came to Old Tucson to lens several episodes. *One Life to Live*, taking their cues from a *Back to the Future*-type plot, many of the cast will go back in time to the old west in 1888. This sequence will occur when Clint Buchanon, currently blind, hits his hard head (he is always trying to prove he can do everything himself, cutting firewood and all) and blacks out. He travels in time back to fictitious Buchanan City, named for the clan whose ever-complicated lives dominate the hour-long show.

Three-time world champion gymnast Kurt Thomas appeared at old Tucson on February 13th through February 15th. Kurt's high-powered entertaining gymnastics show was a cast of seven world-class professional gymnasts.

More than 75 members of the Tucson Sunshine Barbershop Chorus performed at Old Tucson Saturday and Sunday, March 5th and 6th, 1988, for the kickoff of the 50th anniversary of barbershop singing in America. The gentleman appeared in old-fashioned barbershop attire and were heard singing in quartets between some of the shows.

The Alvin and The Chipmunks show. c.1987
(Bob Shelton collection)

Children were able to sing along with the famous cartoon characters, "The Berenstain Bears," as they delighted kids of all ages with three live shows each day during Easter weekend in the Old Tucson Soundstage. The "Bears" 25-minute performances included skits, singing, and greeting Old Tucson's guests. The Berenstain Bears had to solve "The Mystery of the Bumble Bee Boogie" while performing at the Old Tucson Soundstage. The family of four costumed bears sang, acted, and danced in three 20-minute programs each day.

Sesame Street conducted a still shoot of "Big Bird" and other characters for Viewmaster on Tuesday, April 12th, at various park locations.

On May 13th, 1988, Old Tucson closed its doors to the public and opened its streets to 3,500 Tucson 5th graders for the World's Largest Kid's Round-Up. The Pima County Parklands Foundation sponsored the day with lots of activities and lunch for everyone. The round-up was so successful that it became an annual event, which became "Ted Walker day." It has been presented every year through 2020.

Paramount Pictures-TV filmed *Webster* on May 13th, 1988, which starred Emmanuel Lewis, Alex Karas, Susan Clark, and Jack Elam. These were episodes one and two from 1988 entitled *How the West Was Once,* season three. The Papadopoulos's visited Lizard Flats and encounter Dusty and a horse named Moon Hunter. A bad guy stole Moon Hunter, and Webster almost gets killed. The show used Kansas St. and the Sound Stage.

Old Tucson built a new stage near the rodeo arena called Rio Lobo Stage. The first concert on the stage was the rock group, "Sha-Na-Na," on June 14th at 7 PM. The venue contained 3,200 seats and took up part of the rodeo arena.

The park completed a new 640-space parking lot in the summer of 1988, which increased the parking capacity to 1,200 vehicles.

In June 1988, Old Tucson listed the prices charged to movie companies to use our studio and accouterments.

Location prices OLD TUCSON:

Principal photography – exterior	$1500 per day
Soundstage	1000 per day
Combo rate – exterior and Soundstage	2000 per day
Still photography	500 per day
Prep/for exterior or Soundstage	500 per day

MESCAL:

Principal photography	$1250 per day
Still photography	500 per day
Prep/Holding/Strike	200 per day

Additional services:

Antique train and depot on 1,200 ft. of track. The Reno was an 1872 Standard Locomotive & Tender, 4.4.0, passenger coaches, combination baggage and mail car, and crane, and blacksmith cars. Locomotive & Tender were movable but not operative at this time.

Locomotive & Tender	$2000 per day
Individual railroad cars	300 per day

Wardrobe – western costumes	Daily	Weekly
Children	$8.75	$35.00
Mexican peasant (man/woman)	8.75	35.00
Comancheros	14.00	56.00
Mexican well-dressed man	17.25	69.00
Indian	14.00	56.00
Union/Confederate Uniforms	14.00	56.00
Cowboy/Ranch type man	14.00	56.00
Ranch/average type woman	14.00	56.00
Well-dressed man	20.00	80.00
Well-dressed woman	22.00	88.00
Saloon-type woman	20.00	80.00

The prices were based on complete head-to-toe outfits, including accessories. A minimum of $10.00 additional cleaning was charged per outfit for all rentals. Partial costumes were also available for rental. When ten or more head-to-toe costumes were rented, Old Tucson's costumer would work for the production company for eight hours. After eight hours, time and one-half would be charged for the customer's service.

Set dressing and available western rigs: Buggies ($50.00 per day), Farm wagons ($200.00 per day), and western and mud wagon types of Stagecoaches (500.00 per day).

Water trucks with an operator (minimum of 3 hours) $30.00 per hour, Crab Dolly $35.00 per day.

Old Tucson began a concert series sponsored by Budweiser, held mostly in the Rodeo Arena and on the Rio Lobo Stage. The series 1st concert, "The Billy Shearer's Band" in the palace on June 5th and "Sha-Na-Na" on the Rio Lobo stage Saturday night of the 6th, 1988. On Tuesday, June 7th, the Red Dog Palace added a new show, "Billy Buck & The Singing Sweeties" (really Bill Martin, Kim Ronkin, and Kari Kulvinskas) performed four 15-minute shows Tuesday through Sunday. Kim and Kari also did a little waitressing, and all three spent some time on the streets in their costumes for some street atmosphere.

The 18-week Writers Guild strike had a significant impact on Tucson. The number of television productions went way down, and only independent films were in production.

July 1st, 1988, was declared "Western Celebrity Day." Three favorite Western TV celebrities, Henry Darrow (*High Chaparral*), Peter Brown (*Lawman, Laredo*), and Will Hutchins (*Sugarfoot*), paraded around Old Tucson. They signed autographs, had their pictures taken, and shot it out in quick draw contests with Old Tucson's gunfighters.

El Guapo Castle, a leftover from the movie *The Three Amigos*, was torn down for safety reasons.

The Swiss Transportation Museum contracted with Old Tucson to exhibit the Reno during September 1988 in Lucern. They would pay all transportation costs and pay Old Tucson a $20,000 usage fee. They would also insure the engine for $250,000. The Reno would be shipped in early August, be on exhibition for six weeks, and then shipped back to Arizona. The engine arrived at Old Tucson on December 22nd, 1988.

Director Richard Taylor used toy cowboys to film a commercial for Duracell batteries at Old Tucson. Using the "good guy, bad guy" concept, the bad guy's battery runs down at the commercial end.

Old Tucson and KTVW – TV, Channel 52, celebrated Mexican Independence Day 1989 with a full day of family fun, Mexican style. Featured were Mexican food specials, strolling mariachis, and other local Hispanic cultural festivities; this, in addition to old Tucson's regularly scheduled live gunfights, saloon entertainment, and more.

Scenes from an episode of *Highway to Heaven* starred and directed by Michael Landon were filmed at Old Tucson on October 14th and 15th. They used the Soundstage and Silver Lake Park during the two-day filming.

The former Old West Wax Museum, 2500 sq. ft., was converted into a spacious gift shop, complete with a bakery, deli, and wine and cheese shop (Present-day "Last Outpost").

Once this building was the wax museum and was turned into
The Last Outpost in 1988. (Author's collection)

The Greer Garson House in the Mexican Plaza was transformed into the Group Sales office.

In November 1988, Home Box Office filmed a contemporary movie, *Third Degree Burns,* which starred Treat Williams, Virginia Madsen, and Richard Masur. Scott Weston (Williams) is a private investigator hired by a wealthy businessman to determine whether his beautiful wife (Madsen) is fooling around behind his back. During his investigation, Weston begins a steamy affair with the wife. The husband turns up dead, and Weston becomes a prime suspect in an elaborate plot. *Third Degree Burns* filmed with a scene from the bank robbery gunfight show as background action.

Paramount Television, starting November 26th, 1988, filmed a contemporary thriller named *The Laughing Dead.* It starred Tim Sullivan, Wendy Webb, and Premika Eaton. *The Laughing Dead* story centered on a busload of American tourists visiting a remote and ancient ruin in Mexico's interior. The tourists have an encounter with a group of fanatical cult followers, and bizarre things happen. The producers filmed the Old Tucson portion in Mexican Plaza.

Thanksgiving Holiday Weekend brought over 9,000 visitors to Old Tucson to see the "Chinese Golden Dragon Acrobats." They performed three high-energy shows each day on November 27th, 28th, and 29th.

Beginning December 5th and for the next three weeks, Turner Network Television filmed *The Kid* at Old Tucson in the Courthouse, Kansas Street, Soundstage, and Mexican Plaza. It Starred Val Kilmer, Wilford Brimley, and Duncan Regehr. Val Kilmer plays Billy the Kid as a backwoods bumpkin. Another entry in the fictionalizing of this legendary outlaw.

The Red Dog Palace ramada was modified to be open-air, or wholly enclosed, and climate-controlled. The new 2200-sq. ft. kitchen was completed and would be operational by January 1st, 1989. Two attractive snack stands were added in key locations, and the Tres Amigos Mexican Restaurant was created to provide more foodservice variety.

MGM produced, and James Arness starred in *Red River,* filmed from December 8th through the 14th, 1989. It also starred Bruce Boxleitner. This movie is a remake of John Wayne's 1948 classic film of the same name. Arness portrays a rancher at odds with his son during a cattle drive.

Old Tucson Presented "A Storybook Christmas," from December 19th to January 3rd, Old Tucson decorated its streets and shops in a holiday spirit. For the first time, Old Tucson had its own Christmas show. This colorful 45-minute production written expressly for Old Tucson featured eight beautifully costumed professional singers and dancers. The show included everyone's favorite holiday melodies such as "Rudolph the Red-Nosed Reindeer," "Jingle Bells," "Winter Wonderland," "We Wish You A Merry Christmas," and much more.

About a dozen Old Tucson Studios' employees picketed at the studio due to layoffs. They claim they were laid off to make room for out-of-town people. The park's management said there was a shift in focus to music and away from stunts, requiring fewer stunt people.

Identified by his trademark long leather duster and a distinctive flat-crowned hat, "Desperado," a.k.a. Duell McCall, strides down the dusty streets of Old Tucson in a series of made-for-TV feature films that played a significant role in the comeback of the cinematic Western.

Three of the NBC productions have been filmed thus far in Southern Arizona, and Desperado Productions likes what it found around the Old Pueblo. Twenty percent of Sellier's crew was from Tucson, and he was using local wranglers and transportation personnel. "Television has changed the technical image of film productions," Sellier noted. "You don't have that huge union base anymore because TV shows can't afford such a large number of people. The 'ole boy network' is gone. The day when three buddies would get together and put together a production was in the past. Now it is all accountants and balance sheets. Today, costs are everything."

In January, two installments of NBC-TV's *Desperado* movie series were in production at Old Tucson's Mescal location, leaving the ghost town with a few extra buildings that attracted other location directors.

An unusual stunt involved Old Tucson's stagecoach operator Red Wolverton. A stagecoach he is driving is "blown up" during a production scene. He must release its horses at a critical moment.

Western Music Association formed in Tucson in January to promote cowboy songs. It sponsored a get-together on January 26th, 1989, at Old Tucson, which included cowboy poetry, stories, and music.

Though some effects of the 1988s unlamented writers' strike lingered into the fall of 1988, November, December, January, and February showed an increase in the Grand Canyon State's filming activity.

Old Tucson celebrated its 50th year and the nation's 212th year with several "Wild West" activities, including the variety stage show, "How the West Was Fun."

A unique musical tribute show with six cast members was performed for Old Tucson's 50 years as a motion picture location—beginning with "Arizona" in 1939 up through "The Gambler," "Desperado," and "The Three Amigos." Songs, dances, and antics by this talented cast of six filled each 20-minute show with colorful family entertainment. The Entertainment Department scheduled the performances at the Red Dog Palace.

A dusty old cowboy outfit and atomic-powered spurs are ready for a ride to *Planet Texas*. Kenny Rogers and his British film crew, plus the entourage of support people and management from the record company, were in the Tucson area for five days of filming the music video. It was a part of a $600,000 spent for Rogers' *Planet Texas* production. He is abducted by a trio of John Wayne-lookalike space aliens. They put him aboard one of their laser-eyed horses and gallop off to the edge of the universe. The company filmed the video at the Mescal set on March 17th and 18th, 1989.

Grizzly Adams - the Legend Lives On is a wilderness adventure picture scheduled for a fall release. The movie was shot at Old Tucson May 15th through May 21st by Florida-based Bulls on the Run Productions. It starred Gene Edwards as Grizzly Adams, and the bear was played by Acquanetta, the original bear from *The Life and Times of Grizzly Adams*. The story centers on the wilderness adventures of Grizzly Adams, a rough-and-tumble mountain man, and his grizzly bear. It is a sequel to an earlier movie and television series, *The Life and Times of Grizzly Adams*.

Old Tucson opened its new carnival games area at an old-fashioned Memorial Day weekend in the West celebration May 27th through the 29th 1989 in Old Tucson's Silverlake Park. A 1920's theme activity featured bluegrass music by Titan Valley Warheads, strolling barbershop harmonies by Kopper Kings, clowns, and a barbecue.

ABC-TV *The Young Riders* filmed at Mescal and Old Tucson starting on July 17th, 1989. The production company is set for 22 episodes, pumping $9 million into the local community. The pilot was filmed under the name of *The Kid* and accepted into the fall 1989 season. *The Young Riders*, which had been shooting at Old Tucson's Mescal location, shot an episode at Old Tucson December 4th through 8th, and then continue production, chiefly in Mescal, through March 1990. It starred Anthony Zerbe, Ty Miller, Stephen Baldwin, and Josh Brolin. Set just before the Civil War, this series presented a highly fictionalized account of the Pony Express heyday. Its focus was a group of young Express riders based at the way station in Sweetwater, Kansas. Running the station was an ex-Texas Ranger and all-around eccentric, Teaspoon Hunter. Filming was expected to last until November. Old Tucson modified the High Chaparral Ranch house into Fort Recovery for the show.

The *Law at Randado*, a Western by Phoenix Productions Inc., commenced filming at Old Tucson on July 24th for three weeks. Filming locations were Kansas Street, High Chaparral barn, Rio Lobo Cantina, Mexican Plaza, and the Soundstage. The story is about a lawless Arizona Territorial town, which elects a young "puppet" deputy sheriff to do its bidding. The only problem is, the new deputy, played by Cody Glenn, believes in bringing law to Randado. It starred Glenn Ford, Cody Glenn, Charlene Tilton, and Jeff Kaake.

The film business in September 1989 brought in $28 million. Two NBC episodes of *Desperado* were filmed at mescal, as was an Italian bubble gum commercial. The Playboy magazine held a photo shoot and a television promotion for the World Wrestling Federation.

The Legend of Grizzly Adams with Gene Edwards and
Acquanetta, the bear. 1989 (Bob Shelton collection)

John Walsh, host of "America's Most Wanted," was at Old
Tucson on October 7th and 8th. The true-crime series was shooting
a segment about old west crimes honoring the 200th Anniversary of
the U.S. Marshal Service.

The 50th annual homecoming rodeo happened from October
27th through the 29th. This rodeo was the oldest college rodeo in
existence. At noon each day, a special Desert Travel Guide reenactment of the shoot-out at the O.K. Corral was performed. University
of Arizona alumni competed Friday. Students competed the next
two days in the season opener for the Grand Canyon Region (which
includes colleges in Arizona, Nevada, and New Mexico).

University of Arizona rodeo. 1989 (Bob Shelton collection)

The nonprofit Western Music Association, headquartered in Tucson, held its first music festival for an estimated 10,000 fans over four days, November 16th through the 19th. The Western Music Festival featured top Western singers, musicians, yodelers, cowboy poets, and more, with all daytime concerts and events at Old Tucson. Nighttime shows were at the Tucson Convention Center.

The Western movie location will remain open to the public nightly until 9 p.m., offering street shows and rides in an evening atmosphere.

"Probably one of the most spectacular changes is the sound-stage tour," says Dan Aylward. "The Royal Oak Saloon bartender will be chatting with the 'ghost of movies past,' while special effects take

the audience behind the scenes of Old Tucson's colorful film history."
Those special effects include an indoor rainstorm, flaming arrows, a
stampede, and a barroom brawl.

One production to locate at Old Tucson was *El Diablo*, with
Anthony Edwards and Louis Gossett Jr. The El Diablo crew expanded
the train station, built a new cemetery, and remodeled the interior
of the courthouse built for the 1971 Clint Eastwood movie *Joe Kidd*.
El Diablo began filming on Monday, December 11th. The outlaw El
Diablo kidnaps a schoolgirl. Her teacher, a dude named Billy Ray,
enlists the aid of a gunman to help track down El Diablo.

On December 22nd, 1989, Old Tucson officially changed its
name from Old Tucson to Old Tucson Studios. The park employed a
total of 275 people, including about 95 full-time employees.

CHAPTER EIGHT:
Paradise to Ruin

As a sequel to *Young Guns*, the film *Young Guns II* was shot in January of 1990. It starred Emilio Estevez, Kiefer Sutherland, and Lou Diamond Phillips. The movie begins with the aging Bushy Bill Roberts narrating his story to a young historian. He claims that he is the famous outlaw, William H. Bonnie, who was supposedly shot and killed by Pat Garrett in 1881. It is a compelling story on how he and Garrett, along with Arkansas Dave Rudabaugh, Chavez Y Chavez, Doc Scurlock, and a few others, led the outlaw life and managed to avoid the law. Garrett, a friend of Billy's, was paid by John Chisholm, a cattle King, to eliminate the Kid. So, Garrett and Ashman Upson set out on a journey to find Billy the Kid. Bob Shelton Said. "*Young Guns II* is no dirt-cheap production. Do you see all the dirt here in the plaza? Well, we had to haul all of it in because the natural stuff that was here didn't look like New Mexican dirt".

The alliance of theatrical and stage employees erected a picket line to prevent trucks into the set of *Young Guns II*. Department of Public Safety officers escorted the trucks through the picket line in violation of the department regulations about interfering with labor disputes.

The Young Riders continued shooting at Mescal through March 1990, with one scene shot on location at Old Tucson.

Television filming delayed the traffic in Gates Pass from dawn to dusk. Vehicles periodically were stopped, from Gates Pass to Kinney Road, while segments of ABC-TV's "Young Riders" series were filmed.

To provide more entertainment for its guests, Old Tucson enhanced their programs to widen many people's appeal. Still showing live gunfights, for example, they included actresses as well as actors. Also, the park extended the stunt demos to include more daring feats. A petting corral, a rejuvenated haunted Irondoor Mine Ride, plus an expanded games area was added. In addition to expanded food capacity, more public telephones added diaper-changing stations in both the women's and the men's restrooms.

About 100 rare horses, said to be descendants of a breeding herd established by Father Eusebio Francisco Kino in the 1600s, began arriving at Old Tucson in preparation for an adoption and auction program. Horse lovers interested in breeding them received the first choice, but some were auctioned at Old Tucson on June 29th or 30th.

With the completion of all the improvements, Old Tucson had the look of five different towns. There were areas of all adobe buildings, the main street of adobe and board-and-baton western buildings, and a second frame street modeled on a turn-of-the-century Kansas City and St. Louis. Old and present Mexican Villages, including a plaza, adobe cantina, mission, and river, and two photographically isolated ranch sets on the backlot made up the exteriors. Practical interiors included two saloons, barbershop, hotel, three sheriff's offices, stage-coach office, general store, railroad depot, livery stable, a courthouse, and a doctor's office. A soundstage: 12,000 sq. ft. air-conditioned, sound-proofed sound stage with a complete grid system, electrical beds, 2000 amps of 120-volt lighting power, a mill and scene dock full of flats, and adaptable interior sections.

On September 15th and 16th, 1990, NBC Television came to Old Tucson to film *Unsolved Mysteries* with Robert Stack as host. The episode was *Skeleton Canyon Treasure*, about a gold shipment stolen from a cavalry unit and never found.

A new event was initiated in October 1990 with the introduction of "Ghost Town Nights" (AKA: Nightfall I). This production became a yearly tradition from 1990 to 2019. The township of Nightfall, Arizona Territory, was founded in 1842. The asylum took those insane people who could not be held in traditional confinement. After the Civil War, it began housing ex-soldiers who could not adapt to civilian life. Never becoming a boomtown of any sort, the township slowly died off to be all but forgotten by its neighbors and virtually cut off from history.

Dr. Jebediah Hyde runs the township, determined to understand the human psyche with his experimentation and research. Goulliard Asylum houses a variety of critically insane inmates from all over the nation. According to Dr. Hyde, "Rehabilitation, in any case, is never out of the question." It was nearly twenty years after the end of the Civil War, but Hyde managed to find those poor souls who still heard the cries of brother killing brother and brought them to Goulliard. No one seemed to know precisely what happened inside the institution's doors, and those who knew would not speak. But, late at night, muffled cries of terror would pierce the thick adobe walls. They were the cries of a nightmarish war, Hyde explained.

Joe Kidd Courthouse was the main set for the
Nightfall vignette until 1994. (Author's collection)

When the newly elected mayor inquires into these strange emanations of horror, a simple treatment for his recurring headaches, administered by Dr. Jebediah Hyde, made him the dearly departed mayor.

Scheduled to run during October, Nightfall, named at this time "Ghost Town Nights," featuring monsters, madmen, fortunetellers, and special effects. It included a "Gothic West" show, an original live production enacted each evening at 8 in front of the "haunted" courthouse. Shops offered candy spiders, witches' brew, glowing merchandise, and the like. Graveyards came alive, and the entire town resounded with dreaded deeds, including a live guillotine show. Antique cars took guests through a ride of horror.

Expanding its Family Entertainment Kid's Play Area, a multi-level custom-designed area dedicated to families, opened November

1st. The Kids Korral was located near Grandpa Donald's Petting Zoo, featuring a miniature Old Tucson Western Town set with soft-play equipment (Ball Pool, Air Bounce, and Rope Climb) all designed to blend into the rustic park theme. With all edges rounded and padded, the only moving parts were the children. The soft-play concept encouraged a child's interaction while promoting digital and muscular development, fun, and safety.

Refrains of "Tumbling Tumbleweeds" and "Cool Water" drifted through frontier movie sets as Western music legends gathered and performed for the 2nd Annual Western Music Festival, November 15th to 18th, 1990, at Old Tucson Studios. Performers scheduled to play included Rex Allen, Michael Martin Murphey, Riders in the Sky, Patsy Montana, Muzzie Braun & the Little Braun Brothers, The Chambers, Don Edwards, Flying W. Wranglers, Liz Masterson, The Reinsmen, Sons of the San Joaquin, and more.

The annual Western Music Festival presented live bands scattered around the park, playing cowboy music. 1990 (Author's collection)

Old Tucson Studios in December 1990 initiated a program in which Boy Scout and Girl Scout troops could earn a film production patch by participating in a morning series of special studio tours and shows. The program was also available to any youth group with a patch-reward system, such as 4-H, Campfire Girls, or any church organization.

As of January 1991, Old Tucson was alive with all sorts of activities for its guests. Among these activities was a stunt demonstration, showing how various stunts were performed, included was a 21-foot fall from the mission building.

Dr. Wheezer's Medicine Show about the doctor trying to sell his miraculous elixir. Audience members were chosen to help him in his efforts.

In Silverlake Park, guests could ride the carousel, drive antique Stutz-Bearcat miniature cars, take the Irondoor Mine ride, or try their luck at various carnival games.

Also, in Silverlake Park was the train depot where visitors can board the CP Huntington narrow-gauge railroad train for a narrative tour around Old Tucson. They could also check out the Red Dog saloon for some upbeat music and shows or go to the sound stage for a tour and explanation of special effects. Guest could also wander the town to explore the various stores and buildings, see the famous Reno steam train, or go to Simmons' gun museum to see a world-class gun display.

Featured daily was a turn-of-the-century magic show named "The Wizard of the West" beginning in mid-January 1991. This live 25-minute show was presented several times each day in the Courthouse on North Front Street. The illusion performance was created and produced for Old Tucson Studios by Mark Wilson, a Los Angeles illusionist known worldwide for his magic productions. The cast included the illustrious Wizard, a male assistant, and two female assistants.

The Wizard of the West magic show. 1991
(Author's collection)

The first "Celebration of the Wild Horse," which raised funds for the Institute of Range and the American Mustang (IRAM) in South Dakota, was held at Old Tucson Studios, Saturday and Sunday, March 2nd and 3rd. The two-day celebration featured wild horses and burros from the Bureau of Land Management's public adoption program. Fifty horses were adopted for $125 each, and 15 burros at $75 each were sold from Old Tucson's Rodeo Arena.

Gunsmoke III (a television movie) wrapped up a month's worth of filming in Arizona, March 29th, with a series of scenes at Old Tucson, which for the first time since filming began on March 4th, the set was open to the public. These were the final scenes for the two-hour CBS Entertainment production.

Old Tucson built a corral for employee's use. If you had a horse and wished to ride to work, the horse had someplace nice to spend the day.

Old Tucson's famous gunfighters turned in their .45 Ruger revolvers on March 27th, 1991, for more authentic looking .45 replicas, which more closely resemble the 1873 Colt that won the west. With these new guns, the actors used powerful black powder blanks that added more smoke into Old Tucson's gunfights.

In March, Old Tucson introduced a new gunfight show. Called "Raid on Philips Ranch," it was performed on the High Chaparral set. Two outlaws are determined to rob a stagecoach passenger when the stage pulled into the High Chaparral Ranch. Things go wrong when the outlaws are faced with the ranch occupants, and guns ring out. The robbers end up with the short straws.

On April 16th, 1991, a new movie began filming at Old Tucson. Named *Four Eyes and Six Guns*, it starred Judge Reinhold, Patricia Clarkson, and Dan Hedaya. Reinhold plays the part of an optometrist from New York who opens a practice in Tombstone, Arizona. He quickly gets crosswise with a gang of outlaws and must take them on. We see Wyatt Earp as a nearsighted drunk who was not willing to help. Spring in Bisbee changed to winter in New York when a section of Main Street became a scene for the made-for-cable television movie, *Four Eyes*. Snow came in the form of soap suds, and rain (supplied by the Bisbee Fire Department) fell via elevated sprinklers set up on Main Street. Old Tucson doubled for Tombstone.

Willie Nelson and Waylon Jennings finished filming a music video at Mescal, named *The Highway Man*.

Visitors used to see the sign proclaiming "Geronimo III — Grandson of the Famous Apache Chief" just before entering Tucson Mountain Park on Kinney Road. The only problem with the experience, both Indian and non-Indian historians say, is that Geronimo III is bogus. Most of Geronimo's known descendants live near Fort Sill, Okla. Leland Michael Darrow, the tribal historian for the Fort Sill Apache Tribe, said, "As far as we know, he (Geronimo III) has no connection whatsoever to Geronimo." But to millions of guests who watched his presentation at Old Tucson, he will always be Geronimo III.

Old Tucson Studios has acquired thousands of props and wardrobe from the long-running television series *Little House on the Prairie* and *Father Murphy* on May 29th, 1991. Since then, the props have been in storage since *Little House* episodes on the Prairie, and Father Murphy were filmed at Old Tucson from 1977-1983 and were rented to other film companies periodically.

Cancer claims *Bonanza* star Michael Landon, the boyishly handsome actor who battled cancer with the same affability he brought to his television roles in *Bonanza* and *Little House on the Prairie*, died Monday, July 1st, 1991.

The ABC television series *The Young Riders* returned to Old Tucson Studios for its third season. Film production began July 22nd at Old Tucson Studios' Mescal location near Benson. Mescal, formerly depicted as Sweetwater, became the more affluent town of

Rock Creek. The series, which takes place in the 1860s during the Pony Express days, filmed its entire season, 22 episodes, at Mescal (its primary location) and Old Tucson Studios.

The inability of filmmakers to move horses due to the threat of Venezuelan Sleeping Sickness cost the Tucson community and Arizona economy "many, many thousands of dollars," an Old Tucson movie set official reported. His company lost two filming projects so far, but that one of them may be re-gained after the disease problems have passed. Horses could not be moved for an indefinite period unless they are vaccinated. Once that is completed, the animals still could not be moved until 14 days have elapsed, federal health officials said.

Producers said they planned to film segments of a television series *Nichols* at Old Tucson, starring actor James Garner, and a full-length movie, *They Pointed Them North*, were canceled. Shelton said filming further segments of the TV series may happen here later.

Old Tucson Studios names Helaine Diamond as president of the Old Tucson Company.

"Nightfall II: The Legend Continues" features Gothic West, the art of science, "Thing from the Grave" (this happens during the railroad ride), and Death at Dusk (involving a wedding ceremony in front of the mission). Old Tucson presented Nightfall from October 11th through October 31st.

Like the Nightfall residents, Sheriff J.D. Clampett believed the tale of Dr. Lithistrom's disappearance and accepted Hyde's explanations regarding inmates' cries at night. Still, with the mayor's disappearance, he took a second look inside the walls of the asylum. He had heard tales of dismemberment and torture from escaping inmates he had captured and returned to Goulliard but believed, as Hyde suggested, that they were the memories of war as recalled by disturbed minds. Surely, the son of Dr. Lionel Hyde was to be believed. After all, he saved the asylum from closure and restored the future of the township of Nightfall. He went to Hyde with his concerns, only to find himself accused of murdering the mayor. Later, Hyde interrupted the wedding ceremony in which Sheriff Clampett was to wed his beloved Marietta. Hyde hanged the sheriff at the Mission and stole a crazed Marietta for his own. With this, the last vestiges of humanity fled from Nightfall. Hyde proclaimed himself Director Supreme of the township, and those who dared speak against him would invariably "volunteer" to "assist" his metabolic research. He erected a huge new guillotine in the center of the township where a heavy "chunk" could be heard nightly. With the town of Nightfall afraid of his retribution, Hyde was free to harvest the souls of its citizens for the advancement of his ghastly science.

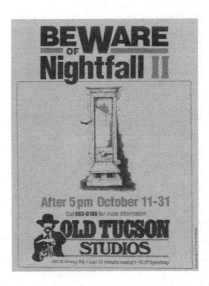

A poster advertisement for the Nightfall shows. 1992

(Author's collection)

As per a news release on November 20th, 1991, employment listed 400 full and part-time employees. Over the past six years, Old Tucson's employment force had steadily increased from 200 employees in 1986. Also, attendance dropped by 5% over 1990 attendance. Theme parks around the country had also seen a dip in attendance. The Gulf War was one explanation for this.

Two new shows made their debut on December 26th at Old Tucson. A new musical performance, "Sapphire Sue's Wild West Musical Revue." Patterned after Annie Oakley, she is a pistol-packing lady who enjoys chatting with the crowd and sharing her years' wisdom. Singing songs such as "You Can't Get a Man With a Gun" and "Go See What the Boys in the Back Room Will Have," Sapphire Sue and her cast of three, two dance hall girls and a rag-time piano player, bring an energy level felt all the way to the border.

The Sapphire Sue Show being performed in the Red Dog Saloon. 1992
(Bob Shelton collection)

The new outside show was "Movie Mayhem." This show demonstrated actual stunts and the process of movie-making with the help of the guests.

Two Old Tucson Studios' gunfighters represented Southern Arizona at the Denmark Travel Show on January 29th thru February 2nd in Copenhagen, Denmark. The gunfighters Jonathan Mincks, 28, of San Francisco, California, and Suede Stevens, 21, of Moorville, Ind., performed western skits four times daily during this Scandinavian travel show, which was attended by approximately 50,000 consumers, travel agents, and tour operators.

As part of its five-year capital improvements plan, Old Tucson Studios began construction on a year-round group banquet facility named "Stage 2." The building would resemble an Old West ranch barn and was to be completed in spring 1992. It was planned to be 65 feet by 120 feet and have an indoor seating capacity of up to 520 people. Sliding exterior walls allow for additional outdoor seating as well.

Filmed in March of 1992, *Stay Tuned* was shot at old Tucson. It starred John Ritter, Pam Dawber, and Jeffrey Jones. After signing up for a new television satellite system (actually, the devil trying to collect souls), sucks a husband and wife into a hellish TV set. To save their souls, they must survive a series of twisted TV shows without dying.

According to Old Tucson Company president Helaine Diamond-Levy, former owner and founder of Old Tucson, Robert Shelton, retired effective May 1st, 1992, after 33 years of commitment to the company. "Working with Old Tucson and all of the people throughout this community has been the pinnacle and joy of my life," said Shelton. He founded Old Tucson in 1959 and remained its primary stockholder until 1979, when the company became affiliated with Westworld Resources Inc., of Houston, Texas. Bob remained CEO and president of Old Tucson until 1985, when he sold the operation to local investors. Since 1985 he had served as executive vice-president of the film department responsible for marketing motion picture, television, and all commercial film projects for Old Tucson.

Imperial Entertainment came to Old Tucson in March to film *Nemesis,* which utilized the Mexican Plaza. The film starred Olivier Gruner, Tim Thomerson, and Cary-Hirroyuki Tagawa. A Futuristic tale about a part man, part robot, police officer. Before leaving the police department, his last assignment is to find and arrest a friend who has stolen some computer data and threatens to destroy the world.

Jack Palance brought a documentary film to Old Tucson. It was released under *Legends of the West* and was about various people in the west, such as George Custer, Sitting Bull, Wild Bill Hickox, and Annie Oakley.

A movie, *Horse Opera,* was filmed at Old Tucson, March 31st through April 13th. It starred Michael Attwell, Gina Bellman, Philip Guy Bromley, and Silas Carson and told the tale about George, a clerk in the tax office and head of the Nottingham Cowboy Society. The movie follows his journey into the old west of his imagination.

Once again, old Tucson Studios was the site for the 3rd Annual Top Gun Competition held August 8th at 3 p.m. The timed quickdraw contest was open to the public and tested the entrants' speed and agility as they drew and fired a .45 caliber handgun.

A contemporary film, *California Dreaming,* came to Old Tucson for lensing. The storyline is that Four Italian men visit the United States on holiday unbeknownst to their wives. The film follows the group as they encounter many troubles on their journey. Bo Derek played herself in the movie, which was filmed on October 9th and 10th.

The Mission being used for the main venue for Nightfall. 1992
(Author's collection)

"Nightfall III: The Awakening" saw Goulliard inmates rebelling against Dr. Hyde in front of the church. The inmates rampage through the town to a climactic show at the courthouse. There were no more questions from the citizens of Nightfall, and their allegiance had replaced their doubts. The townspeople's hope for prosperity became a hope for survival. The walls of the asylum had grown to surround the township itself. Those citizens unfortunate enough to catch Hyde's eye were separated from friends and family and, later, from their arms and legs as well. With the nightfall population diminishing, Hyde turned his attention to the inmates who had been enjoying a brief respite from his experimentation. Spoiled by their temporary taste of freedom, they rebelled at the idea of becoming Hyde's "white mice" once again and took matters into their own re-attached hands.

A bloody confrontation ensued, and a fleeing Hyde fell from the asylum's parapets into a vat of bubbling acid. Convinced that Hyde's grasp had finally dissolved, the inmates were frozen in their tracks when they heard his wretched voice come out of the darkness, his face melted to the skull, guns blazing. In the battle that followed, two large explosions ripped apart Hyde's mansion, and the resulting fires consuming the inmates hiding within. Only the sick laughter of Hyde, from the second-story balcony, could be heard as the flames' orange glow licked upward.

On November 4th, 1992, Polygram Film Entertainment brought their newest film to the studios. Entitled *Posse,* it starred Mario Van Peebles, Stephen Baldwin, and Charles Lane. A group of mostly black soldiers returns from the Spanish-American War with a large catch of gold. They form an all-black community in the west. The neighboring white settlements are resentful, and in one act, they brutally killed a white settler sympathetic to the Blacks' cause. The Steinfeld Mansion in downtown Tucson, Arizona, was a lawyer's office until the movie folks from *Posse* took over and transformed the place into a turn-of-the-century bordello and gambling house.

The ABC network morning show, *Good Morning America* stopped in Tucson on November 17th to tape one of eight segments in its Great American Southwest Bus Tour. Host Joan Lunden anchored the broadcast from Canyon Ranch Resort and Spa, while her co-host Charles Gibson and weather forecaster Spencer Christian were at Old Tucson Studios.

In December 1992, Old Tucson introduced a new gunfight show. In this drama, "The Last Wish," Billy Sinclaire has takin' a liking to the local drink purveyor, Lily, and would do just about anything to call her his own. Two amigos of Billy show up, and they plan to rob the bank. Lily goes into the saloon with the sheriff, and Billy, in anger, goes to the saloon while his two friends rob the bank. They shoot the banker and run out just as the sheriff runs out. A gunfight takes place, and the two guys are shot, as is Billy. Lily runs out and gets shot. Billy knows that she is dying and goes to her side. "Even the simplest of hopes and dreams are often shattered in an instant ... for it is only the living who can fulfill "The Last Wish." The show utilized the White Oaks set.

When traveling the streets of Old Tucson, guests needed to beware of the "not-so-wise" Professor Magillicutty and his very able assistant, T.H. Dremin. These two washed-up carnival men professed to read minds and cure-all, but their only trick was surviving the wrath of their poor innocent victims. Professor Magillicutty performed his type of trickery daily in Silverlake Park.

Old Tucson's legends and history are examined in *Hollywood in the Desert*, narrated by Tucson actor Don Collier, and premiered in December 1992. This documentary traced Old Tucson's colorful history from its inception in 1939 through more than 50 years of movie-making magic and old west fun. The show was screened every half hour in the Arizona Theater.

The park introduced two new rides in December. First was the "Rio Bravo" canoe ride. Small children were sure to enjoy riding these miniature canoes through a desert setting. The pint-sized canoes were propelled along a water trough aided by water jets. The second one was the "Iron Pony" Hand Car ride, a pump-a-round hand car that was kid-powered.

Old Tucson opened a few new attractions in January 1992. The new Fire House Exhibit featured an antique fire pumper and fire-fighting equipment; and an authentic Kachina Doll Exhibit located in one of Old Tucson's newly constructed buildings. The exhibit featured more than 30 native Navajo Kachina dolls collected by Old Tucson throughout the years.

Front Street presented two new displays, a reproduction of an Assay Office and an Apothecary Office, and next to the Red Dog Saloon, a new Red Dog Hotel display. A new store appropriately named the Old West Shop opened near the Western Wear Shop. The Old West Shop featured Western and leather goods instead of western clothing offered by its neighboring store.

The new firehouse and collection of fire equipment located on the north end of Main Street. 1992 (Author's collection)

A new show began in mid-January in which Old Tucson's entertainers offered a "Silver Screen Adventure" in the 12,800 square foot Soundstage. The two-part show started with a tour and discussion about the Soundstage, but the real adventure began when selected audience members performed in an Old West film. The scene involved Old Tucson's gunfighters, and with special movie-making effects, put the "innocent" audience members into the movie. The scene was then replayed to the audience, giving them a real taste of Hollywood moviemaking.

Governor Fife Symington's tax relief bill for production companies remained in effect in March 1993. Companies spending $1 million or more in state on tangible goods and services were eligible to apply for a 50% aid on those goods and services.

The Arizona town of Tombstone claims to be "Too Tough to Die" mainly due to its infamous reputation as home to lawman Wyatt Earp and the Gunfight at the O.K. Corral. Millions saw this story in the motion picture *Tombstone*, filmed entirely in Southern Arizona, May through August 1993.

Main Street Mescal during the filming of *Tombstone*.
The town reached its pinnacle with this movie. The film experienced several days of rain. 1993 (author's collection)

Most of the filming took place at Old Tucson Studios and its second set in Mescal, Ariz. The film starred: Kurt Russell, Val Kilmer, Sam Elliott, and Bill Paxton. Visitors were encouraged to observe all exterior filming on the streets of Old Tucson. However, interior filming in the Soundstage was closed to the public. Unlike Old Tucson, Mescal was solely a filming location and was not open to the public. A replica of the Bird Cage Theatre was built in the Soundstage with construction and prep also taking place at the Red Dog Hotel and Reno train depot. *Tombstone* was filmed at Old Tucson in June. Set construction also took place in Mescal, Arizona, where the crew built a replica of the O.K. Corral. Filming used shredded plastic to simulate snow at the Joe Kidd Court House for Tombstone's last scene. If that is not enough, Russell's father, Bing Russell, played a deputy in 1957's *Gunfight at the O.K. Corral*. (And son of a gun if Russell's little boy's name isn't Wyatt.)

Video Wizards and The Nashville Network, Nashville, Tennessee, filmed a one-hour music special, *The Music of the Wild West*, featuring John McEuen (Nitty Gritty Dirt Band), Marty Stuart, Michael Martin Murphey, and Jennifer Warnes from May 10th through May 14th, 1993. Filming was done on Kansas Street, Mexican Plaza, the soundstage's Royal Oak Saloon, and various street locations.

Other 1993 projects included filming a television pilot titled *Marshal Charley*; however, no information could be found on this production.

Management made a few changes as the 53-year-old location, improving and upgrading its Old West buildings. One new feature is the reconstruction of Old Tucson's main entrance, where the front gate area was razed in July. The new building was built with stabilized adobe and looked remarkably similar to the original entrance.

The front gate after it was upgraded to handle
more people at one time. 1993 (Author's collection)

It housed six ticket windows, turnstiles, restrooms, the Guest Relations department, an Information Center, and Lost and Found. Crews completed the project in the fall of 1993.

Under construction was the Emporium, which formerly housed movie memorabilia and the Old West photoshop, became the Arizona Theatre, which showed the *Hollywood in the Desert* video. The new facility housed a Wall of Fame and exhibition area and a theater seating 116 upon completion in September. The old Arizona Theatre housed an expanded Old West photoshop.

The next film shot at Old Tucson was *Geronimo*, a TNT movie of the week, which started filming on August 13th, 1993. It starred Joseph Runningfox, Nick Ramus, and Michele T. John. This story is about the life and legend of the Apache Chief Geronimo.

As of August 14th, the park added a guided tour of the town.

Newly added guided tour of Old Tucson, seen here at the bridge on Main street. These were very popular, and they lasted until 2020. 1993 (Author's collection)

Lightning Jack, a $25 million comedy western, filmed at Old Tucson Studios and its second western set in Mescal, Ariz., September 7th through September 20th. It starred Paul Hogan, Cuba Gooding Junior, and Beverly D'Angelo. Jack Kane is an Australian outlaw in the wild west. During a bungled bank robbery, he picks up a mute, Ben Doyle, as a hostage. They become good friends, with Jack teaching Ben how to rob banks, they plan Jack's last heist.

The 6th annual kids' day at the park occurred on September 21st. This event was renamed Ted Walker Day to honor the late County official who helped found the celebration. The day drew 6,000 kids from around Tucson.

Gunsmoke V starring James Arness and Produced by Caroline Film Productions of Studio City, Calif., for CBS, was filmed October 4th–8th, 1993. It utilized Old Tucson Studios' locations, the Reno, Train Depot, Kansas Street Saloon, Rio Lobo Cantina, Mexican Plaza, and the Livery Stables. It also featured Bruce Boxleitner and was scheduled to air on CBS in February 1994.

"Nightfall IV" ran from October 8th through the 31st, 1993. Following the revolution of inmates in "Nightfall III," the town of Nightfall has been deserted for almost two years. A cavalry unit, attached to the Indian Wars, mysteriously disappears in the vicinity of Nightfall. A team of Army officers is sent to investigate. They arrive on the Reno and begin their examination of the township. They narrowly miss the horrors that occur throughout the evening and can only learn of the activities through Nightfall visitors' interrogations. Some of their methods are questionable (shoot-a-guest).

Meanwhile, Dr. Hyde uses the "members" of the cavalry unit to regenerate his features and repair the physical damage the inmate's revolt caused him in "Nightfall III." With each disgusting new procedure, he becomes more powerful and more dangerous than ever before. The plot uses three shows, "The Arrival," "Ghastly Science," and the evening's final presentation, "The Conflict," to explore the circumstances.

Action on the hanging scaffold in this scene
from Nightfall. 1993 (Author's collection)

The movie *The Quick and the Dead* was filmed by Tristar Pictures through February on a closed set at Mescal The movie, directed by Sam Raimi, stars Gene Hackman and Sharon Stone. John Harod (Hackman) is holding a gunfighter competition with no holds barred. He tries to force an ex-gunfighter, turned preacher, to compete. A female stranger (Stone) shows up and tries to enter the contest. This movie company built the Devil's Plate Saloon in Mescal, which became a favorite set for movies in the future.

More than half of the movie's extras hired were out of work and drawing state welfare or while on other assistance.

Death on the set on January 26th brought the whole cast closer. An extra, Frank Pilney, 68, who retired from a sales job in the Chicago area and moved to Tucson, collapsed on the set from a heart attack.

There were some explosive moments on the Quick and the Dead set during the last week of filming, but it was not stars Sharon Stone and Gene Hackman duking it out. The film company at Mescal wrapped up production by blowing up various parts of the set, including Gene Hackman's house.

A scene from *The Quick and The Dead* along
Main Street in Mescal. 1995 (Author's collection)

Old Tucson Cowboy Christmas included Christmas music and a dinner party and was held December 4th through the 18th.

Old Tucson Studios premiered four new shows on December 26th, which traditionally marks the new season's start.

"The Belle of the West": in this action-packed stunt demonstration show, "Lightning" and "Dynamite" fought it out with "Duke" and "Belle" twice daily in the Mexican Plaza. Duke managed to hilariously outwit and out battle the quick and explosive antics of Lightning and Dynamite with Belle at his side. Audience members played an essential role in the story as they portrayed the town's mayor, under-taker, and schoolmarm, complete with a roomful of school chil-dren. A Master of Ceremonies explained the stunt techniques used during "The Belle of the West" and kept the audience on the edge of their seats as they watch the action unfold.

"Lilly's Red Dog Revue" – Madam Lilly brought her favor-ite gals around four times a day to entertain guests at the Red Dog Saloon. "Lucy," "Georgie," and "Jewel" provided Lilly with a beautiful backdrop as she sang and danced her way into the audiences' hearts.

"Wonders of the West" – A command performance of the famous Old West illusion show featured ten new illusions that left the audience dazed and amazed.

In the "Big Picture Adventure," visitors to Old Tucson experi-enced the film-making process from casting to cues during this show. This production was videotaped six times a day in the Soundstage and turned some lucky visitors into Old Tucson's biggest stars.

Starring Richard Dean Anderson, John de Lancie, and Mark Adair-Rios, *Legend* was "a lighthearted western adventure series set in the closing decades of the 19th century, an age in which the inven-tion and imagination of America changed the world forever."

Anderson, known for his character on the television series *MacGyver* and various made-for-television movies, plays The Legend. The story started with some cowboys on their first cattle-drive. They hook up with a gambler, and during a card game, a fight ensues. During the fight, one of the cowboys is killed, and the gambler is taken to jail. Meanwhile, in a different gunfight, the gambler escaped from jail. A wretch of a dime novelist who, with the aid of an eccen-tric European scientist, reluctantly assumes the role of his fictitious literary hero, Nicodemus Legend. In the end, the sheriff, the judge, and one of the original cowboys are the only men left alive. The company scheduled filming to continue both at Old Tucson and Mescal through May 1995.

While local Tucsonans ran for cover during a rainstorm, the movie crew from *Terminal Velocity* ran for its "cover sets" located inside Old Tucson's 12,000 square foot Soundstage. The Soundstage housed three different sets to use in case of rain. The company will use the soundstage until the crew heads to Phoenix to film exterior shots. The movie featured Charlie Sheen, Nastassja, James Gandolfini, and Christopher McDonald. Sheen's character, Ditch Brodie (Sheen), is a maverick sky diving instructor. When a female student's chute does not open, the authorities accused him of murder. He starts investigating the circumstances and finds himself caught between the KGB and the Russian Mafia trying to steal a plane full of gold.

There was always something shooting out at old Tucson, and March 1994 was no exception. That month, old Tucson hosted a production crew from Los Angeles shooting a McDonald's TV commercial, a unit shooting a TV commercial for Stella beer. A team from Miami wrapped up after snapping some photographs for a German catalog.

The most unusual projects shot at Old Tucson were two video games. *The Last Bounty Hunter* was an action-packed western videogame that shows off not only the streets of Old Tucson but also prominently featured Old Tucson gunslingers doing what they do best, fighting off the bad guys. American laser games out of Albuquerque produced *The Last Bounty Hunter*.

March 28th, 1994 saw the production of the first-ever CD-ROM videogame, appropriately titled *Shoot Out at Old Tucson,* and while this included some great scenes of Old Tucson, it did not come close to matching the shoot up action found in *The Last Bounty Hunter*.

The Mescal set was used for a science fiction film that started lensing on May 2nd, 1994, called *Timemasters*. It starred Jesse Glickenhaus and Pat Morita. Young Jesse is traveling through time to stop some evil virtual-reality fighters from a parallel universe from destroying the earth.

Tracy Lawrence's latest music video wrapped up on May 17th, but not before the crew blew up Old Tucson's bank building. In the scene, Tracy grabbed the damsel in distress, who happens to be his wife, and they barely escape the flames as the building blows behind them. Look for it all in his video *Renegades, Rebels and Rogues*.

Also, red-hot country dual Brooks & Dunn shot publicity stills for their latest album on May 9th, 1994. They had just won their second consecutive duet of the year award during the Academy of Country Music Awards.

The new Wardrobe building was built to house Old Tucson's extensive collection of costumes. 1994 (Author's collection)

Until this spring, the wardrobe and props were in a trailer in Old Tucson's backlot. But the 24-year-old collection outgrew this location. As part of its 1994 construction plans, Old Tucson Studios built an expanded wardrobe and props facility at the west end of Kansas Street. This new building housed the $1 million collection of approximately 20,000 pieces of costuming items and multi-thousands of props ranging from dishware to wagon wheels. Construction began in April and was completed by mid-summer. The building was open during the park's operating hours for public viewing. Visitors to the park could walk through the complex to see the extensive prop and wardrobe inventories. Displays lined the building's entryway. The first floor served as Old Tucson's working wardrobe department, along with the storing of costumes and props. A mezzanine held additional wardrobe items.

The Old Tucson costume collection began in 1970 when the company purchased hundreds of pieces at an auction of Metro-Goldwyn-Mayer Studios' wardrobe collection. Old Tucson then added various pieces throughout the years, and in 1991 the company purchased thousands of more costume pieces from the two NBC television series *Little House on the Prairie* and *Father Murphy*. Also, Old Tucson's collection featured costumes from television shows such as *Bonanza* and *Death Valley Days*.

Many unique items were on display in the Arizona Theatre located inside Old Tucson's front entrance. Three pieces included a wedding dress worn by Melissa Gilbert, who portrayed Laura Ingalls in *Little House on the Prairie*. Also, a dress worn by Barbara Stanwyck in the opening credits of *Big Valley* and a hat worn by Dan Blocker, who portrayed Hoss in the *Bonanza* TV series. It also demonstrated to out-of-town visitors that Old Tucson remained an active film location.

The Reward, a 20th Century Fox motion picture, went into production on June 19th. Old Tucson underwent a face-lift as George Chan, Fox art director, had designed a small Mexican village for the movie's set. A completely new street took form just northwest of the Mission. The crew remodeled the adobe mission church and built a typical Mexican cantina and poolroom. Also, there was a fountain and plaza in the town square, several homes, and a rundown filling station.

On August 13th, 1994, the long time Old Tucson railroad engineer, Eugene Smith, died at 88 years of age. He retired from Southern Pacific in 1971 and went to work piloting the Reno engine.

As of September 1994, activities available to park visitors were: "Wizard of the West" Illusion Show, "Movie Mayhem" audience participation show, "Hollywood in the Desert" informational video, "The Last Wish" action drama, "Professor McGillicutty's Astounding Transfiction Show," and "Sapphire Sue's Musical Revue" in the Red Dog Palace.

The park undertook many improvements to Silverlake Park during fall 1994. The remote-control boats were replaced, and the air bounce was also replaced with a soft play area for one to five-year-olds. "The Old Tucson Jail" featured a foam and vinyl "jail" with a net climb that dropped down into a "canyon" of plastic balls. Outside the "jail" were rocking saguaros, cows, and horses. The entire area was foam covered and well-cushioned.

The watermill in Silverlake. 1995 (Author's collection)

In the fall of 1994, the park undertook to remodel the Red Dog Hotel to add additional seating and an expanded performance area. As a result, the saloon's seating more than doubled from 100 to 230 seats. The expansion also allowed for an increase in banquet seating. "We can now accommodate two banquets at one time by holding one in Big Jake's and another in the saloon, both served by an enlarged common bar," said director of operations, Bruce Meekin. Meanwhile, across the street at the Wells Fargo Bank, the first aid center and executive offices had been upgraded. A new conference room had also been added.

Periscope Pictures brought their film, *Under the Hula Moon*, to Old Tucson in the fall of 1994. It starred Stephen Baldwin, Emily Lloyd, and Chris Penn. In the desert outside Cactus Gulch, Arizona, Buzzard and Betty Jeanne Wall lived in a trailer decorated in Hawaiian themes. Betty Jeanne was trying to get pregnant. Buzz wanted to market "Cammo," a sunblock lotion that looks like camouflage makeup, but financing is tough to find, and Betty thinks he should get a real job. Moses' half-brother, Turkey, a murdering psychopath, escaped from jail, went to the trailer, tied up Buzz, kidnapped Betty, stole

$10,000 they have just won from Publisher's Clearinghouse's lucky loser drawing, and headed for Mexico. Buzz was untied by Maya, an ex-girlfriend who was now a TV reporter searching for a story. They pick up Turk's trail and set out to rescue Betty. Filming took place in Old Tucson's backlot near Phillip's Ranch set and the Soundstage.

"Nightfall V" was presented from October 7th through the 31st, 1994. Attempting to end years of rumors and rumblings, the U.S. military had sent an inspector and a "professor of the mind" to investigate Nightfall atrocities. Professor Mortimer and his "gang" come to take over the asylum, and Hyde fights back. The story of Nightfall begins, with "The Arrival." In 1994, more than 25,000 people attended.

The 20 United Post Office stamps, "Legends of the West," made their national debut at Old Tucson on October 16th, 1994. Help was supplied by the Park's entertainers who attended the ceremony in character as the legends. The First Company of the Arizona Governor's Horse Guard presented the colors, while the Tucson Arizona Boys Chorus sang the National Anthem and entertained the crowd of about 600 people. The ceremony was attended by U.S. Postal employees and dignitaries, avid stamp collectors, and the public. Actor Stephen Baldwin, who portrayed "Buffalo Bill" Cody in the television series "The Young Riders," helped unveil the stamps during the ceremony.

The post office initially planned to recall and destroy more than 5 million sheets of the stamps after discovering that one stamp, honoring black cowboy Bill Pickett, had a picture of Pickett's brother. But once it was determined that some of the sheets had already been sold, the post office announced that it would sell 150,000 more to maintain a policy of never deliberately creating a stamp rarity.

December kicked off the new season of shows, starting with two new gunfight shows, "The Crime" and "The Trial," presented at the White Oaks set. Also planned was the "Bell of the West" stunt show in Mexican Plaza.

"The Crime" involved two cowboys coming to town and running afoul of a gambler. When it becomes apparent that the gambler is cheating, a fight ensues, and the gambler knocks one of the cowboys to the ground. The gambler then draws his gun and shoots the cowboy on the ground. The other cowboy runs away. The Sheriff then arrives and challenges the gambler to a duel. The gambler loses.

Starting December 26th, the park offered trail rides along the outskirts of the park. Included in the price of admission, these rides lasted about 30 minutes. Groups of riders led by a wrangler took one of three trails. Plans included operating the rides out of the High Chaparral ranch set. Along with the trail rides, Old Tucson was also adding wagon rides. The wagon, which can seat up to 20 people, took guests to Philip's Ranch, just outside of the public park area. The ride lasted 30 minutes. Changes were also underway for the stagecoach, and there would no longer be a fee. The trail, wagon, and stagecoach rides operated daily.

Thirty bull riders locked horns with 30 of the meanest bulls around during the second bull rider shoot out at Old Tucson Studios, January 7th at 1 PM.

The United Paramount Network television series *Legend*, which starred Richard Dean Anderson, was filmed at the north end of town by the courthouse, sheriff's office, and the Reno train station. The series also used the Mescal set.

Five crew members of the television show *Legend* were injured when a balcony on a movie set collapsed at the Mescal location near Benson, authorities said.

The men were standing on a balcony when it collapsed, said Jackie Hammock, a spokeswoman with the Cochise County Sheriff's Department. Hammock said the men fell about 15 to 20 feet and were taken to Benson Hospital for treatment and released.

April 24th, 1995, started just like all other days. But things were not as normal as they seemed. Someone was out to destroy Old Tucson Studios. At about 6:30 p.m., with about 300 guests still in the park and the mission show, "Belle of the West," just ending, the first flames were seen coming from the last building on the northwest side of Kansas Street.

Security responded and made the first 911 call to Drexel Heights Fire Department at 6:47 p.m. Meanwhile, one of the security personnel attempted to extinguish the flames with a fire extinguisher, to no effect. On loan from Drexel Heights, the park's fire engine was driven to the scene, but lack of knowledge kept it from operating correctly. The only trained person on duty that day was busy evacuating the park.

By the time Drexel Heights, which responded to a full alarm, arrived, several buildings were burning. The firefighters immediately requested mutual aid from Pascua Fire Department and Picture Rocks Fire.

Firefighters cut the power due to the possibility of electrocution, which disabled the main pump for the park's water supply. They tried to use the diesel-powered auxiliary pump and found that it was down for repairs. With the pump out of order, 20,000 gallons of water was unusable. At about this time, a propane tank vented, sending flame 30 feet in the air. The firemen had to pull back until the tank burned itself out.

Fire consuming sheriff's office on Front Street. 1995 (Author's collection)

As this was happening, water tenders arrived with additional water. Fire personnel placed a call to Tucson Fire and South Tucson Fire Departments for more aid. During this time, park employees were busy escorting guests into the front parking lot and evacuating the animals from the petting zoo. Due to their effort, no guests were seriously hurt, and all the animals were rescued.

Lack of water was still a problem until Davis Monthan Airforce, and the National Guard emergency tankers arrived. The fire force was then divided into four areas of responsibility, and the attack on the fire commenced in an organized manner and was declared controlled at 9:40 p.m. The fire consumed over 9,000 gallons of water before the fire was declared out. A total of 200 firefighters, using 60 pieces of equipment from 14 area fire departments, were utilized. Several pieces of equipment were left on the scene when the various departments returned to their stations. These engines were on standby to put out little hotspot fires that flared up in the burn area.

Firefighters trying to battle the flames. 1995 (Author's collection)

Ironically, the responding fire engines passed busses carrying about 200 insurance agents heading to a party at Old Tucson.

Front Street damage from the air. 1995 (Author's collection)

Early the next morning, 12 arson investigators, including seven from The Bureau of Alcohol, Tobacco, and Firearms, responded to commence a detailed investigation of the fire scene.

An eighth Alcohol, Tobacco, and Firearms agent from Phoenix responded who was a financial expert. His job was to research Old Tucson's books for any financial motive on the part of the park. After his investigation was complete, he found no evidence of any economic motive.

Starting at the outside of the burn area and working inwards, the investigators found only one point of origin. This spot had been the interior of a small building, which was the westmost building on the north side of Kansas Street. This building did not have any electricity, nor did it contain any chemicals which could spontaneously combust. Due to the quick spreading of the fire, it appeared that something aided its spread. An analysis of the wood fragments showed no accelerant was used. After the investigators ruled out all natural and accidental causes, it was declared arson.

Investigators examined all photos and film of the incident but noted nothing suspicious. Officers interviewed several hundred people, identified several people of interest, and suspected one particular person of being the arsonist. However, no hard evidence was found to definitely tie him to the fire. After six months of investigations, officers put the case on a back burner until more information could be developed.

Old Tucson Studios open the Last Outpost visitor center and gift shop just three weeks after a fire swept through part of town.

The only company filming at Old Tucson Studios was keeping a "show-must-go-on" attitude after the fire destroyed 40 percent of the famous Southern Arizona tourist attraction.

In a testament to the movie industry's flexibility, the film crew for *Legend*, an off-beat western adventure television series that aired on the United Paramount Network, was able to leapfrog the problems created by the fire. The film company adjusted quickly to the fire and moved some of its shooting to similar facilities at Mescal.

View of damage along Front Street. 1995 (Author's collection)

The fire, said by investigators as having a 99 percent chance of being arson, caused an estimated $10 million to $14 million in property damage. However, insurance investigators sifted through the ashes to determine the actual cost.

Based on 1994 revenues of $8.5 million, the park was losing an estimated $23,000 daily in revenues from film production and visitors, although officials declined to estimate potential revenue losses.

The April 24th fire that damaged 40 percent of Old Tucson also claimed $60,000 worth of equipment, costumes, and instruments about to be used by the Twilight Band.

The performers were not Old Tucson employees; instead, they were under contract with Twilight Productions, which provided entertainment for conventions and corporate functions. Twilight's musicians and dancers were about to begin a private dinner show for employees of an insurance company when the fire started.

For sale in the park's gift shop, the Last Outpost, were small vials containing ash from the fire. A large number of visitors wanted the keepsake from the studios.

In June 1995, Old Tucson Studios laid off 23 of its remaining 58 workers as the company waits for an insurance settlement to continue the redevelopment of the fire-damaged attraction. "I cannot tell you how deeply saddened I am to see these people go," said general manager Bob Kenniston. "It has been a difficult and emotional day. We will do everything we can to assist them." Kenniston said the workers laid off included staff from management, maintenance, security, and other areas. About 200 of the park's workers were laid off immediately after the fire.

The studio held a job fair that drew 80 local companies offering to hire the fire-displaced employees. Kenniston said Old Tucson contacted those companies and provided the laid-off workers with a list of opportunities with those firms. Kenniston said it took longer than initially expected to resolve the insurance claim and rebuild the movie studio.

CHAPTER NINE:
The Phoenix

Old Tucson was no closer to a public reopening, but the outdoor movie studio's rebirth already had begun. The general manager for the location said August 1st, 1995, "I think the pendulum has finally swung to the far end," said Bob Kenniston, who in June had to lay off an additional 23 employees, reducing his staff to 35. "We're coming along here." Plans got underway to improve the mobile kitchen stored at Stage 2, and a dance floor was slated to be placed outdoors on the north side of Stage 2.

Map of Old Tucson showing the damage. 1995 (Arizona Daily Star)

By the end of August, the park considered reopening to private corporate parties in areas unscathed by the April 24th arson-caused fire. "It forced the park to shut down and cancel all 192 of its group bookings through September, worth more than 8,000 visitors and $400,000," Kenniston said. The fire also decimated a payroll of close to 300 people. Meanwhile, efforts to draw up a master plan for the park's rebuild began.

A team of industry experts came to town on July 24th to analyze the marketplace and determine if the "new" Old Tucson should reposition itself or if the park was moving in the right direction before the fire. Planners would use that information to develop reconstruction plans. The intent was to reopen as a theme park/movie studio because management saw the strength of being a movie studio on the park's marketing.

The annual "Sundown at the Pass" run from the Wildlife Museum to Front Street at old Tucson happened as planned on September 13th, 1995.

For a small town, Mescal, Ariz., had certainly seen its share of movie stars. Located 40 miles southeast of Tucson, Mescal is home to Old Tucson's second western movie set situated off Interstate 10 at the Mescal exit. While mountains and desert surround old Tucson, Mescal's terrain resembles a prairie town of rolling hills and tall grasses, giving producers an entirely different "look" for their production.

Old Tucson purchased the location in 1961 from CBS after the network completed filming the movie *Monte Walsh* which featured Lee Marvin. The Mescal set is located on 60 acres of land, and Old Tucson Company is currently leasing from the Arizona State Land Department. An additional 2,400 acres of state-owned open grazing land surrounds the Mescal set.

Mescal in 2001. (Author's collection)

Mescal has been featured in approximately 80 television, motion picture, and still photography productions ranging from the 1972 movie *Life and Times of Judge Roy Bean* starring Paul Newman to the 2016 film Tombstone Rashomon. In the 1990s, it was featured in *Tombstone* (1993) and *The Quick and the Dead* (1994). In 1991, for the third season of the television series *The Young Riders*, MGM invested more than $200,000 in the location. Construction crews added new storefronts and second stories to existing buildings in addition to building complete new sets. Mescal was being used through May by United Paramount Network for the television series *Legend* starring Richard Dean Anderson.

On October 18th, 1995, Old Tucson was again open for group events and banquets utilizing Stage 2.

On December 6th, 1995, the owners hired Burns and Wald-Hopkins Architects and Engineering Inc. to design the exterior's town layout and landscape.

The Pima County Board of Supervisors, on February 21st, 1996, voted to renew a 25-year lease with the company, Diamond

Ventures, that owns Old Tucson Studios. Under the new lease agreement approved by the board, the minimum rent paid to the county increased from $38,000 annually to $300,000. Raul Grijalva, who opposed the lease renewal and fellow Democrat Dan Eckstrom, said the board should have sought bids nationally to see if other companies could better manage the theme park.

All new structures were to be equipped with sprinklers, and the park installed fire hydrants throughout the park. All the facilities had to meet the state fire code. Under the new lease agreement, the park would be better insured against fire and natural disasters.

Grand Palace under construction. 1995 (Author's collection)

The park set a quarterly payment schedule, which would carry a $1,250 fine for late payments. Any amount paid to the county above the minimum rent due was based, in part, on company earnings. In 1995 that payment was about $600,000, he said. The contract will be effective from Jan. 1st, 1999, to Dec. 31st, 2023. It can be renegotiated in 12 years, but the minimum rent amount can vary by no more than $60,000.

As of February 1996, Old Tucson Studios worked on a master plan for redevelopment. This plan was finalized within a month and put the park on track to return to action by the end of the year. According to Old Tucson's vision statement, the new park's basic plan was to create an interpretive entertainment experience that blends the reality and the myth of the Old West as portrayed by the "Western film." "The park would be geared toward families and highly interactive. We're trying to reproduce the period between the late 1800s and early 1900s," said Ms. Levy, CEO of Old Tucson Company.

The 13,000 square-foot sound stage attracted a lot of attention, but it was rarely used and would not be rebuilt.

Construction at the park would start as early as April. "We look forward to a grand opening at the end of this year," said Bob Kenniston, the park's general manager. Old Tucson hired the local architectural firm of Burns and Wald-Hopkins to plan the design. The engineering firms Turner Structural Engineering Co., Jerome E. McGetrick & Associates, and RS Engineering to plan the rebuilding., The local general contractor, Adams & Associates, was brought on board about the end of April.

When the park reopens, there will be a staff of 250 to 300 people.

Old Tucson started a new tour that took visitors through the park, explaining the fire's aftermath and plans. The three-hour tour, which offered a train ride, a meal, and a video on the studios' history, already had 70 groups booked through the fall.

Front entrance of the Last Outpost to the left in the distance. 1998
(Author's collection)

Greeting the visitors coming into the park's south entrance were the familiar adobe-like territorial structures. However, as they progressed northward, the architecture will act as a timeline tracing various styles spanning the 1800s. Among the most significant buildings was a town hall, split up into a courthouse, a sheriff's office and a land office, and a show venue with the character of the courthouse in Tombstone.

The construction company erected a large building disguised as a hotel and cantina to house stage shows and a Mexican restaurant, which became the Palace Hotel.

Also erected was a large circus tent for featuring traditional dog-and-pony shows.

The company built a theater with a round interior to host Native American storytelling.

A new sound system helped make some of the exhibits "less passive," such as the noise of a class in session at the schoolhouse or the sound of metalworking in the blacksmith's shop.

This rebuild would create long-lasting architecture with a movie-set flair that would last long past the park's scheduled opening at the end of the year.

The Last Outpost Gift Shop remained open, selling local arts and crafts, souvenirs, and little vials of ash from the fire.

In addition to the lake, Old Tucson would have a new water system with 180,000 gallons on-site and sprinklers in all the buildings in case of future fires. That was a significant increase from the 67,000 gallons of water in two tanks at that time. Fire hydrants were installed throughout the park.

There were no plans to add amusement park rides to Old Tucson. The children's play area with its half-dozen kiddie rides remained. The play area, which was not damaged in the fire, included a mine ride, a small log ride, an antique car ride, a pump car ride, a carousel, train, and a petting zoo.

The Board of Supervisors agreed that Pima County was to put up $2.75 million over seven years toward rebuilding Old Tucson on county land. The money would come from the county's share of ticket and concession revenues at the movie studio and theme park, not from taxes. Old Tucson Co., which leases 360 acres from the county in the Tucson Mountain Park, wanted to build a more extensive amusement park than the nearly destroyed one.

The company would duplicate the more than 40 percent of Old Tucson that burned with the $4.4 million insurance settlement they received. The expanded version of Old Tucson has a $9.9 million price tag. Company officials borrowed the extra $5.5 million they needed to complete the park. Old Tucson told the supervisors that county participation was necessary for the company to get the loan.

Once paying the minimum rent, the company would keep a portion of the county's share of Old Tucson profits to pay off its share of the construction loan. Next year the company would keep the county's total share above the minimum rent. Each succeeding year the company would keep an increasingly smaller portion of the county's share of the profits for up to seven years.

Stage Two, a party venue and auxiliary location
for shows and exhibits. 1998 (Author's collection)

Stage II was used extensively for banquets and parties since the fire. A semi-trailer was rigged to serve as a portable kitchen that could serve up to 1500 people. In August, Old Tucson hosted its first activity, a wedding reception. Since then, they served 30,000 people at various functions, and over 800 people stopped at the Last Outpost each day.

The company broke ground on May 5th, 1996, for the multimillion-dollar rebuild, and what Old Tucson states will be a better, safer version of Old Tucson by early next year.

It will continue to be a western-themed, family entertainment park; and, at the same time, a location for Hollywood to film movie and television westerns.

Old Tucson Art Department and construction crews started to arrive for the latest edition of *Duell McCall* (released under *the Desperado V)* motion picture filmed at Mescal and Old Tucson. Set construction commenced on Monday, November 24th, and continued throughout December at Mescal. Principal filming began in December.

In November 1996, Old Tucson Studios introduced the Annual Pass Program. As a special pre-Grand Opening promotion discounted the $34.95 individual pass to $29.95. Passes provide access to the park every day of the year as well as these value-added benefits: ten percent discount on all in-park food and beverage, 15 percent discount on park merchandise, 15 percent discount on general admission tickets for guests, a quarterly newsletter, and special previews not available to the public. Passes were valid for one year from the grand opening date.

More than 30 films, television, and print productions utilized the company's facilities since the devastating fire in April 1995. Through October of 1996, movie companies have filmed 17 productions at Old Tucson Studios. These included television projects, print advertisements, and movie projects. "We've always had a nice mix of film, television, and still photography at both locations," Jay Cole, Director of Operations, said. "Old Tucson provides a lot of different looks for all types of productions," he said.

Notable productions at the studio in 1996 include:

- The completion of the UPN series *Legend*.

- The television movie *Blue Rodeo* starred Kris Kristofferson and Ann Margaret.

- Three national Coors commercials.

- Truly Nolen's first national television commercial.

- Ben Fold's Five, an up-and-coming music act, taped a music video that received heavy rotation on MTV.

Old Tucson Studios held job fairs on November 16th and November 23rd in the cafeteria of Pima Community College, West Campus. With cooperation from both Pima Community College and the Department of Economic Security's Job Services, Old Tucson Studios interviewed applicants for jobs in all areas of the park. Karen Morrow, manager of human resources for Old Tucson Studios, estimated over 200 employees would be needed to complete the park's staffing when it reopened in January 1997.

Old Tucson introduced a new logo of a coiled rope spelling out Studios placed under "Old Tucson."

Old Tucson Studio's Entertainment Department began rehearsals for six new shows in preparation for its grand re-opening. Old Tucson Studios had rededicated itself to quality entertainment with "live" performances, an all-new wardrobe, a state-of-the-art sound system, and a professional troupe of performers. Although Old Tucson retained its signature gunfight and stunt shows, the park hired 17 women and 20 men to perform new shows that portray a western town's a-day-in-the-life.

On December 18th, on what was predicted to be the coldest day of the month, Old Tucson Studios planned to flood its river and lake in preparation for its grand re-opening in January. After 20 months of drought, the re-landscaped Rio Lobo and Silverlake were filled by fire hoses at 9 a.m. It took approximately 70,000 gallons of water to fill the river and lake. After filling the waterway, the water was recirculated at a rate of 800 gallons per minute.

The Rio Lobo and Silverlake areas have been re-landscaped to include 8-foot, 4-foot, and 3-foot waterfalls, a waterwheel, and a water tower. Crews planted hundreds of indigenous trees and more than 2,000 bushes to provide shaded areas for rest along the new waterways.

Old Tucson Studios re-opened January 2nd, 1997, for the first time since it suffered a devastating fire on April 24th, 1995. Reconstruction of the park included developing a master plan to ensure compatibility between film production and park guests. The master plan struck a balance between preserving the park's late 1800's western charm that attracted film producers and the excitement of themed entertainment that drew approximately 500,000 people to the park each year.

Striking that balance had cost Old Tucson Studios over 13 million dollars in reconstruction, landscaping, and infrastructure upgrades. The new construction included six major buildings that housed restaurants, live entertainment and served as interior/exterior film locations. Among those buildings were the Grand Palace Saloon and Hotel, the Town Hall, a reconstructed Mexican Mission, and the underground Storyteller Theater.

Grand Palace Saloon was the primary location
for the inside shows. 1998 (Author's collection)

The company upgraded the park's infrastructure with new electrical, plumbing, cooling equipment, a state-of-the-art audio system, and all new food and beverage equipment. Old Tucson Studios also installed a new fire protection system.

The Fire Inspector issued an interim permit that was good for 60 days, giving the park time to finish the Arizona Theater, Cowboy Café, and El Dorado Mine.

Some of the opening day shows were:

- Murder in Town Hall – The town gossip witnesses the murder of the judge's twin brother. A bumbling deputy arrests the gossip and puts her on trial. The actors choose audience members to be the jury, judge, prosecuting attorney, and defense attorney. They must decide if the gossip is guilty or innocent.

- Storyteller Theater – Girard Sinaugua relates the tale of how Rattlesnake got its beaded skin. Shows illustrated by pantomime.

- The Jailbreak Show was about two brothers, one in jail and the other determined to free the first brother. They were up against Sheriff Diamond Lil and her girls. The show took place in Town Square, and after a lot of shooting, both brothers end up dead.

A former Tucson resident from Florida visiting her mom in Tucson stopped by the park in January and presented Wardrobe Supervisor Kathy Murphy with a period dress. In the early 1970s, Old Tucson Studios held a prop and wardrobe sale where the woman bought the dress. Sixteen years old at the time, she removed the tag in the dress but recalled that it was said to have been worn by June Allyson (who played Jo in the 1949 film production of Louisa May Allcott's novel Little Women). She donated the dress to Old Tucson because she had bought it here and knew that we had lost wardrobe items in the 1995 fire.

Old Tucson Studios continued its commitment to quality, family entertainment with the opening of its Storytellers Theater on Sunday, Feb. 9th. The Storytellers Theater is an underground show venue that celebrates the traditional art of storytelling with the ancient story of "Tsitsikgwes," the rattlesnake. The opening celebration began at 9 a.m., included ten presentations throughout the day, and the opportunity to meet Gerard Tsonakwa, author and narrator of the story.

The new town square, an open area in the middle of town.
Used heavily for outside shows. 1999 (Author's collection)

In honor of National Tourism Week, Old Tucson Studios had a memorable week planned for Tucson residents. The park discounted admission prices from Sunday, May 4th through Mother's Day, Sunday, May 11th.

The week's events included behind-the-Scenes tours with pyrotechnic demonstrations and stunt workshops, an ice cream social, a screening day featuring various movies filmed at Old Tucson, a half-price Senior Citizens Day, and many other in-the-park activities.

Sunday, May 4th – Music in the Park with a youth Mariachi Band, a strolling guitarist, and country-style fiddlers performing, in addition to gunfights and stunt shows.

Monday, May 5th – Behind-the-Scenes Day. Behind the scenes tours, stunt workshops, pyrotechnic demonstrations, and open rehearsals

Tuesday, May 6th – Seniors Day. Adults 50 years and older got 50% off the general admission price.

Wednesday, May 7th – Hollywood Screening Day. The park showed old westerns filmed at Old Tucson.

Thursday, May 8th – Student Day. With I.D, students received up to four admissions at half price.

Friday, May 9th – Old Tucson's Lady's Quilters Guild presented a free ice cream social from 1 to 3 p.m., complete with make-your-own sundaes, a cakewalk, games, and music.

Saturday, May 10th – Visitors brought a picnic lunch and listened to the Brass Marching Band as they performed throughout the day at the gazebo in Old Tucson's Mesquite Grove.

Sunday, May 11th – Mother's Day. Mom gets in free when you bring her to Old Tucson.

In a news release on December 6th, 1997, Old Tucson gave a first quarterly report. Since its grand re-opening, Old Tucson Studios has seen more than 150,000 visitors from all over the world, employed more than 400 people, both full and part-time, and signed two significant productions to film at its Mescal property.

Opening day 1997 view in town square.
(Author's collection)

Turner Network Television's (TNT) brought its made for television movie, *The Buffalo Soldiers,* to Old Tucson and Mescal to film. The movie starred Danny Glover, Lamont Bentley, and Tom Bower. The 9th US Cavalry (the Buffalo Soldiers) are in the southwest trying to subdue Victorio and his Apaches band.

CBS Television brought the filming to Old Tucson of their pilot *Magnificent Seven,* a television series which ran from 1998 to 2000. The television show starred Michael Biehn, Eric Close, Andrew Kavovit, and Dale Midkiff. Based on the 1970 film *The Magnificent Seven,* this pilot follows seven gunfighters, each with a unique talent. They are recruited to save an Indian village.

On June 28th, Old Tucson Studios and the Tucson lesbian and gay community presented, The Gay West, a Pride Week Fund Raiser, to benefit the gay community non-profit organizations. The festivities included all Old Tucson Studios' rides, shows, and attractions, plus a Country & Western dance under the stars. A high energy dance in the Grand Palace featured Wet Dog Promotions and the 100 Families/One Family exhibit, and Desert Voices' performance.

The Rocky Autograph Picture Show and Memorabilia Sale featuring secondary cast members of the *High Chaparral* television show occurred Saturday, June 14th and 15th. The event's highlight was the reunion of many High Chaparral cast members, from the 1966-1971 television series filmed at Old Tucson Studios and the High Chaparral ranch house. Don Collier, Bobby Hoy, Ted Markland, Roberto Contreras, and others were available to meet and greet the Western series fans. The event included an exhibition and sale of movie memorabilia, wardrobe, posters, Hollywood collectibles, toys, comics, and sports memorabilia from dealers worldwide.

The Sunset Dance Party will be presented each week in the Grand Palace Saloon at 7:00 p.m.:

August 16th: The Billy Shears Band.

August 23rd: Latin Traditions.

September 6th: Trick Rider.

September 13th: Bad News Blues Band.

Paramounts Berenstain Bears brought their unique brand of family entertainment to Old Tucson Studios on August 9th and 10th. Based on the original Hanna-Barbera animation, the costumed characters, Mama Bear, Papa Bear, Sister Bear, and Brother Bear performed four 20-minute song and dance shows in the park's Grand Palace Hotel. A five-minute photo session followed each performance.

The Star Trek Enterprise crew beamed down to Old Tucson Studios to learn about life in the old west. Shows performed throughout the day. Paramount Pictures' Starfleet characters Lieutenant Mhalchc (Klingon), Ensign Tabbar (Vulcan), and Commander Kir-Toch (Bajoran) will beam down to Old Tucson Studios on Sunday, Aug. 31st and Monday, Sept. 1st, to perform four shows and interact with 20th Century earthlings.

Old Tucson resurrects its Halloween production "Nightfall VI." After a two-year hiatus, Old Tucson Studios reintroduces Nightfall. "The Doomed," a battle for survival erupts in the Town Square when Dr. Hyde discovers four outsiders snooping around the town of Nightfall, a judge, a sheriff, a bounty hunter, and a reporter, each equally determined to find Hyde for their purposes. They must now join forces to stop him in this fatal face-off at the guillotine and gallows. Judge Baily is beheaded so that his brain could be used in his new creature. The Condemned Hyde unveils his most ambitious experiment of metabolic reassembly in the desecrated Santa Maria Mission. His fight to maintain control of Nightfall and his blood-thirsty creature bursts into flames of horrific destruction.

Santa arrived by train every day from December 20th to the 24th. Bring any Fuji film product and get free admission with a paid admission through December 24th.

On December 25th, 1997, Old Tucson buried a time capsule containing a cell phone, a pager, and local newspapers. The Arizona Film Commission did this to commemorate *The Postman*. It was supposed to be dug up in 2013; however, the location was forgotten. Old Tucson has an officially lost treasure.

Production crews took over Old Tucson Studios' Mescal location in July to shoot a national television commercial that featured the Lincoln-Mercury's 1999 Sable. The spot featured national actors in the lead roles with several local actors as the townsfolk. The commercial also featured two actresses from Old Tucson Studios. As the rumbling of horses echoed through the deserted town, four dangerous desperados appeared on the horizon, ready for a showdown. The featured car, which was not allowed to be shown at the time, rolls through the dusty streets while the townsfolk run for cover.

Country singer Joe Diffie shot a music video for his latest release, *Poor Me* at the park, on Wednesday, October 7th. Fans of western movies and Old Tucson Studios are sure to notice some familiar shots of the Phillip's Ranch set. The video aired on The Nashville Network and Country Music Television.

Old Tucson Studio's first step in its educational goals was to feature three main exhibits: mining and minerals, Native American art, and movie history in the park's Townhall. The exhibition of minerals from the Copper Queen Mine highlighted Bisbee's rich history in mining. Gerald Tsonakwa did interpretive Indian stories among Abenaki art, entitled "Shamanism, Magic Busy Spider" and "The Busy Spider." The third wing contained a collection of costumes and movie memorabilia. (Some of the collection is now in Shelton Hall).

A chill passes through the October air as Dr. Jebediah Hyde and his evil horde return just in time for "Nightfall VII" at Old Tucson Studios. A ghastly scream pierces the silence as Hyde appears cloaked in the darkness of evil. A wail of pain, a ground-quaking explosion, and a Gatling gun's rapid cracking punctuate the beginning of another October filled with the sounds of Nightfall. In this episode, the United States Cavalry was sent to Nightfall to investigate Judge Bailey's disappearance. Wounded in a sword fight, Sergeant Benteen is able to fire a cannon that destroys Dr. Hyde's creature. Hyde gets revenge by ripping out Benteen's heart and providing many new thrills, including the impressive "Human Torch" stunt. The torch features veteran stuntman Rob Jensen, and with flames quickly engulfing his entire upper body, there is no room for error. Once ignited, the fuel burns rapidly, allowing the stuntman 30 to 50 seconds to do his part in the performance before being extinguished out of the audience's view.

The cast of Nightfall. 1998 (Author's collection)

The second annual "Rocky's Autograph Picture Show" was presented on November 28th and 29th at Old Tucson Studios. Saturday's celebrities included Linda Cristal, along with fellow *High Chaparral* stars Henry Darrow and Don Collier. Celebrities who appeared both days included Brandon Cruz (Eddie on *The Courtship of Eddie's Father*), *American Graffiti's* Bo Hopkins and Paul LeMat (celebrating the movie's 25th anniversary), Andrew Prine *(Chisum and Star Trek),* pro wrestling's "Honky Tonk Man," and others.

Child-oriented activities included the International Tour of Mad Science with fun-filled educational science experiments and the stories of Tsonakwa featuring snakes and spiders.

About a dozen entertainers at Old Tucson Studios planned to picket on December 26th because they say they were unfairly fired or had their hours cut. They claim that they were being replaced to make room for out-of-town actors brought to the Western theme park for the peak season, which started in February. But Thomas R. Moulton, the park's general manager, said there were only a handful of layoffs because the park's new shows relied more on musical talent than stunts. The stunts, including gunfights, staged several times daily. "It's unfortunate that the new season started on Dec. 31st," Moulton said.

About 30 part-time entertainers at the park, 201 S. Kinney Road, were affected by the changes. Moulton said the park this year used 15 full-time actors instead of 30 to 40 part-timers. "That gave the park a more consistent crew for shows," he said. "About 15 part-time and on-call entertainers supplemented the full-time crew", Moulton said. "Some employees were complaining about the staff changes were disgruntled about not getting rehired. Not everyone can sing and dance," said Moulton, who has been running the park for 13 months. Moulton said, "the 15 full-time entertainers hired consisted of former part-time workers, new local hires, and hiring half-dozen actors through an Indiana company. Three workers offered part-time jobs declined, and three others were laid off.

Stuntman takes a gunshot and falls from the Apothecary roof in the show "The Last Reckoning." 2000 (Author's collection)

Sparked by sagging attendance, Old Tucson Studio moved away from its roots as a movie set for Western motion pictures. Instead, it started promoting and expanding its live shows, including mock gunfights, musical reviews, and concerts. "We're not the same park we used to be," said Thomas Moulton "while we remain conscious of our historical roots, day to day we're a live entertainment park." The park also added three new live shows and aggressively courted performers to fill out the concert schedule at the park's Budweiser rodeo arena through the summer. The effort was aimed at attracting more locals to the park. Last year, local visitors' attendance shot up 20 percent, but it still could not offset the overall downturn in attendance, which dropped by about 10 percent from the previous year.

On February 12th, 1999, Presidents' Day weekend, premiered a new stage show, "Sing Our Songs America," a performance of beloved songs from America's past, presented in the Carousel Theatre.

"Raise a ruckus," a rousing can-can show continued in the Grand Palace with Diamond Lil', the queen of Old Tucson.

Jack and Silas ride into town to rob the bank, and nothing goes right in "The Last Reckoning." They tie up their horses out front of the bank. Silas enters the bank by the front door, and Jack goes up to the second floor, the safe's location. An old drunk man happens by and takes in what is happening. He unties the robbers' horses and then goes into the Doc's office to get a shotgun. Jim and Laura McKay were already inside the bank. Silas yells for them to throw their hands in the air. Silas shoots the banker and runs out the front door, followed by Jim McKay. They fight, and Silas shoots McKay. Jack runs out onto the balcony of the bank and yells for Silas to get down. An explosion occurs inside the bank. Jack runs in the door and immediately returns with a bag of money. He throws the bag down to Silas and sees the horses are gone. The old man sees Silas and, raising the shotgun, kills him. Jack exchanges bullets with the old man and Laura McKay runs out of the bank, grabbing Jim's gun, shoots Jack off the roof.

The park introduced a new Mission stunt show entitled "Lost Treasure of Santa Maria." A Deputy and Sheriff must defend the treasure from the Jenkins Gang with pratfalls and stunts.

Old Tucson's Can-Can show with lots of
dancing and songs. 1999 (Author's collection)

The Wizard of the West was a magic show performed on stage at the Grand Palace.

Festival Folklorico March 6th-7th and March 13th-14th, presented Ballet Folklorico in a concert, "Viva Arizona," a dance history of Arizona from Spanish history to the present.

Old Tucson Studios' Mescal location came to life when filming began for *South of Heaven, West of Hell*. A theatrical feature film starring country music star Dwight Yoakam, Vince Vaughn, Billy Bob Thornton, Bridget Fonda, and Peter Fonda. Filming was scheduled to continue through June. The local action is considered a coup since work in Hollywood was down dramatically as studios continue to tighten their belts by turning out fewer projects.

A major studio did not back *South of Heaven, West of Hell*, instead, getting its backing from smaller production companies, including one tied to Yoakam. Valentine Casey is a Marshal in the desolate Tucson Territory in the early 1900s. On Christmas Eve, his outlaw family visits him, and he must confront the sins of his past.

He and his partner, U.S. Christmas, journey to a small town that the ruthless Henry Clan controls to save his love interest.

Wild West Fest rode into Old Tucson Studios on April 10th for an old west celebration weekend, which featured an intercollegiate rodeo, a world-famous trick roper, cowboy poets, old-fashioned fiddlers, and authentic rope makers. Wild West Fest became an annual tradition that continued until 2020.

Country music artist Kenny Chesney performed at 7 p.m., Friday, May 6th, followed by a Classic Rock All-Stars concert on Saturday, May 7th. The featured performers were band members from Iron Butterfly, Sugar Loaf, Rare Earth, Cannibal, and The Headhunters. Both concerts were held at Old Tucson Studios Budweiser arena. A dust storm of sorts shrouded the Rio Lobo stage as 3,000-plus fans danced, whirled and boogied with Kenny Chesney.

"Richard Scary's Busytown Express," an interactive traveling experience, was at Old Tucson Studios Saturday, May 28th, 1999, through Monday, May 30th. The national tour was based on Scary's books and "The Busy World of Richard Scary," animated series popular with preschoolers. There were activity stations, a musical stage show featuring safety tips, and character appearances.

Old Tucson Studios hosted the Budweiser Entertainment Series, which featured Jan and Dean plus The Association on Saturday, June 5th. Jan & Dean were becoming hot again on the retro rock circuit, cranking out such '60s classics as "Surf City," "The Little Old Lady (From Pasadena)," and "Drag City." To audiences often too young to know how tragically apropos their hit "Dead Man's Curve" really was. The duo brought their feel-good show to Old Tucson Studios' outdoor Rio Lobo Stage. The Association featured its pop singles "Cherish" and "Never My Love."

Longtime rock 'n' roller Eddie Money was on stage June 19th, 1999. Money and his trademark guitar riffs had been around for some three decades. He was touring again, this time in support of his new CD, "Ready Eddie."

The opening act was Tucson's own LeeAnne Savage and Shockadelica. The wind whipped up suddenly during the show, toppling the 15-foot-high light fixture on the left side of the stage as LeeAnne Savage was finishing her version of the artist formerly known as Prince's "Kiss."

The wind quickly died down. But it took stagehands 45 minutes to tie down the towering tresses on either side of the stage before Savage and her band, Shockadelica, could finish their opening act and Money could take the stage. The fans, more than 2,200 of them, hooted, howled, and got anxious waiting it out. But it was worth the wait when the Moneyman emerged in blue jeans, a black shirt, and straw cowboy hat - a fitting outfit given the location.

The *Wild Wild West* movie Starring Will Smith and Kevin Kline was an updated rendition of the television series and took on a "Steampunk" look. It was filmed in New Mexico. The producers also used Old Tucson's locomotive, Reno, which had been destroyed in the disastrous 1995 fire. The producers rented other fancy locomotives but needed one they could blow up. They refurbished the Reno, trashed it, and then re-refurbished it.

As of July 9th, 1999, a newly designed logo went into effect and used a gunfighter partially hidden by the words "Old Tucson" and using the slogan "Were Legends Come Alive."

Sounds of the 60s from the Lovin' Spoonful and Felix Cavaliere's Rascals rolled into Old Tucson on July 10th. Members Steve Boone and Joe Butler, along with Jeny Yester, after joining the Spoonful in 1967, were slated to be on Old Tucson's Rio Lobo Stage in the Budweiser High Noon Arena. The group, Desert Cadillacs, opened the concert.

The Magic School Bus was live on July 17th and 18th. Ms. Frizzle, Liz, and her class made a stop at Old Tucson Studios for two days of fun, music, and problem-solving as they taught the importance of recycling. The popular Fox Kids' program based on the Scholastic book series of the same name was on the road that summer with two shows: "Recycling" (which came here) and "A Bright Idea." "Magic Bus" taught kids about science through songs, dances, and skits featuring Ms. Frizzle and Liz and her classmates.

The 13th annual Great Tucson Reader Festival benefit got rolling at Old Tucson Studios on Sept. 25th, 1999. The event, which benefited Sun Sounds Radio Reading Service, features a chili, salsa, wings, guacamole cook-off, and a massive beer-tasting event. Also on the schedule were live entertainment and a silent auction. Sun Sounds is a Tucson-based group that reads printed materials to blind and physically disabled people via a closed broadcast radio station. The organization was funded solely by grants, donations, and fundraisers.

The saga of Dr. Hyde continued at "Nightfall VIII," 1999, as the spider-web-draped park was spooky from attraction to attraction. Without question, the scariest place was the haunted house, Dr. Hyde's Hall of Horror, where visitors make their way through a maze of power-tool-wielding killers, snarling monsters, raging prisoners, and much, much more.

Dr. Hyde experimenting with one of
his inmates. 1999 (Author's collection)

Other new attractions include *Nightfall: A History of Horror*,
a video that details the unimaginable abuses endured by one small
desert town, and the Abra-Cadaver Magic Show, which featured the
not-so-Great Mordecai as he attempts to bring back his long-lost
brother.

Nightfall VIII's centerpiece was the continuing story of Dr. Hyde.
Two new installments add to the saga: "The Hidden Fury," which
took place in the Town Square, and "Vengeance Unleashed," which
occurred in the courtyard of Mission Santa Maria. The plot involved
two interlopers who steal Dr. Hyde's secret book with a magic stone
that has the power to bring the dead back to life. But Dr. Hyde does not
let the stone go without a furious and flame-filled fight.

On October 13th Rolles Rance Farm Production Company
brought its film *Legend of the Phantom Rider* to Mescal for filming. It
starred Denise Crosby, Robert McRay, and Stefan Gierasch. The setting of this fantasy movie is an old ghost town. Two ancient entities
are reincarnated to fight over a lost soul once again. The film, which

has a budget of less than 91 million, is the latest project brought to town by independent filmmaker Patrick Roddy.

In December, Old Tucson was aglow with 30,000 Christmas lights in the inaugural "Winter West Fest." The celebration ran from November 26th through January 1st, 2000. In the palace was a stage show, "Christmas Memories," and at the mission was the show, "Edwin the Elf Saves Christmas."

Winter West Fest's show "Edwin the Elf" presented
at the Mission set. 1999 (Author's collection)

The Easter weekend 2000 program introduced the new show: "Celebration" in the carousel theater. A song and dance spectacular with popular songs and several costume changes.

Also introduced for the high season were two new stunt shows, "Trail of the Bounty Hunter." A bounty hunter arrives at the High Chaparral Ranch looking for two wanted fugitives. He finds them both staying at the ranch. A confrontation takes place, and gunfire erupts.

And the "Behind the Scenes Stunt Spectacular," presented at the Mission set, is a humorous look at how stunts are performed.

The 2000 Budweiser Entertainment Series churned out classic rock and country shows. Sammy Kershaw, Steppenwolf, Eric Burton, Blue Oyster Cult, Doug Stone, and Mark Chesnutt are some of the stars who performed at the park. On May 13th, the first concert of the season was Eddie Money, on his third trip to Old Tucson.

"Parachute Express," a kid's band, played their music on May 19th and 20th.

Scooby Doo's "live review" appeared with Fred Flintstone and Yogi Bear's Young Riders round Up. Which included Winnie the Pooh, a jumping castle, King Putt, Pepsi challenge, Pikachu and Michigan J Frog, Sandy Sidewinder, Teletubbies, Jeffrey Giraffe, Elmo, and Cookie Monster, Mickey and Minnie Mouse, and Cinderella held a stage show on May 21st and 22nd in Stage 2.

A professional wrestling showdown occurred on July 15th, 2000. "Summer Stomp" showcased Yokozuna, the world's heaviest wrestler at 600 pounds against Jimmy "Super Fly" Snuka. It was a full card with the appearance of "Doink the Clown."

Proclaiming that "Bigger is Better," the Discovery Institute, an interactive science program for kids, hit Old Tucson on October 1. They demonstrated numerous scientific principles with the overriding theme that "Bigger is Better."

"Nightfall IX" 2000 comes alive October 6th through October 31st. Nightfall included a stunt show "Genesis" that began with a wedding that Hyde interrupts; "Exodus of the Doomed" details an inmate uprising. The main Nightfall shows included plenty of high falls, a few gunfights, and explosions. Early in the show, the evil psychopath breaks up a wedding in the worst way. Hyde's antics at Nightfall are not anything new. The diabolical doc has been causing havoc at Old Tucson Studios for the better part of a decade. The main stunt shows occurred in the town square.

Nightfall IX Dr. Hyde on the porch of
his laboratory. 2000 (Author's collection)

Starting December 15th, the second Winter West Festival kicked off. Old Tucson had a drive-through light show for automobiles that was about 1 mile long. A 30-foot-tall Christmas tree graced Town Square, and the presentation of stunt shows and music shows with a Christmas theme.

Starting on January 27th, 2001, every last Thursday of the month through December were "Golden Days." Old Tucson Studios treated seniors to a day of fun-filled live music, bingo competitions, prize drawings, and informational exhibits, including health care, recreation, and community services. Visitors ages 50 and older received 50 percent off regular admission. The "Green Valley Stage Band," which is a 15-piece band, provided entertainment.

"Give My Regards" premiered on March 1st and was a rousing revue of timeless Broadway hits of then and now, including Cabaret,

Oklahoma, Lullaby of Broadway, Grease, and Phantom of the Opera. In all, more than 21 Broadway favorites from some of the biggest Tony Award-winning musicals were showcased. The 30-minute show took place daily in the Carousel Theater. The production included lavish costumes and stunning sets.

Zorro, the dashing defender of justice, rode into Old Tucson Studios for two new live-action thrill spectaculars March 18th through May 31st. "Diamond Lil and her girls" played host to Don Diego, and the badman Mondecero showed up at the Palace in "The Blade of Zorro," set in 1824, as the famed hero swooped in to thwart the evil Mondecero. "Zorro and the Desert of Deception" was a 20-minute stunt show presented at the Mission set, which featured Capitan Montecero's efforts to steal the land deed to a local church and use the land to mine for silver.

More than 30 top-tier BMX pros competed in the first desert dirt jumping challenge on March 31st and April 1st and competed for a $10,000 purse.

The alternative bands "Aggressive Sound Session" and "PH 8" performed in concert on April 1st.

The Tombstone Vigilantes took first place in Old Tucson Studio's first Annual Gunfight, and Stunt Competition held on April 7th and 8th. Five Old West reenactment groups from California, Arizona, and Texas participated in the two-day event.

Old Tucson had scheduled a "rave," a music concert that ran all night and had a reputation for drug use. The county was opposed to holding it on county property. The producers, "Perfecto To Work 2001", argued that the concert on April 27th was not a rave but a concert featuring "trance" music. Regardless, the event was canceled.

On Wednesdays and Fridays through Aug. 31st, the Tucson Parks and Recreation offered the "Summer Kids Camp," which featured numerous activities for little cowgirls and cowboys. It included daily shows, storytelling, art classes, and gang prevention.

The Budweiser concert series included: Ty Herndon, Patty Loveless, Clay Walker, Pat Benatar, John Kay and Steppenwolf, Kenny Rogers, and the Charlie Daniels Band.

A charlatan and huckster claimed he could make it rain in "The Rainmaker." The crowd-pleasing blend of comedic antics and special effects took the edge off the heat in more than one way.

In addition to "The Rainmaker," one other new show premiered on August 3rd, 2001, a dancing and singing extravaganza called "Gun Belts & Garters" was presented in the Palace Hotel and Saloon.

Then, the classic gunfight, which helped make Old Tucson famous, was showcased in "Terror in a Small Town." Jack and Big Ed Callahan are the law in a lawless town. They started an extortion ring to shake downtown businesses for money. Jack goes into the Doc's office to collect extortion money and ends up beating Doc. Cassidy, of the Arizona Rangers, shows up and confronts Jack, and a fight occurs. The marshal shows up and turns out to be Big Ed Callahan. The Ranger gives both 12 hours of leave town. A gunfight begins when they start shooting at the Ranger. Jack and Ed Callahan run into the bank as the Ranger runs into Doc's office for a shotgun, and he demands that Jack and Big Ed surrender. Big Ed sends Jack around the back to get behind the Ranger. Big Ed runs out of the bank and fires at the Ranger, who fires back and kills Big Ed. The Ranger then runs into the street, where Jack fires on him on the roof. The Ranger then shoots Jack off the roof. This show is the reprisal of a presentation from the 1960s.

The third show to premiere was "the "Hollywood Stunt Demonstration," which offered a behind-the-scenes look at movie action mechanics and stunts.

High fall from Mission during a
stunt show. 2001 (Author's collection)

For ten years running, Dr. Jebediah Hyde and his ghoulish minions have been descending upon Old Tucson Studios each October like an ominous blanket of fog, transforming the much-loved attraction into the frightening town of Nightfall. For 2001, Old Tucson expects more than 80,000 brave souls to enter the Haunted Mansion and Creepy Catacombs of "Nightfall X." Josey McFarland and Phaidon, the spirit of the dead, takes on Hyde and his minions. After defeating the minions, Hyde teleports to his lair atop the Palace and his transmuter. McFarland and Crazy Sam had previously booby-trapped the machine. Hyde throws Sam off the tower. McFarland and Phaidon blow up the device, and Hyde high falls off the tower.

The Creepy Catacombs, a haunted walk-through version of the park's Iron Door Mine Adventure, has quite a few surprises that may frighten children younger than 5 or 6. The Discovery Institute's family science show provides lighthearted and educational relief from the rest of the Nightfall's eerie atmosphere.

A truck explosion during the north end show. 2001
(Author's collection)

Opening on December 6th, 2001, Old Tucson Studios' Town Hall Museum featured exhibits celebrating Arizona's rich history and the American West's culture. A History of the Movies exhibit told the story of a deserted landscape becoming America's premier Western film studio. Photographs, costumes, and movie posters told an engaging tale of Old West action from Arizona's "Hollywood in the Desert." In partnership with the Arizona-Sonora Desert Museum and the Bisbee Mining and Historical Museum, the park presented Minerals of Bisbee.

Third annual Winter West Fest, a Festival of Faiths, meant to appeal to church groups. The Tucson Jewish youth choir sang on Sundays starting December 7th, the first night of Hanukkah. The event included stories, Kosher food, lighting the first candle on the menorah, and an annual Las Posadas celebration. Specialty shows included "A Christmas to Remember" (stage show), a live Nativity scene, "Little Outhouse on the Prairie" (a humorous stunt show), and storyteller Thaddeus Appleby telling old English tales.

January 2002 saw the opening of several new shows. The first "American Anthem" took a musical trip through popular and patriotic music from the last hundred years.

Old Tucson presented "Little Outhouse on the Prairie." The bad guys, Stinky and Cletus, decide they will steal the Christmas money from the Mayor. The good guys, Billy and Abby, try to stop them. There was a running gag about Granny and a woodpecker. While trying to carry the safe down a ladder, Stinky falls with the ladder. Then the safe is dropped on him. Some comedic foot chases occur while Stinky hid in the outhouse. A stick of dynamite is thrown in, and the outhouse exploded. Stinky and Cletus are both captured.

"Little Outhouse on the Prairie" showing a comedic
chase scene. 2002 (Author's collection)

Finally, in "Day of the Hunter," a bounty hunter runs down a fugitive who has changed his way, the Sheriff, a friend of the criminal, must choose between duty and friendship. A bounty hunter, Tanner, confronts the marshal. He tells the marshal that the storekeeper, Jeb, is wanted for murder, and he intends to take Jeb in dead or alive. The marshal disarms the hunter and tells him he can have his gun back when he is ready to leave town. Jeb comes out, and a fight takes place, and Tanner is beaten. Tanner goes to the marshal and says that he is leaving town and needs his gun back. Jeb faces Tanner and confesses that he is wanted. They each draw, and Jeb kills the hunter. The marshal arrives, and Jeb says he will not surrender, so the marshal kills him. This show was a reprisal of one from the 1960s.

The "Rip Roaring Roundup" was presented on March 30th -31st and April 6th-7th. Highlights included "Six Shooter Smoke Off" held the 2nd weekend, the 6th and 7th, sanctioned by the Kansas City Barbecue Society. The purse was $6000. Other events included gunfighter competition, mountain men, a costume contest, cowboy poets, and Kowboy Kal and his horse Easy Dancer.

"Ranching in Arizona," an exhibit that chronicles the cattle industry's history started on April 26th, 2002, at Old Tucson Studios' Town Hall Museum. The new exhibition covered ranching from the introduction of Andalusian cattle by Spanish conquistadors to the way cattle ranching is conducted in Arizona today.

Old Tucson Studios lined up a star-studded ensemble of performers for its 2002 Budweiser Concert Series. The Budweiser High Noon arena hosted eight concerts that ran throughout the summer, providing concertgoers with Tucson's premier concert venue. This 4,400-seat outdoor arena featured the Rio Lobo Stage with its stunning backdrop of Tucson Mountain Park and cool summer evenings.

The concerts include:

Eddie Money in concert June 7th

Aaron Tippin in concert June 9th

Gary Allen on July 6th, along with Troy Olson.

"Blue Oyster Cult" performed on July 19th

Tracy Byrd along with Mark Wills on August 25th

Chad Brock in concert on August 16th along
with "Titan Valley Warhead."

Pat Benatar in concert with Neil Giraldo August 30th

Rock West featuring "L. A. Guns," "Warrant," "Ratt,"
"Dokken," And "Firehouse" on September 13th

A concert being set up on the
Rio Lobo stage. 2003 (Author's collection)

Old Tucson Studios announced that the park would close for
the summer. Tours to accommodate its guests on Tuesdays and
Wednesdays would be held throughout the summer. Effective May
30th, every hour, on the hour from 10 a.m. through 2 p.m., guests

could enjoy the park scenery and relive Old Tucson Studios' movie history. The tour was five dollars for adults, three dollars for children. The cost could be used towards a regular admission when the park usually is open.

As visitation fell off after an unsolved fire in 1995 and the national drop in travel after September 11th, 2001, left Old Tucson to consider bankruptcy protection, and its county landlords threatened foreclosure over back rent. The County signed a new lease, which allowed the company to gradually restore more than 60 full-time jobs or equivalent positions it had eliminated. It also restored operating hours cut over the summer because of the financial woes. The company's full-time workforce before the cutbacks was 125.

Hollywood Returned to Old Tucson Studios with *Via The Ghost Rock Trail* (released under the title *Ghost Rock). The Ghost Rock Trail* started filming on July 29th, 2002, and the Old Tucson Studios streets were alive with thundering horse hooves, blazing six-shooters, and the classic conflicts of good vs. evil. The veteran actor Michael Worth, Director Dustin Rikert, and the Temple Hill Entertainment group brought their feature film production of *The Ghost Rock Trail* to Southern Arizona. It starred: Gary Busey, Michael Worth, and Jeff Fahey. The film begins with a flashback to a family's massacre by outlaws, then cuts to the present time (the 1880s), and the same outlaws control the town. John Slaughter and Company show up to take the town back with Kung Fu fighting and a ghost's help.

Once a closed-to-the-public movie set, Mescal was opened for public tours, starting September 27th, 2002. Guided photo and walking tours were given every hour on Tuesdays, Thursdays, and Saturdays from 10 a.m. to 2 p.m. The fee was $8.

Nightfall X ended in 1924 with the death of Dr. Hyde. In "Forbidden Passage" "Nightfall XI," a truckload of kids invade the town. They run into a sinister character that blows up their car. The two women are involved in physical stunts, a roof role, and a tramp explosion. One of the men is set on fire and runs around the set. The kids are killed off by the end of the vignette. Also available in the park are two heckling gargoyles. For comic relief is "Nightfall: On Location," about two clueless filmmakers. "Fright Mare: The Music of the Night" was a stage show presented in the Palace Hotel.

Explosion at the Palace Nightfall. 2002 (Author's collection)

As part of the Christmas celebration running from November 29th through January 5th, some 400-holiday light displays ran around Old Tucson's perimeter, creating more than a mile-long winter light driving tour.

The Grand Palace Hotel & Saloon featured three all-new musical revues, including "Holiday Hoedown," "For Unto Y'all," and "Holiday Cheer."

"Thaddeus P. Appleby" and his tales from Victorian times returned to the Arizona Theater.

Town Hall was converted to a Western version of the North Pole as Santa took over the judge's chambers, joined by "Elf Troup II" and "Santa's Workshop for Little Elves" in the Town Hall anterooms.

Two new gunfight shows kicked off on December 26th, which ran for the full season. "Billy the Kid, Scourge of New Mexico" and "The Gold of Santa Maria." The signature live-action gunfight show, created by Old Tucson's Entertainment Manager, Rob Jensen, told the story of how "Billy the Kid" and "Dirty" Dave Rudabaugh formed their notorious alliance and went on to terrorize New Mexico! Kids of all ages loved the good ole' fashion gunfight!

"The Gold of Santa Maria," also inspired by Jensen, was a behind-the-scenes look at how the actors performed the stunts. But the show took a bit of an unplanned detour when two outlaws show up to steal the treasure, and the sheriff and his deputy must stop them. But not to worry, our fearless sheriff and Deputy saved the day.

The new lineup also featured the old-time favorite saloon musical "Miss Kitty's Cowboy Christmas," the holiday version of Miss Kitty's world-famous Can-Can show.

Miss Kitty's Can-Can Show performed in the
Palace Hotel and Saloon. 2004 (Author's collection)

Old Tucson Studios hosted the 24th annual ChiliHeads Wild West Chili Cook-Off on Feb. 8, which featured more than 30 vendors who prepared a variety of different chilies. The Chili Appreciation Society International was on hand to dole out awards for the chilies in various categories. Proceeds benefitted the Asthma Foundation of Southern Arizona.

Old Tucson's debt and lease were back on the county's agenda. Nearly eight months after county officials declared Old Tucson Studios in default of its rent, the Pima County Board of Supervisors tried to decide what to do about it. The supervisors met behind closed doors on March 9th, 2003, to get advice from County Administrator Chuck Huckleberry and the County Attorney's Office on collecting $124,000 in back rent and dealing with Old Tucson officials' concerns about the viability of the lease. Officials of the ailing theme park had warned they might close if the county sued to collect the money. They say they meant to pay the rent once the county had formally sent out notices seeking bidders on a new lease. The county owns the Old Tucson property and leases it to the Old Tucson Company.

On May 3rd, the Budweiser Rock Band Tour with "Pat Benatar," "Judas Priest," "Cheap Trick," "Led Zeppelin," and "AC/DC" was brought back to old Tucson. Included with these artists were Rick Springfield in concert on the Rio Lobo stage May 11th, "Diamond Rio" on May 23rd, Gary Allan on July 5th, "Garcia Brothers" on June 14th, 2003, "Joan Jett and The Blackhearts" were in concert on June 28th, for Gay West VII. Also playing were the "Motels" with Martha Davis, Clay Walker played on June 29th. Old Tucson presented a rock show with "Lynch Mob," LA Guns," and Swedish rocker Yngwie Malmsteen on August 16th, and the Honky Tonk Tailgate Party with Chad Brock was held on September 20th.

Old Tucson Studios reduced its workweek by about 75 percent, leaving a core group of about 30 people to run limited operations throughout the summer, a company official said. The company told employees at a meeting, May 30th, 2003, that they could go to seasonal, on-call status or accept being laid off if Old Tucson drastically cut its hours and operations at least through the summer.

Available entertainment included a behind-the-scenes one-hour guided tour. It originated just inside the front gate and left on the hour from 10 a.m., with the last tour starting at 2 p.m.

The Last Outpost gift shop remained open. Banquets, weddings, private parties, educational activities, school field trips, and all other on-going and special events either booked or in the planning phase will be unaffected by this change.

Unaffected were all concerts, musical events, and nighttime activities, including the Budweiser Concert Series.

Old Tucson Studios got a new lease on September 19th that allowed it to restore jobs and hours of operation cut because of financial difficulties. The Board of Supervisors decided to grant the Western theme park and movie set a new lease, hoping that it would benefit the county treasury in the long term. Old Tucson Studios, built-in 1939, had struggled since a devastating fire in 1995, a situation made worse by a drop in tourism after the September 11th, 2001, terrorist attacks. The county had threatened to foreclose because of unpaid rent. But the new lease would allow Old Tucson to gradually restore more than 60 full-time jobs and operating hours cut over the summer. The new lease would delay ten years repayment of $222,000 to $240,000 in back rent to Pima County, although the county would earn interest. It also reduced the park's annual rent payments to $50,000 from $300,000.

The Halloween season did not include the annual "Nightfall" event. The park canceled the popular month-long event because of delays in reinstating the lease Old Tucson had with Pima County. This would have been the 14th year for Nightfall, that Old Tucson turns into a ghost town and the performance of scary Halloween shows. Pete Mangelsdorf, CEO of Old Tucson, said the new lease would allow Old Tucson to operate a slightly smaller Halloween attraction called "Fright Fest" on October weekends and Winter West Fest in December.

The new entertainment would include "The Scary Slinger Show," a ghoulish take on trash-talk television. The Chinese alley turns into the home of "the diabolical and dreaded Dr. Kiyuu,"; according to the park's website, "The Tortured Train Ride" transformed the park's railroad attraction into the lost wanderings of Old Unlucky No. 13. Coming back this year are the musical revues "Frightmares" with a new production called "Dead Again," the Iron Door Mine's Creepy Catacomb, vicious "Manimal," and gargoyle tricksters.

Nightfall show "Torture Time" performed in the
Storyteller Theater. 2004 (Author's collection)

With the lease in full operating mode, the park hours returned to 10 AM to 6 PM seven days a week starting January 28th, 2004.

Starting on September 5th, 2004, Star Pass Hotel and Resort offered a 2 ½ hour, 6-mile horseback ride from Starr Pass Resort to Old Tucson Studios. After the ride, visitors' can enjoy the park and could be bussed back to Starr Pass.

In 2004, "Nightfall" was back and scarier than ever. The main stunt show was "Evil Flame," in which several young people arrive at Nightfall with their college professor trying to summon up the spirit of Dr. Hyde. They have an altar set up, and the professor has them bring forth a mysterious box containing robes and a magical amulet. The professor summons up a large tongue of flame, and a creature comes out of the ground and fights the kids. One of the kids becomes a zombie. He and the creature throw another student into a woodchopper.

The female student appears in an upper room window. She throws dynamite and blows up the zombie. She throws another at the monster, who throws it into the building's first floor and blows up the building. The professor has climbed to the palace tower's roof and is shot off with an arrow. He does a high fall. He then comes out of the gate very much alive. He and the creature have a fight, and the professor wins and summons the spirit to make the creature go back into the ground. The professor shows himself to be Dr. Hyde.

Two creatures of the night fighting
to the death. 2004 (Author's collection)

Inside are two shows, "Frightmares: Zombies Alive," a singing and dancing show presented in the Palace, and "Torture Time,"
presented in the Kachina Theater, where Mistress Helga tortures her
lovely assistant.

In October 2004, the Tucson Convention Center was being
used as a soundstage when a fire broke out during the filming of
Stephen King's Desperation. The city told the production to go elsewhere. The producers brought the movie to Old Tucson and finished
their interior filming in Stage 2.

Starting on December 17th, Old Tucson Company began working alongside Spirit Horse Productions, a California based production development company, initiating a revitalization of the film
and television industry at Old Tucson Studios and its sister site,
Mescal. This arrangement allowed Old Tucson Company to culti-
vate its active studio status and leverage its promotional efforts by
working with an established production company with strong ties
to the Hollywood film community. According to Michelle Hartly,
co-producer of Spirit Horse Productions, "This is an expansion of
our commitment to keeping film production in the United States."

Co-producer Shari Hamrick agrees, "We've been working on a studio project in Southern California and are very happy to bring additional opportunities to Arizona."

Spirit Horse confirmed the History Channel's *Wild West Tech,* which featured host David Carradine for January 2005, followed by an independent feature titled *Miracle at Sage Creek,* based on Western author Thadd Turner's script. Spirit Horse negotiated production services for Dream Work's newest series *Into the West,* which utilized the Historic Reno train.

Setting up a shot for the production of
Wild West Tech: Gang Technology. 2005 (Author's collection)

The first Spirit Horse production was *Wild West Tech: Gang Technology,* which starred David Carradine, Jacqui Allen, Amos Carver, and "Ace" Martinez. A television series explaining different technologies of the old West. This episode (season 2, episode 12) chronicles several gangs in the old West.

The Tucson based movie *Cutoff* concluded in Town Square with 20 or so police cars drawn up before the Palace Hotel for the final shootout. It Starred Amanda Brooks and Thomas Ian Nicholas. A spoiled rich girl and her boyfriend rob a check-cashing business. They steal an ambulance, get in a high-speed chase with the police, and end up in Townsquare.

In the second Spirit Horse production, the movie *Miracle at Sage Creek* was lensed at the Mescal Facility for the Hallmark Channel. Starring Tim Abell, Sarah Aldrich, Marissa Bock, and David Carradine, this was a film about two families overcoming prejudice and tragedy in 1888 Wyoming when an extraordinary Christmas miracle saves a small boy's life.

A Movie, *Duel,* was filmed in 2005, at the Mescal facility. Starring Michael Worth and Tim Thomerson. A man wanders into a small town where he finds every person dead. He must track down and face the person responsible for the slaughter.

Honky Tonk Saturday Night, a weekly event, featured live music in the Palace Hotel and Saloon. The first night, July 9th, saw Jesse Alexander and John Randall entertaining.

The park also presented karaoke in Rosas Cantina and opened the new El Vaquero restaurant in the previous Cowboy Café.

Clay Walker was in concert on August 3rd on the Rio Lobo stage. As he celebrated the 10th anniversary of his platinum-selling debut album on August 3rd, he was thinking ahead to September, when his RCA debut album would be released, and his career started afresh.

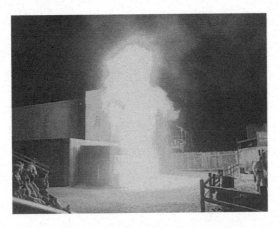

An explosion on the set of Nightfall XIII at the
north end of town. 2004 (Author's collection)

"Nightfall XIII" ran during October. This year it was called "Nightfall: The Gathering." The main stunt show was titled "Evil Unbound." A man and a woman arrive on set dressed as Goths. Hyde explains he needs to build an army to defend Nightfall. Hyde attacks them until they agree to help him. They leave the set at the sound of engines when a motorcycle and a Quad four-wheeler drive onto the scene. The two males' dismount and discuss the haunted place. Just then, Hyde appears on the roof of the Palace and speaks with the two men. He then uses a zip line to slide onto the bathhouse roof. The male Goth comes out of the bathhouse door and attacks the two males. He knocks one out, kills the other, and then raises him from death to be a zombie. The Goth guy and the zombie drag the second male and feed him into a woodchipper. The two Goths decide to take on Hyde, who blows the girl off the bathhouse's roof.

Meanwhile, the male Goth has climbed on top of the Palace and sets off a bazooka, blowing up a gas truck. He is then shot off the roof by Dr. Hyde. The flames burn their way across the set to boxes of dynamite stacked on set with Hyde standing next to them. The boxes explode, and Hyde is apparently killed.

December 22nd, 2005, the Christmas celebration included "Christmas Time is Here," a play and music show in the Palace.

The 16th annual Ted Walker day was scheduled for February 9th, 2006, and was open to 4th, 5th, and 6th-grade classes. The attendance was limited to approximately 3000 kids.

In March, BBC TV filmed *The Wild and The West* at Old Tucson Studios. It Starred Peter J. Brown, Joe Demmi, Tanya Turner, and Thadd Turner and compared Western films seen in the myth of Hollywood vs. the real west.

Old Tucson presented the annual Girl Scout Jamboree at Old Tucson Studios on May 3rd. Activities included camping and other Girl Scout skills; plus, the usual daily activities of the park.

The second movie of the year was *The Decoy* with Justin Kreinbrink, Howard Allen, and Susan Arnold. Cooper (Kreinbrink) must arrest an old friend and bring him to town for hanging. He must fight off a gang of desperados and his conscience.

Old Tucson Studios celebrated John Wayne on May 26th, 2006, with the premiere of a documentary about Wayne's involvement with Old Tucson entitled *Remembering John Wayne*. It was filmed at the park and highlighted the John Wayne films shot at the park.

Honky Tonk Saturday Night returned with the "The Wyatt's" kicking things off and would be presented throughout the summer from May 27th to September 2nd, 2006. "Kevin Pakulis and Ranch Deluxe" played June 3rd and "Greg Spivey and Wild Ride" on June 10th.

"Nightfall: Dark Asylum" started October 5th, 2006. Included: "Dark Asylum," the stunt show, "Vampire Nightmare," an inside musical performance, and "Zambora," in which a woman turns into a gorilla.

The brother of Josie and a friend shows up in Nightfall to find Josie's brother. He meets up with Marietta, and they fight. Cavanaugh comes on set and fights the friend of Josie's brother. Dr. Hyde makes his entrance and fights with everyone. At the end of the fight, Josie's brother throws Hyde down a fracture in the earth, causing Marietta and Cavanaugh's destruction.

The actor's on the set of "Evil Flame" trying to summon a beast. 2005 (Author's collection)

Another Movie for 2006 was *The Seven Mummies,* about a gang of six escaped convicts. They kidnap a woman and head for Mexico. In route, they discover a quantity of gold. While crossing the hot Arizona desert, they come across a small town where the residents seem very friendly. They all turn out to be zombies and vampires.

The first film of 2007 was *Al's Beef*, starring Dean Stockwell, Jordan Ladd, and Liam O'Neil. A small western town run by a corrupt sheriff who has killed several townspeople to keep his power. He has his comeuppance when he faces off with a woman.

Old Tucson Studios kicked off "Honky Tonk Saturday Nights" on May 26th, 2007. The grand opening featured special events celebrating John Wayne's 100th birthday, including a "Rough Stock Rodeo." While dining at the "Chuck Wagon," guests could tap their toes to a live theatrical entertainment show starring "Miss Kitty's Can-Can Review," a roof-raising ruckus. A live band, "Mamie Chastain and The John Wayne Band," played well into the night.

"Nightfall" started its 16th run on September 29th, 2007, with "Darkness Rising." The shows included Cannibal House, Gross Anatomy, Vampire Nightmare (a musical), Zambora (a girl turns into a guerrilla), Caverns of Despair, and the Transylvanian Twins.

The main attraction, the "Darkness Rising" stunt show, depicts Dr. Hyde's dangerous decision to resurrect Kain, the Vampire King, to capture the vampire's power. To complicate the situation, Van Helsing, the vampire hunter, enters the set. Van Helsing fights with Lilith, who is also a vampire. As Kain re-emerges, things quickly get out of hand, and he and Hyde fight to the death in a dramatic showdown. The Darkness Rising Stunt Show incorporated more than 30 pyrotechnic explosions and a 35-foot fall taken by a stuntman on fire.

BBC/Film West Productions brought their production *The Wild West* to Old Tucson Studios. Narrated by Michael Praed, this documentary series was about gunfights in the old west. This episode chronicled The Gunfight at the OK Corral.

Jason Wade standing on the porch of the Palace Hotel and Saloon,
anticipating a gunfight in the movie *Dead West*. 2008 (Author's collection)

The next movie up, which was filmed during both the 2006
and 2008 Nightfall shows, was shot under the name of *Ghost Town*
and released under the name of *Dead West*. Starring Jason Wade and
Angelica Celaya. Johnny Dust (Wade) is the head stuntman at Old
Tucson Studios. A new management group takes over the park and
produces "Nightfall," a Halloween celebration. Johnny soon finds out
the town is populated with vampires, and a struggle ensues between
Dust and the vampires. This movie used the Nightfall theme and
used some stunts and pyrotechnics of the Northend show in the film,

In a first for Old Tucson, was filming of a music video in
Russian. The band Diskoteca Avaria, a well-known band in Russia,
came to Arizona to film a music video and short film based on their
song "Four Guys." Directed by Hindrek Maasik and starred Igor
Krutoi, Alexi Serov, Alexi Ryzov, and Nikolai Timofeev. Done in a
"The Good, The Bad, and The Ugly" format, it is about three bad
guys and a sheriff out to get them.

This summer celebrated a series dedicated to the American ideal. The themes were: May 24th celebrate patriotism, July 5th celebrate freedom, August celebrate friendship, and September 6th, 2008 celebrate family with the band, "Little Joe Y La Familia."

The comic western, *Mad, Mad Wagon Party* came to Old Tucson Studios, Mon. July 21st for four days of shooting. Starring George Kennedy, Roger Holston, and Sandy Cooper, the movie is a spoof of a wagon train heading to California. The cast and crew filmed at the park during regular operating hours and offered the public a chance to watch the shoot.

To celebrate Harley-Davidson's 105th birthday on August 23rd, a Harley motorcycle was a raffle prize, plus live music by "Little Joe Y La Familia."

"Nightfall XVI" returned to Old Tucson Studios from October 3rd through October 31st, 2008. As "Release the Beast" opens, the audience hears various animals sounding like they are in distress. An explosion throws various animal parts onto the set. Hyde appears on the mansion's balcony and tells the two half-men/ half animals on the set that they were changing into hybrid animals. As Hyde disappears, they open two cages releasing Sam and Isabelle. Isabelle explains that she is a scientist and helped Dr. Hyde in his project to cross breed people with desert creatures. A "Manimal" appears on the palace roof. He slides down to the set and begins fighting Sam and the other two subjects. Isabelle injures a second bad guy with an electric shock and shot the "manimal" off the bathhouse's roof. Hyde descends to the ground and confronts Sam, Isabel, and Cavanaugh. A fire consumes Cavanaugh for letting Hyde Down. Hyde flies to the top of the Palace and begins to destroy the electrometer (the machine used to transform people into animals). Amid gunfire,

Hyde catches fire and does a roof fall. Dr. Hyde comes on set, and Isabelle forces him into a cage and announces that she will be taking over the asylum.

For the production of *Blood Moon*, Triboro Pictures came to Old Tucson to film. The cast included Naomi Jones, Cuyle Carvin, and Tim Intravia. A big bad wolf stalks a stagecoach and its passengers.

On the Road Weekly, "For Everything Country" presented itself as the West Coast's foremost authority on entertainment news with a Western Theme. It comprised the most comprehensive, engaging coverage of local and global entertainment news from concerts and movies. It also covered sports and recreation, dining and shopping, along with fashion and celebrity news. The show was seen weekly throughout the 2009 season starting Saturday, March 28th, 2009.

Old Tucson Studios announced that it was going to sponsor a western cowboy music sampler. Each Sunday, beginning March 8th and lasting through April 26th, 2009, guests could head out to Old Tucson Studios for a series of intimate performances by some of Western folk music's most cherished and original acts. The performances staged in the Grand Palace Saloon began at 1 pm. Each artist in the line-up featured their unique blend of cowboy music that embodies the American West's true spirit.

The Duet "Call of the West" combines unique harmonizing and top-notch musicianship with some good old-fashioned fun and showmanship! The series wound up Sunday, April 26th, with Arizona singer/songwriter Jon Messenger whose original Folk and Western tunes have entertained audiences throughout the West.

Date	Artist
March 8th	Joe Green
March 15th	Dennis Jay
March 22nd	Call of the West
March 29th	Mike Moutoux
April 5th	Journey West
April 12th	Katy Creek
April 19th	Jeff Harrison
April 26th	Jon Messenger

Old Tucson Studios was pleased to announce corporate sponsorship of The Single Action Shooting Society or SASS. This group is an international organization created to preserve and promote the sport of Cowboy Action Shooting. According to Old Tucson Studios CEO Pete Mangelsdorf, "Old Tucson is proud to support SASS and its members as both organizations are committed to preserving and promoting the spirit and traditions of the Old West." Free admission was offered to SASS members dressed in 1880's western period costume and presented a valid SASS ID and badge.

Old Tucson Studios 2009 "Nightfall: Harvest of Fear," which opened October 1st and ran throughout October, featured a live performance on Wednesday, October 21st by the alternative rock group Saosin (say-oh-sin) in the Palace. The Virgin Records artists will rock the house with the tracks from their latest CD, "In Search of Solid Ground." There was also a live performance of hip-hop superstar Flo Rida on Thursday, October 29th.

The town of Nightfall was once again terrorized by the extraordinarily evil Dr. Jebediah Hyde, in "Nightfall: Harvest of Evil." Hyde had apparently been killed last year along with the equally wicked Isabel. Both of them come back this year in "Dead Reckoning." Isabel steals Hyde's records and tries to repair the Electromonator Hyde created to crossbreed animals and people. Zombies come on the set and again after a big fight, and pyro explosions destroy Isabel and presumably Hyde.

The monsters were out and looking for victims
at Nightfall. 2009 (Author's collection)

The stage show "Necrosis: Party of Six" is centered on a group of hip-hop dancers who get locked in Hyde's palace followed by strange events.

Members of the cast and crew (many cast members including Don Collier, Henry Darrow, Bob Hoy, and Ted Markland) of the long-running television series *High Chaparral* gathered to meet friends of the show. The show aired on NBC from 1967 to 1971, held a reunion at Old Tucson Studios on October 17th, 2009. Visiting the set was the highlight of the 3-day reunion of *High Chaparral* fans. Attendees gathered at a Question-and-Answer session with cast and crew in the Grand Palace Saloon that afternoon.

On November 5th, 2009, Pima Rotary Club held a "City Slicker Rodeo." A safe city slicker rodeo event has carnival booths, a chuck-wagon dinner, and a barn dance.

A full day of fun events greeted guests at Old Tucson Studios on Saturday, November 21st, 2009, as "Arizona's Hollywood in the Desert" marks its 70th Anniversary. A special concert by country music superstar Darryl Worley, sponsored by KIIM-FM, headlined the day's events. Old Tucson presented a fireworks display immediately following the show.

Old Tucson Studios and Pima County Natural Resources, Parks and Recreation hosted the 20th Annual Ted Walker Youth Day. Old Tucson Studios hosted over 3,000 fourth, fifth and sixth graders from Tucson and Pima County school districts.

The *American Experience* is a long-running television series covering historical events from our past and presented by Public Broadcasting. The series came to Old Tucson for the episode on *Wyatt Earp*, with the narration and interviews done by Bob Boze Bell, Michael Murphy, and Anne Butler.

Guests were able to travel back to the simpler times of the 1880s at Wild West Days at Old Tucson Studios, March 25th through 28th, 2010. Each day from 10 am to 6 pm, this special event featured shows and musical performances that honor and recreate frontier life in the thrilling old days of the Wild West circa the 1880s.

The headlining performance at the Wild West Days occurred Saturday, March 27th, when Pistol Packin' Paula (World Champion Lady Six Gun Spinner) and Hot Shot Johnny Tuscadero squared off in a pistol spinning contest. A portion of the Wild West Days' proceeds was directed towards repairing buildings that house The Tucson Rodeo Parade Museum's priceless collection of horse-drawn vehicles. Many vehicles from "The Tucson Rodeo Museum" have appeared in movies filmed at Old Tucson Studios and displayed during this event.

Guests to Wild West Days took in our new comedy stunt show, "Wild, Wild West: Night of the Deadly Tycoon." Based on the popular television show of the same name from the 1960s, the series spawned two television movies filmed at Old Tucson Studios and a feature film about two Secret Service Agents roaming the west solving crimes.

Some actors waiting for the call to set for the pilot
Stardust and the Bandit. 2010 (Author's collection)

A production company filmed a pilot for a potential television show between August 23rd and August 30th. *Stardust and the Bandit* starred Scott Martin Thomas, Shanna Brock, Douglas Mitchell, and Wayne Spencer. The accountant for a mob boss testifies in a trial and is placed in the witness protection program. He is a timid bookkeeper offered a job at an amusement park. One day, the mob boss and his family show up at the park, and things get crazy.

Starting September 30th, 2010, "Nightfall XX: 20 years of Terror" began its annual October run. The main stunt show began with McFarland, a former inmate and a present-day inmate fighting on the set. Hyde enters from the bathhouse roof and announces the reversal of the transmutations. Samantha and the second inmate go up the rock crusher, and Samantha throws him in. Hyde and McFarland fight, and McFarland throws Hyde into the flaming pit. At last, the cavalry arrives and kills McFarland and Samantha.

Old Tucson Studios held A Waila Festival on November 11th, 2010. Instruments included in the band are a button accordion, guitar, bass, drums, and sax. This music is unique to the Tohono O'Odham Nation.

Old Tucson sponsored a concert on Thanksgiving weekend, November 26th, 27th, and 28th, when JD Norris opened for Larry King and The Legends of Country. All proceeds went to the Food Bank.

Old Tucson Studios presented Wild West Con on March 4th through the 6th. For this event, the town was renamed "Rusted Gear," and guests were invited to dress in steampunk costumes for the weekend. "Steam Punk" is a mixture of Victorian-era costumes and what it would be like if steam was the highest form of energy achieved by humankind.

Actors dressed up for Wild West Fest in 2011. (Author's collection)

Cameras were rolling for *Ambush at Dark Canyon,* an independent movie during the week of May 23rd to May 31st. A sheriff, convicted of a robbery, is sent to Yuma prison. While in prison, he learns that his wife is in danger from his ex-partner. He escapes from the prison and heads out to save his wife. Directed by Dustin Richert and starred Kix Brooks, Ernie Hudson, and Ronnie Blevins. It filmed under the title of *To Kill a Memory.*

The television mini-documentary, *Legends and Lies,* came to Old Tucson. Based on a Bill O'Reilly book, the series looks at the old West's myths and gives an accurate account of the incidents portrayed. The first of the series to film at Old Tucson was *Billy the Kid: Escape Artist.* This episode tells about the escape of Billy, the Kid, from the Lincoln County Jail.

In June 2011, Old Tucson Studio constructed the "Heritage Square Project." The park built this addition in the middle of the old town square, a wide-open space in the town center. The foundation of the project were steel shipping containers with false fronted façades. These buildings created three new streets to the existing town.

The new buildings in the town square were added as part of
the Heritage Square Project. 2011 (Author's collection)

Producers brought another new film to Old Tucson for lensing. *The Gundown*, produced by Freewill Films, starred Andrew Walker, Peter Coyote, and Sheree J. Wilson. A man seeking justice and revenge ends up in the small town of Dead River. He is faced with a showdown to protect a saloon and a woman.

The year 2011 saw the "Nightfall" show, "Dead of Night." The scene is a junkyard run by Pappy, A grizzly, old curmudgeon and populated by his son and daughter, Lyle and Loretta. Brad and Janet show up at the scrap yard looking for a t-shirt left in a car by Janet. Janet recognizes the shirt worn by Loretta as hers and demands it back. A fight ensues among the five of them. Janet pushes Loretta into a baling machine while Brad blows Lyle's head off with a shotgun. Brad then shoots Janet, saying to Pappy that he needed blood. He then kills Pappy and lights a book of matches, revealing he is the matchbook killer.

Sponsored by the Ruger Arms Company, the park held a gunfighter competition on January 14th, 2012. The Single Action Shooting Society sanctioned the event, and several groups from around the state competed in live-action gunfights.

The gunfighter competition was followed the next weekend by the Old West Roundup Cowboy Collectibles sale at Old Tucson.

The Food Channel's program *Chopped* held its competition at Old Tucson in March 2012. This is the first time *Chopped* filmed somewhere other than in New York. They shot five episodes of the show entitled *Grill Masters Summer Battle*, a competition using outdoor grills and cowboy pots and pans. The total prize money was $50,000. The hosts for the show were Ted Allen, Amanda Freitag, and Marc Murphy.

Old Tucson Studios and Western Music Association presented "The Cowboy Music Festival," which included "The Sons of the Pioneers," "Bill Ganz Western Band," and "Tumbling Tumbleweeds." "The Cowboy Music Festival" occurred on April 28th and 29th.

Marshal Vance Dillinger makes a shocking discovery when he finds out that his twin brother, who was presumed dead, was alive and believed to be the "Lucky Bandit." This is the plot for *Hot Bath and a Stiff Drink,* which starred Granger Hines, Rex Linn, William Shockley, and Jeffrey Patterson.

Old Tucson Studios went on hiatus starting June 1st until Nightfall began on October 1st. The winter average monthly attendance was 40,000, and in the summer, it was less than 4000.

Eva Daniels Production Company filmed part of their motion picture, *Goats,* at the Phillips Ranch set on Old Tucson's backlot. Starring David Duchovny, Vera Farmiga, and Graham Phillips, this is the story of a young man preparing to leave home to go to school back east. He faces separation from his flaky hippy mother and the only father he has ever known, Goatman.

Marty Freeze is showing school children how to make
adobe bricks. 2012 (Author's collection)

Offering an additional educational dimension, Old Tucson added living history talks. These talks were about Chuckwagon cooking and trail drives, Sheriffs of the old west, general stores, transportation in the old west, and saloons. Also added was a Tohono O'Odham village mockup where members of the tribe could demonstrate cooking native foods and native crafts.

What could you expect from "Nightfall XXII, 2012"? Unsettling encounters of horror lurk around every corner. Murder and mayhem reign with renegade freaks, and the walking dead were on the loose, claiming victims without remorse. The Gargoyles were back cracking sarcasm and were hysterical equal opportunity hecklers, hurling nightly verbal assaults.

The Ringmaster welcomed guests to the madness and kicked things off for the night when Pappy showed up to disrupt the plan. Pappy's Practically Perfect Prototypes Mission Hobart Gainey, the serial killer better known as "Pappy," served multiple life sentences in the Maricopa County Prison. In his showcase forum, he tested a full line of personal hygiene products for effectiveness and consumer safety on unfortunate "Volunteers."

In "Death Before the Dawn," Justin and Becky investigate an abandoned amusement park with a dark and mysterious past. Suddenly, Justin's arm is severed. A few seconds later, his head comes off. The ringmaster then enters, holding a whip. He drags Becky into the park. Then the scene swings to two workers busy tearing down the place. Their supervisor shows up and tries to hurry them up. The Ringmaster appears and tells them that they are tearing down his only home, and he intends to kill them. He pulls his whip out and slices them into pieces. Becky comes into the scene and cozies up to the

Ringmaster. Without him seeing, she had picked up the gun, killing the supervisor. As she hugs the Ringmaster, she shoots and kills him.

Returning for a sequel to *Hot Bath and a Stiff Drink*, Once Upon a Dream Production Company came to Old Tucson to film *Hot Bath and a Stiff Drink II* on January 14th, 2013. The movie, starring Granger Hines, Rex Linn, and William Shockley, is about two twin brothers, one a marshal and one an outlaw, who must team up to bring another outlaw to justice.

Gunfighter groups from throughout Arizona came to Old Tucson for a gunfighter competition at the High Chaparral set. The shootout occurred on February 16th and 17th.

The steam age meets the old west at the second annual Wild West Con Steampunk Convention on March 8th through the 10th. Attendance was over 2,000 people. Hundreds of guests attended dressed in their finest Steampunk outfits. Regular guests to the park did not know how to react to the Steampunkers.

The streets became alive with music on March 14th and 15th when the Western Music Association sponsored the "Old Tucson Cowboy Music and Arts Festival." While headlining group played on the main stage in the Palace, various other groups played and sang in other venues scattered about the park.

Probably the largest gunfight in Old Tucson history occurred on March 16th. This date commemorated the 50th anniversary of gunfight shows at Old Tucson. Gunfighters and Can-Can Girls from years past got together to share memories and entertain the visitors. The ladies put on a music show drawing from songs and dances occurring at Old Tucson for the last 67 years (going back to 1946 when the Jayceettes performed the Can-Can for visitors.).

Can-Can girls welcoming a studio visitor. 2013
(Author's collection)

Then in an action-packed ending, the stuntmen, and yes, stunt-women, from the present and years back, held a huge gunfight on the Northend set. The show's highlight was Jack Young firing a cannon. Mr. Young was the entertainment manager who introduced gunfight shows at Old Tucson way back in 1963.

Poster advertising the 50th anniversary of Old Tucson. 2013
(Author's collection)

The *American Experience* television series was back at Old Tucson in 2013 to film a second episode about Wyatt Earp's life.

The annual Wild West Days went off as planned on March 23rd and 24th, 2013. Some of the activities included an opening ceremony and flag raising, a Gatling gun demonstration, an encampment of the Mormon Column, Buffalo Soldiers showing and explaining military equipment from the 19th century, a mountain man camp demonstration, and reenactors demonstrating some of the equipment from the Civil War. The regular daily shows went off simultaneously, and the annual *High Chaparral* reunion took place at the ranch house.

The Wild West Performing Arts Society Championships were held at Old Tucson, which included trick roper's, trick and fancy gun handling, knife and tomahawk throwers, bullwhip, trick riders, and stuntmen on April 12th through the 14th.

"Nightfall XXI: 2013" ran during October. The main stunt show this year was titled "Kindred of the Dust." It takes place in a post-apocalyptic world where water is very scarce. "Kaos" leads the first group, and they possess a large tank of water. Pappy Scrap runs the second gang. The scene is a stronghold held by "Kaos." Pappy's group attacks the compound, and a series of gunfights, many stunts, and explosions, Pappy's group wins.

From November 29th through December 1st, the park hosted the Heritage Harvest Festival, presenting Native American culture and Southwest culture, including the Buffalo Soldiers, Future Farmers of America demonstrations, White Elementary School mariachis and Folklorico group, food, and Santa arrives.

"The newly established **Arizona Sonora Western Heritage Foundation** entered discussions with Pima County to take over the lease from the park within the next six months," said Old Tucson Co. CEO Pete Mangelsdorf. The foundation would help the park move toward an educational mission; a move the park hopes will make it more financially sustainable. Moving to a nonprofit-foundation model also lets the park pay a lower rate to lease the county property. It enables the park to apply for federal grants and solicit private donations.

Old Tucson Company paid $64,000 a year to Pima County to lease land in Tucson Mountain Park. If the foundation were to take over the lease agreement, the for-profit company would continue to operate the park in a deal with the foundation. Old Tucson announced plans to "expand Old Tucson into a multicultural Western heritage center." The main attractions would be interactive living-history programs, the announcement stated. "County leaders are interested in the concept and are awaiting a more detailed plan before negotiating a new lease with the park," said Tom Moulton, Pima County economic development and tourism director.

The park began offering living-history programs three years ago and has expanded to seven programs, five of which are available each day. The programs mixed lessons and laughs about life in 1880s Arizona and feature characters including a rough-and-rowdy sheriff, a gold prospector, and a schoolmarm. The park would feature interactive exhibits, entertainment, food, and crafts from various cultures, including Native American, Mexican, Spanish, Anglo, African, Asian, Mormon, and Jewish, the park's announcement said." It's an exciting concept because Western Heritage and culture always has been a part of the park," Moulton said, "but the new plan would create a visitor experience in true history rather than in Hollywood movies."

Old Tucson started giving talks about living in the old west.
The author is explaining the life of a mountain man. 2014
(Author's collection)

The foundation uses the Arizona-Sonora Desert Museum as a model for its business side and Virginia's Colonial Williamsburg as a model for its programming, he said. The foundation, which plans to hire a development director in the next few months, also is establishing relationships with the University of Arizona and the Arizona Historical Society. Historical re-enactment groups said they are excited about the possibility of a new venue and said demand for such programming is healthy.

Team 2 Entertainment, in conjunction with Dustin Rickert, utilized Old Tucson to film the music video of Randy Howser's latest hit song, *Like a Cowboy*.

The Wild West meets the steam era during the Wild West Steam Punk Con March 7th through the 9th. Enjoy watching participants as they wander through town dressed in costume and participate in several steampunk activities. Guests could walk through the vendors' area and shop for their own steampunk accouterments.

The year 2014 was the 75th anniversary of the building of Old Tucson Studios. This celebration reached its peak on March 15th. One highlight was once again a gathering of past stuntmen and women to perform a show which debuted in 1963. Also, ladies from the past performed a Can-Can Show.

75th anniversary of the building of Old Tucson. 2014
(Author's collection)

The Native American Arts Festival was presented on November 23rd, in which Native Americans demonstrated making their crafts. The following weekend the Heritage and Harvest Festival when Native Americans talk about their culture and the use of native plants.

October 2014 saw the presentation of "Nightfall XXII." The scene is the desert somewhere in Arizona. Four military people find a glowing round object in a hole in the ground. As one of the men, "Kodak," with a video camera gets close, he disappears. Another object flies from the sky and fires some shots at the men. As this is happening, Kodak reappears. As the craft leaves, several aliens come out of the round object. A female begins talking in a strange language and communicates in English with the men through the camera's speaker.

A running gun battle takes place. In the end, the alien leader ends up next to Milkman. She doesn't kill him, and he explains he is with the aliens. At this, the Sergeant starts to fight with the other aliens and defeats them. The alien woman double deals Milkman and kills him. She then walks to the round object, and everything disappears.

Old Tucson Studios presented "Old Time Holidays" for the Christmas season that benefitted the Community Food Bank, November 28th to January 1st.

There was plenty of gunfighter action at the annual "Shoot out at Chaparral" gunfighter and stunt show competition held on February 21st and 22nd, 2015. Groups from around the state met to determine which group presented the best gunfight show and which person exhibited the most skillful stunts.

The television series *American Experience* returned to Old Tucson to film another episode in the American history series for the third time. This episode was titled *Black Bart: Gentleman Bandit.*

The park's guests traveled back in time when they attended the annual Wild West Days. Held on March 20th, 21st, and 22nd, "Wild West Days" included an opening ceremony, Civil War Reenactors, Buffalo Soldiers, and other Wild West activities.

Visitors got to shop for fleas at the "Big Heap" vintage, antique, and handmade show. About 50 vendors met at Old Tucson's Stage 2 area to set up a large flea market from April 11th to April 12th.

April 16th, 2015, was the start of the Old Tucson Studios bluegrass weekend featuring "Cadillac Mountain," "Crucial Country," and "Buck and Friends." Many bluegrass groups played for the visitors' pleasure at various venues around the park.

Old Tucson Studios presented the Western Music Festival sponsored by the Western Music Association. Guests were entertained by Bill Ganz, Jon Messenger, and "43 Miles North" on May 1st and 2nd. The weekend included other groups scattered around the park, playing western and cowboy music.

The Bill O'Reilly television series, *Legends and Lies,* returned to Old Tucson to film three more episodes on old west myths. These episodes were *Butch Cassidy: The Last Man Standing, James "Wild Bill" Hickok: Plains Justice, and Jesse James: Bloody Politics.*

"Nightfall XXIII" returned to Old Tucson during October 2015 with "Dead End," a tale of deadly hauntings. Five kids arrive at an old farmstead around midnight. One of the kids tells the others that the place is haunted. Just then, the barn door opens, and one of the kids is grabbed by the killer and stabbed to death. The other kids run to the ATVs, but the machines will not run. A fight breaks out between the killer and one of the male kids, apparently drowning the killer. One teen is violently pulled into the cornfield from which a lot of voices are coming. A second male kid is stabbed to death by the killer, who then drags the body into the cornfield. The body is seen being erected on a pole to form a scarecrow.

Waila bands entertained visitors during the 22nd Waila Festival on November 28th, 2015. The music is a blend of guitar, accordion, and saxophone and is native to the Tohono O'Odham.

The famous western band, "Sons of the Pioneers," entertained the guests and visitors in a concert on January 30th, 2016, in the Palace.

The hawker for the medicine show is trying to sell the "Miracle Elixir" to the audience. 2016 (Author's collection)

As of April 3rd, 2016, the Miracle Elixir Show was running. This outside show features a professor who is selling a miracle medicine with help from the audience. They get chased out of town by vigilantes.

A movie company brought a new film to Old Tucson in the spring of 2016. Buffalo and Mustang Studios presented *No Sunday West of Newton*, starring Austin Buchanon, Aaron Johnson Araza, Tad Sallee, and Jesse Pickering. Mclauskie has killed Bailey in self-defense. He must get his adopted son, with tuberculosis, James Riley, and Riley's girl, out of Newton before Bailey's brothers get to town and exact their revenge.

The film *Tombstone Rashomon* was based on a Japanese movie in which a crime is seen through three pairs of eyes. This movie starred Eric Schumacher, Richard Anderson, and Benny Lee Kennedy. The movie plot was based upon the "Gunfight at the O.K. Corral" as seen by the gunfight's various participants. The movie premiered at the Loft Film Festival on November 9th through the 13th, 2016.

Old Tucson Studios and the Arizona Sonoran Western Heritage Foundation presented an old-fashioned 4th of July celebration. Patriotic music, games for kids, a pie-eating contest, and beer tasting occurred from July 2nd through the 4th.

The third movie in 2016, *The West and the Ruthless*, was brought to Old Tucson by Naisanceb Production Company. A group of misfits get involved in a bloody shootout and end up running for their lives; it starred Danny Brown, Dan Fowlks, and Paul Hapaiemi.

The "Dog Days of Summer" dog adoption program sponsored by the Pima Animal Control Center from September 3rd through the 5th was held at the park. Potential buyers paid a $17 licensing fee, and all the adoptions were free. McGruff, the crime dog, made an appearance. This year, for the "Dog Days of Summer," there were two competitions. In the first competition, a dog must run a 40-foot plank and dive into a pool of water with the object of reaching the other side in the quickest time possible. The second competition was a costume contest.

Robert Shelton, the founder of Old Tucson Studios and the longtime owner, died on December 15th, 2016, at the age of 95.

The first production of 2017 was *Cassidy Red,* which starred: Abby Eiland, Rick Cramer, and David Thomas Jenkins. When a corrupt Sheriff kills her lover, Josephine Cassidy seeks retribution.

Kix Brooks premiered his music video *Your Gonna Miss Me When I'm Gone* on May 13th. Brooks played an acoustic concert in the Palace Hotel and Saloon following the premiere.

The second movie to be filmed in 2017 was *Amazed By You,* which involved a man who has only his faith to get him through circumstances involving a group of dysfunctional cowboys. *Amazed By*

You starred Richard Pryor Jr., Chuck Williams, Wade Everette, and Jessica Lynch.

Arclight Pictures brought another movie to Old Tucson in 2017. *The Bequest* is about a mentally ill woman who becomes the victim of a conspiracy by her best friends. They conspire to steal her husband's only asset, a civil war rifle. The film starred Richard Pines, Gia Gerardo, and Eric Schumacher.

Lights come up on a gas station, and old diner as "Nightfall XXV" for October 2017 begins. This year's program is called "Eddie's 'Die'ner," about a small restaurant owned by three women. A vehicle pulls up in front of the gas station and diner. It is obvious that the three men in the car are wanted for murder, heard in a radio report. They capture a woman pumping gas and then a woman who comes out of the diner. After they are tied up, two of the men go off, one to search for another car and the other to find the third woman. While alone with the women, the third woman kills the guard and unties the other two women. They then go off the find the other two men. Both men come back on set, and the women kill them. After the killings, the owner of the gas station and diner kills the other two women. Her plan all along was to sell the land and move on.

A new gunfight premiered called "The Last Ride to Wilcox." Two known outlaws, John and Phil, ride into town and go into the saloon. Two sheriffs walk onto the set discussing how to arrest the outlaws. They decide one would go around back and flush them into the street. They set the plan in motion. Suddenly the inside sheriff commands them to put up their hands; instead, both outlaws run for the door. As they run into the street, the sheriff watching the front commands them to throw up their hands. A gunfight erupts, and one bandit goes down, and the other surrendered.

A scene from *September Gun,* the movie on which the new
north end show was based. 2018 (Author's collection)

Another show to premier in 2018 was "September Gun," based
on the movie of the same name. A nun comes to town with a group
of orphans to start an orphanage in the old mission building. She
finds out that the church is now a saloon. Ben Sundy, a known gunfighter, decides to help the nun who has hidden the children in a
barn. Ben confronts the saloon owner's boyfriend and throws him
out of the saloon, and a fistfight ensues. The saloon owner, Mama,
decides to close the saloon, which causes the bad guys to kidnap the
children. Ben, followed by the nun, went into the saloon to confront
the boyfriend and his son. A gunfight occurs, in which the boyfriend
and his son are killed.

October 1st, 2018, saw the opening of the "Nightfall XXVI"
show "Ranchero Motel." The play starts with people checking into
the Ranchero Motel. A biker couple and a man and woman with
a mentally disturbed young man. The biker chick starts acting violently, and when she comes to her senses, she cannot remember anything. Sid, the motel owner, starts talking to an invisible entity. We
find out that the entity was summoned forth during a satanic ritual.

He needs souls to stay active, and Sid provides the souls to the entity. In the form of a motel guest, the entity kills the other guests until there is only one left, the biker chick. She shoots Sid apparently to death and tries to shoot the entity. The entity kills her as it steals her soul. The entity then picks Sid up, and as the lights fade, says," Let's get you fixed up so you can reopen the motel tonight."

The new year saw the making of *The Legend of Five Mile Cave*. Produced by INSP Productions, the film shot at Old Tucson starred Adam Baldwin, Jeremy Sumpter, Jill Wagner, and Alexandria DeBerry. A stranger comes into a widow's life and her young son and tells the son about Shooter Green, a character in one of the son's pulp fiction books. We see the story play out in a series of flashbacks.

In February 2019, a new attraction, a zip line, opens. It runs from next to the sheriff's office to Silverlake. As a person slides done, he/she shoots at targets with a laser gun.

Nightfall XXVII opened on September 27th and ran until October 31st, 2019. The main stunt show was entitled "The Neighbors," an eviction notice is received by all the residents in the local run-down trailer park. Everyone is upset and out for blood when the manager drives up. Everyone starts yelling, and things get physical. Gunfire erupts until only a woman, and her husband are alive. When they get into a vehicle, the wife shoots her husband in the back. The woman gets on a Polaris ATV and starts to leave. She stops by an old shack and thanks an old man for helping her set the whole thing up to get away from her husband.

CHAPTER TEN:
That's a Wrap

Over the past 80 years, Old Tucson Studios has taken a long and winding route to get to its present-day self. No one could tell back in 1939 that the adobe movie town intended for one-time use would grow and become the historical park it became. Many elements and circumstances came together to mark the evolution of Old Tucson Studios. As the park grew, it kept its unique style of being at once an amusement park and a movie studio. It eventually became the second most visited attraction in Arizona, second only to the Grand Canyon. Its major fundraiser has always been the guests from all over the world. Admissions are in a symbiotic relationship with the movie industry.

When the Junior Chamber of Commerce first took over the town, they had the vision to use the existing building as a fundraiser for their association. With them as caretakers, Old Tucson was preserved and did not melt back into the desert. They instituted an entertainment legacy that would later become a professional facet of the park. The Jaycees developed the park as a piece of the old west, which drew people from all over and laid the foundation of fun, which would carry on.

Bob Shelton was not impressed at his first sight of the town. But he came to see the potential in the place and stuck his head in the loop, hoping that it would lead him to prosperity rather than hang him. Fortunately, Shelton had an easy-going personality, which would cause people to want to get involved in his risky venture. He could pick competent people to fill essential roles in the organization. Most of all, he kept his vision in front of him and pushed it along.

When the fire hit in 1995, most organizations would have cut and run. But the DRD Ventures Corporation kept their belief in Old Tucson to rebuild and see it through. The finances were thin for a couple of years, but they kept the faith that people would come to the park and insisted that only the best people were employed and knew that they needed to keep the customer at the forefront of their efforts. They had many talented people to write and produce inside and outside shows, which is the foundation of the professional attitudes that infused the shows.

Finally, when the Arizona Sonoran Western Heritage Foundation was formed and staffed, they started an era that let the park grow. The foundation helped to find another direction to entertain and educate the adults and children who rely on Old Tucson Studios to enrich their vacations and daily outings.

As a person walks the Old Tucson Studios streets, it is easy to see and hear moviemaking visions. Over 500 productions have been filmed or photographed here and at its sister site in Mescal.

In March 2020, a virus spread over the world and forced the shutdown of Old Tucson. There was a lack of funds to continue the operation of the park. In July of 2020, the county took over the park for nonpayment of rent. The future of the park is uncertain.

At night, walking down Main Street in the quiet of the desert, it is easy to hear the voices of past movies. One prominent voice calls out, "That's a wrap."